THE AMISTAD MUTINY

During the month of August 1839, reports were circulating up and down the eastern coast of the United States about a "mysterious long black schooner" sighted at sea. This ship was a Spanish schooner, *Amistad,* which had sailed from Havana for Port Príncipe, Cuba, on June 28, 1839. The *Amistad* carried, in addition to its crew, fifty-four African slaves. Four nights after leaving Havana the Africans, led by Cinqué, mutinied, killing the captain and three of the crew. For nearly two months the Africans attempted to force the remaining members of the crew to sail the *Amistad* back to Africa. On August 26, 1839, Cinqué and a few other Africans went ashore for supplies near Montauk Point on Long Island, New York. Soon after, the *Amistad* was illegally seized by the United States Navy. Cinqué and his fellow countrymen were imprisoned and taken to New Haven to await trial before the next Circuit Court at Hartford.

In New York City a committee headed by Lewis Tappan, Simeon Jocelyn, and Joshua Leavitt employed legal counsel consisting of Seth Staples and Theodore Sedgwick of New York and Roger S. Baldwin of New Haven.

The case against the Africans was argued by United States District Attorney Holabird whose position was that of the Spanish Government and American proslavery interests—that the Africans were slaves (property), and had committed murder.

The Circuit Court at Hartford ruled that the *Amistad* had been taken on the high seas, and that therefore the Africans could not be charged with murder. The Spanish, who had argued since the *Amistad* had been captured that the ship and the Africans were their property, then sent a letter to President Martin Van Buren, denying the rights of United States courts in the case. The Spanish also asked the President to return the Africans to Cuba in a government boat. President Van Buren ordered the naval officer who had captured the *Amistad* to stand ready to transport the Africans from New Haven. This order was sent before the court could assemble at New Haven on January 7, 1840, to further consider the *Amistad* case. When the New Haven court affirmed the decision of the Hartford court—that the Africans were freemen (not property or criminals) who had fought to regain their lost freedom—the United States Secretary of State ordered an appeal. Now the case was before the United States Supreme Court.

The legal counsel for the Africans, sensing the broad historical significance of this fight for freedom, realized the necessity of enlisting the aid of an individual who epitomized many of the idealistic qualities associated with the best of American character. They found this person in former President John Quincy Adams. Adams, then a Congressman from Massachusetts, eloquently argued the case before the Supreme Court and on March 8, 1841, the Africans were set free. The next year the Africans returned to their homeland, Sierra Leone.

Amistad 1

Edited by

JOHN A. WILLIAMS and CHARLES F. HARRIS

 VINTAGE BOOKS A Division of Random House, New York

Amistad

Editors: JOHN A. WILLIAMS AND CHARLES F. HARRIS
Designer: KENNETH A. MIYAMOTO

VINTAGE BOOKS EDITION, February 1970
FIRST EDITION

Copyright © 1970 by John A. Williams
Copyright © 1970 by Vincent Harding
Copyright © 1970 by C. L. R. James
Copyright © 1970 by Ishmael Reed
Copyright © 1970 by Addison Gayle
Copyright © 1970 by Calvin Hernton
Copyright © 1970 by Oliver Jackman
Copyright © 1970 by Verta Grosvenor
Copyright © 1970 by George Davis

Library of Congress Catalog Card Number: 75-107196

"The Negro Artist and the Racial Mountain" by Langston Hughes first appeared in *The Nation* and is reprinted by permission of Harold Ober Associates Incorporated. Copyright 1926 by Langston Hughes.

Manufactured in the United States of America

To Langston Hughes

INTRODUCTION

The word *amistad* means friendship in Spanish. The Amistad Mutiny of 1839 stands for revolt, self-determination, justice and freedom. With these meanings always firmly in mind, we have designed this publication primarily for use in college courses in literature, history, sociology, psychology, education, political science and government, and the arts. In addition to college use, *Amistad* should have meaning and relevance for anyone interested in knowing and understanding the bases, workings, and implications of Western (especially American) culture and civilization, past and present. The main purpose of this publication is to present penetrating analytical and interpretive essays and new fiction that will lead to a multidisciplinary understanding of the humanities and the social sciences. An integral part of this magazine will be to select essays and fiction in a way that will permit *Amistad* to serve as a systematic cohesive body of basic material for Black Studies courses.

The emergence of Black Studies as an intellectual

discipline is a direct result of the racism that has pervaded American higher education since its inception. Since the founding of the first college, most academicians have understood that their "search for truth" meant, in fact, a continuous search for new and interesting theories and philosophies that could be used to justify or obscure the heinous crimes that many of the religious, political and business leaders of this country have committed in denying other men —black, brown, and red men—their *human* and civil rights. Granted, there are and have been many academicians of high principle who have unknowingly participated in the suppression of truth and enlightenment. But these unwilling or unknowledgeable co-conspirators have had a negative influence equal to that of their more insidious colleagues.

The humanities and social sciences are the major divisions of the university that must bear the responsibility for the inculcation of "intellectual" racism. If a student learns and accepts what he is taught in the first courses in American history and American literature, he will have acquired enough sophisticated racism to carry him through a doctoral program, and/or through life. Since almost all college students at some time or another must take some courses in the humanities and social sciences, one can easily see how "intellectual" racism can be rapidly infused into this society simply by examining the number of persons who graduate from college each year. When we see how much these college graduates, especially teachers, influence other people, we realize that the effect of "plausible and logical racism" can be, to say the least, devastating.

This publication is going to show what the world is really like. To this end we are proud to present in this first issue an interview with the redoubtable Chester Himes on writing, publishing and his life. C. L. R. James—a contemporary and associate of the brilliant George Padmore, Eric Williams and Richard

Wright—discusses the significance of slavery and the slave trade in the development of Europe and the United States. Vincent Harding probes the meaning of black history, and Addison Gayle's *Cultural Hegemony* explores the influence of white Southern writers on the literary scene.

Our fiction comes from the young satirist Ishmael Reed, the imaginative writer-diplomat Oliver Jackman, and a veteran of Vietnam, George Davis.

Amistad deals in relevance. We know that the truth of Western civilization lies in precisely what has previously been omitted in its teachings. We propose to answer some of the questions that so many of the young are asking. We know that those answers lie in revealing what so many of us have long thought and known about ourselves, our forebears, our institutions.

A final two words in this introduction to the first issue of *Amistad*. Right on!

Charles F. Harris and John A. Williams

CONTENTS

CONTENTS

Amistad 1

Cultural Hegemony
The Southern White Writer and American Letters

by Addison Gayle, Jr.

MOVEMENTS IN LITERARY HISTORY are difficult to discern, and the influences which give rise to and sustain them are not easy to trace. The movement from Classicism to Neo-Classicism in seventeenth- and eighteenth-century English literature cannot be traced to one particular work, although Dryden's *Essay of Dramatic Poesy*, Samuel Johnson's "Preface to Shakespeare" and Gotthold Lessing's essay "Laocoön" must be noted. The movement from Neo-Classicism to Romanticism is equally difficult to pinpoint, despite the poetry of Thomas Gray, Oliver Goldsmith and William Blake which reflects the theories of Romanticism enunciated by Samuel Coleridge in *Biographia Literaria*, William Wordsworth in the preface to *Lyrical Ballads* and Shelley in his "Defence of Poetry."

In America, where little of a national literature existed until the latter part of the eighteenth century, any discussion of literary history centers upon the established traditions of Germany, France and England. So great was the foreign influence on American letters, that Nathaniel Appleton, Noah Webster, David Ram-

say and others demanded a literature of their own.
John Trumbull summed up their nationalistic arguments in couplet form:

> This land her Swift and Addison shall view
> The former honors equalled by the new
> Here shall some Shakespear charm the rising age
> And hold in magic chain the listening stage.

David Ramsay demanded a decisive break with the
Old World. The models to be followed were those of
nations that had existed on the shores of the Aegean
long ago: "It is hoped that the free government of
America will produce poets, orators, critics, and historians equal to the most celebrated of the ancient
commonwealths of Greece and Italy." Ramsay's call
for an indigenous literature based upon the Greek
ideal was not answered until 1830. Cooper's two
novels *The Spy* and *The Last of the Mohicans* moved
the American novel away from the influence of Samuel Richardson and Henry Fielding; Philip Freneau,
"the first real poetic voice to be heard in the U.S.,"
broke new grounds in the field of poetry; and the
Transcendentalists attempted to lay a philosophical
foundation for a national literature. Yet, despite these
specific movements in Northern literature, the literary
tradition destined to survive the influence of Walt
Whitman and William Dean Howells was brought into
being by Southern writers who, in crossing Aristotle
and Plato with Sir Walter Scott, produced a tradition
which not only, in Dr. Johnson's words, stood the test
of time, but has dominated American cultural thought
from 1830 to the present.

The Plantation Movement occurred almost simultaneously with the Transcendental Movement. The
latter, dying with Emerson, never reached the status
of a tradition, while the former continued to grow
and develop. The rise of the Plantation Movement and
the demise of the Transcendental can be attributed to
the fact that the latter went back, as Ramsay had

suggested, to the Aegean "for confirmaion of its faith," while the former went back to Germany for the same reason. Between Immanuel Kant and Plato lay a world of difference, not only in philosophical approaches, but in views of man and society. The voice of Kant calling upon men to be open-minded, to be inquisitive, to approach the complex problems of men in humanitarian terms fell on deaf ears in a nation where prejudice, dogmatism and simplistic approaches to problems, human and social, were and still are the norm. Given the choice between Platonic idealism and Kantian transcendentalism, the South chose to ally itself with the Greek mind, and thus became the embodiment of the American myth.

The earliest proponent of this myth was the statesman-philosopher John C. Calhoun; and American cultural thought is more indebted to Calhoun than critics and teachers care to admit. In defending the plantation system, Calhoun championed a republic modeled on the Greek ideal—that is, Platonic idealism—one in which classes predominated. He devoted himself, according to Vernon Parrington, to setting "class economics above abstract humanitarianism . . . He undid for the plantation South the work of his old master [Jefferson]. Speaking in the name of democracy, he attacked the foundations on which the democratic movement in America had rested, substituting for its libertarian and equalitarian doctrines conceptions wholly alien and antagonist to western democracy, wholly Greek in their underlying spirit."

With Calhoun, the defense of the plantation system passed from Virginia to South Carolina. Virginia, the intellectual seat of the Confederacy, inoculated with the philosophy of Thomas Jefferson, her plantation system working at peak performance, had settled down to the complacency of an affluent Greek city-state. With abolitionism on the rise in the North, the *Appeal* of the black writer David Walker, flooding the South with its call for slave insurrections, and the plantation system under daily attack, Calhoun presented the rationale for what Thomas Nelson Page called "the purest sweetest life ever lived."

In "A Disquisition on Government," Calhoun declared: ". . . it is a great and dangerous error to suppose that all people are equally entitled to liberty. It is a reward to be earned, not a blessing to be gratuitously lavished on all alike—a reward reserved for the intelligent, the patriotic, the virtuous and deserving—and not a boon to be bestowed on a people too ignorant, degraded and vicious, to be capable either of appreciating or of enjoying it . . . Nor is it any disparagement to liberty that such is and ought to be the case. On the contrary, its greatest praise—its proudest distinction is, that an all-wise providence has reserved it, as the noblest and highest reward for the development of our faculties, moral and intellectual." Having carried us thus far in pursuit of the Greek ideal, having paid his debt to the early Plato of *The Republic*, Calhoun turns to invoke the spirit of the later Plato whose last dialogue, *The Laws*, is a treatise on despotism: "A reward more appropriate than liberty could not be conferred on the deserving—nor punishment inflicted on the undeserving more just, than to be subject to lawless and despotic rule."

For an accurate summation of Calhoun's thought on this point, one must turn to Vernon Parrington: "Democracy is possible only in a society that recognizes inequality as a law of nature, but in which the virtuous and capable enter into a voluntary co-partnership for the common good, accepting wardship of the incompetent in the interests of society. This was the Greek ideal and this ideal had created Greek civilization."

In "Remarks on the States Rights Resolutions in Regard to Abolition," Calhoun describes the new republic: "The southern states are an aggregate, in fact, of communities, not of individuals. Every plantation is a little community, with the master at its head, who concentrates in himself the united interests of capital and labor, of which he is the common representative. These small communities aggregated make the State in all, whose action, labor, and capital is equally represented and perfectly harmonized. Hence the harmony, the union, the stability of that section which is rarely disturbed, except through the action of this government."

John Pendleton Kennedy, William Alexander Caruthers and Nathaniel Beverley Tucker, among the South's earliest literary lights, accepted the Calhoun sociological doctrine in total, and lent their talents to extolling the virtues of the plantation system. Contrary to popular belief, their major efforts were not spent in defending the institution of slavery, but in praising the virtue of the concept upon which the plantation system rested. Slavery was defended in the social, political and theological realms by Calhoun and Albert Taylor Bledsoe, but its defense was not undertaken in earnest by poets and writers until after the publication of *Uncle Tom's Cabin* in 1852. Until that time, men of letters were content to propagandize the virtues of the Greek ideal.

The Southern mind was attracted to the Greek ideal partly because of the justification for slavery offered by the world's first "democracy"; it was not attracted by what Matthew Arnold called the "humane principles" handed down from the Aegean through Greece's most famous sons—principles which distinguished man by placing him at the center of the universe. To the Southern mind, historically incapable of dealing with complexity, seeking a stable, ordered society free from the disruption occasioned by the intrusion of enlightened ideas, Greece offered a model of the agrarian society. Athens was a universe wherein each man, awarded his place in society, lived by a set of norms which defined his daily existence, and by extension defined him.

Plato's *The Republic* and Aristotle's *Politics*, not the

King James version of the Bible, are the ancient tracts
from which the Southerners gleaned their theology.
Central to each of these works is the idea of the
planned society in which men and women function
as a unit—a world of superiors and inferiors, each
cognizant of his particular niche in the social, political
and cultural hierarchy. Having laid down the sociological and political basis for such a utopia, John C.
Calhoun turned his attention to the coming break
between North and South, and left the task of singing
the glories of this utopia—of recording it in verse,
prose and song—to poets and novelists. When these
"legislators of the world," as Shelley called them,
took up their pens to describe Calhoun's world, the
plantation system became the model for the Plantation
School of writers.

In prose, poetry and fiction one finds almost everywhere the dramatization of the perfect society for
whose structure the ancient theory of the "Great
Chain of Being" is the closest analogue. At the
apex of the chain was the master of the greatest plantations, God's vice-regent on earth, Solon and Christ
combined—bold, generous and philanthropic, bending man and beast to his will with cajolery if possible,
with the whip if necessary. The lesser plantation
owner, whose wealth, calculated in terms of number
of slaves, was insufficient to grant him top status, was
next. Next came the farmer, and following him were
the peasants, the poor whites who, due to lack of
ingenuity, were incapable of surviving in a Darwin-
ian world. At the bottom were the slaves upon whose
shoulders the task of maintaining the planation system rested. They were the inferior element, and a
modern-day supporter of the plantation system, John
Gould Fletcher, has justified their existence at the
lower rung of the hierarchy: "The inferior, whether in
life or in education, should exist only for the sake of
the superior. We feed and clothe and exercise our
bodies, for example, in order to be able to do some-

thing with our minds. We employ our minds in order to achieve character, to become the balanced personalities, the 'superior men' of Confucius' text, the 'Gentlemen' of the old south."

The " 'superior men' of Confucius' text" remain the heroes of plantation literature. Their most important characteristics are devotion to region, duty, and loved ones. The loved ones are often fair damsels, ladies whose material possessions are fans, musical boxes, billets-doux and perfumed handkerchiefs. In addition to the influence of Plato and Aristotle, that of Sir Walter Scott, Samuel Richardson and Alexander Pope is apparent everywhere. The idyllic utopia, the paradise on earth, is recreated in poetry and fiction with the authenticity vouchsafed it by the rhetoric of John C. Calhoun.

Calhoun died in 1850, two years before the plantation tradition came under assault by Harriet Beecher Stowe. Although the plantation system was based upon the institution of slavery, one must not think of them as one and the same. In doing so, critics have attributed motives to Harriet Beecher Stowe which she did not entertain. Mrs. Stowe had no intention of "starting the big war," nor did she seek to do away with the slave system. Unlike her father, Lyman Beecher, and her brother, Henry, she was not an abolitionist. What bothered her was not slavery but the immorality of the institution which offended her Quaker sensitivity and led her, without realizing it, to explode the myth upon which the plantation system rested.

The society of Southern mythology could be justified by its apologists only if it rested on a high plane of morality. The inferiors had to be treated humanely or proved deserving of the punishment inflicted upon them by loving masters pushed beyond the limits of patience. Rewarding instead of abusing those who "stayed in their places" was an unwritten law of the ideal republic which, when violated, introduced chaos into the system. No slave was more conscious of his position than Tom, none accepted so readily the "place" to which providence and ill fortune had doomed him, and none was more obedient, loving or submissive.

Tom's treatment at the hands of Simon Legree—who, as Edmund Wilson points out, is the plantation owner, a Yankee, not an overseer and a Southerner as many have been led to believe—does irreparable injury to the ideal which Southern writers had been propagating, and reveals the plantation system to have been modeled less upon Plato and Aristotle than upon Epicurus and Heraclitus. He is not the victim of "the most pernicious institution known to man," but the victim of an imperfect social order, one which fails to live up to its promise. Whatever others might make of *Uncle Tom's Cabin* for abolitionist ends, Mrs. Stowe would have settled for a world in which the justice and humanity espoused by Southern writers was an actuality, in which an "inferior" like Tom who never violates the norms of his condition is accorded due treatment for loyalty, devotion and piety.

Southern writers have always been aware of the underlying thesis of Mrs. Stowe's novel. Their counter-attack was ostensibly not based upon a defense of the plantation system. They went to great lengths to prove that the Simon Legrees were anomalies, and that the black Toms of the South fared better than the white Toms of the North. The tenacious zeal that had been displayed in articulating the virtues of Calhoun's "near-perfect society" was now marshaled to defend it.

Less than one year after the publication of *Uncle Tom's Cabin*, William John Grayson, who with George Fitzhugh formed a two-man truth squad dedicated to correcting the falsehoods of Mrs. Stowe, used the heroic couplet as the medium for his rebuttal. Black slaves in the South, he argued in "The Hireling and the Slave," fare far better than the Northern poor; and after cataloguing the abuses of the poor in the North, he contrasts their plight with that of the slaves in the South:

> If bound to daily labor while he lives,
> His the daily bread that labor gives;
> Guarded from want, from beggary secure,
> He never feels what hireling crowds endure,
> Nor knows like them, in hopeless want to crave,
> For wife and child, the comforts of the slave,
> Or the sad thought that, when about to die
> He leaves them to the cold world's charity
> And sees them slowly seek the poor-house door—
> The last, vile, hated refuge of the poor.

George Fitzhugh in *Cannibals All/or Slaves Without Masters*, choosing to mount his defense in prose, based his argument on the same theme. In "Slavery— Its Effects on the Free," he meets the moral argument posed by Mrs. Stowe without retreating one step from the Greek ideal: "Now at first view it [slavery] elevates . . . whites; for it makes them not the bottom of society, as at the North—not the menials, the hired day laborers, the work scavengers and scullions— but privileged citizens, like Greek and Roman citizens, with a numerous class far beneath them." And reminiscent of Grayson, Fitzhugh concludes: "Our slaves till the land, do the coarse and hard labor on our roads and canals, sweep our streets, cook our food, brush our boots, wait on our tables, hold our horses, do all hard work, and fill all menial offices. Your freemen at the North do the same work and fill the same offices. The only difference is, we love our slaves, and are ready to defend, assist and protect them . . ."

Such gallant defenses proved of no avail against the juggernaut now poised to move in the North. Three years after Fitzhugh's *Cannibals All*, "the irrepressible conflict" erupted into a violent conflagration wherein men like William Tecumseh Sherman, riding the whirlwind of the apocalypse, burned to ashes the

physical props upon which the literature of the South
had rested. When chaos came, when peace and tranquility were disrupted, all that would survive of the
Greek ideal was a record of what men believed had
once existed.

Writers after Reconstruction such as Thomas Nelson Page, Thomas Dixon and Joel Chandler Harris
brooded over the past and attempted to resurrect it in
fiction and poetry, to create once again the Garden
of Eden. The paradise lost haunted them all of their
lives, and they died, pitiable old men, clinging to
the dream of ancient Greece which had once flowered
anew on American soil. The dream would not die
with them. They lived during the years of "the bloody
shirt," when every Northern politician singled out the
South as villain, when John Brown replaced Davy
Crockett as the national hero, and when the best
literary talents of the North were celebrating the virtues of "old New England."

When the days of Northern vindictiveness were
over, when the railroad men discovered new routes in
the South, when the Supreme Court had struck down
the last of the Reconstruction legislation, and when
President Hayes had withdrawn the last troops from
the South, other men, dreaming the dreams of the
post-Reconstruction writers, awakened to ask with
Fletcher: "How can we preserve what little is now left
to us of the traditions of leisure, of culture, of intellectual tolerance and sane kindliness, which are all
that our fathers had to give us as a legacy from the
past that was broken in the civil war?"

The Southern writer was no longer the interpreter
of the system nor its defender; his task was now, to
paraphrase James Joyce, to forge from the smithy of
his soul the uncreated conscience of the race. He set
out at first to justify the ways of John C. Calhoun to
his Southern brethren; and he was oblivious of the
fact, until much later, that his appeal was listened to
and applauded by those in the ranks of the enemy.

Despite Parrington's attempt to subordinate the influence of the Plantation School to that of the Transcendentalists and the Realists, the Plantation School with its simplistic view of man and the world remains dominant in American letters.

Men like John Gould Fletcher, better educated and more sophisticated than their predecessors, discovered Matthew Arnold's truth—that great creative epochs demand great ideas to propel them into being and that to accomplish this task an era of literary criticism is necessary. Such men, apostles of a modern romanticism who refused to believe that the Southern Athens was gone beyond recall, set out to seize the reins of literary criticism in America, to force it into new and different channels and to posit a romanticism far less humane than that which they set out to destroy.

The New Critics appeared at a time when complexity was the norm in American life. In the late nineteen twenties and early thirties, the society was undergoing spasms from sources as varied as race riots and industrial expansion. The influence and power of the priest had been dissipated; the politician had lost favor through perversion of his art. The social institutions seemed incapable of confronting the complexity of life in the twentieth century. There was an overwhelming moral and social void and, like the men of the middle ages, the men of twentieth-century America turned to the university, calling on it to wage war in the interests of progress, to construct the formulas by which a nation might rise or fall.

Men who held such naive faith in the universities learned the lesson that young college students are learning today: The most reactionary institution in the American society is the university, and the last place that one will find Enlightenment, morality or redemption is within its ivy-covered walls. Nowhere is the Southern myth of the simplistic universe more pervasive than in the university, nowhere is the aristocratic

ideal held so dear, nowhere the vision of John C.
Calhoun clung to so tenaciously, and nowhere are
the Greeks regarded with more condescension as the
accurate prophets of man's existence. The American
university has not changed essentially since the
founding of Harvard College in 1636. Its purpose then
as now was "to provide for young gentlemen a body
of knowledge that would assure entrance into a community of educated leaders."

Toward these ends the university channeled its
energy and its resources. Obsessed with the idea of
establishing an educational aristocracy, the men of
the university hastened to defend the validity of the
American tradition, despite the precarious position
upon which it rested. Despite the efforts of a few
professors—outcasts among their peers—the tracts,
books and articles supporting the institution of slavery, and perpetuating the nonsense that the black man
is inferior poured out of universities, North as well as
South. For a while the historians were the chief vil-
lains in this comedy of errors, but soon the torch was
passed on to the teachers of literature.

The English departments were ready for the New
Critics who, in the later 1920's began to remodel literary criticism in their own agrarian (read plantation)
image. They left the Southern universities, took up
residence at the University of Chicago, and proceeded
to construct a republic in letters based upon the social
republic which they outlined in *I'll Take My Stand:
The South and the Agrarian Tradition, by Twelve
Southerners* (1930).

Sometimes called "the Bible of agrarianism," *I'll
Take My Stand* is a racist, fascist document, equaled
in the twentieth century only by Hitler's *Mein Kampf*.
Among its contributors are men whose names are
legend in the field of American literary criticism. Included are articles by Donald Davidson, who in 1954
became chairman of the Tennessee Federation for
Constitutional Government, a right-wing organization

"formed to oppose desegregation on the principle of states rights"; Allen Tate, whose introduction to *Libretto for the Republic of Liberia* by Melvin B. Tolson surpasses William Dean Howells' preface to *The Complete Works of Paul Laurence Dunbar* in racial bigotry and arrogant, Aryan superiority; and Robert Penn Warren, who has denounced his contribution to *I'll Take My Stand*, admitting that "it was written in support of segregation." However, in his conclusion to *Who Speaks for the Negro?*, published in 1965, Warren evidences how far along the road to rehabilitation he has traveled—which proves to be not very far at all.

In *I'll Take My Stand* the major thesis is a reiteration of the social thesis propounded by John C. Calhoun in the 1830's. We are called to a rebirth of the republic of Athens; asked to reconstruct the society formed along class lines which existed in the South before the modern evils, progress and industrialism, intervened; invited to follow the agrarians back to the time when ". . . the even-poised and leisurely life of the Greeks, their oratory, their philosophy, their art . . . appealed to the South. The Greek tradition became partly grafted upon the Anglo-Saxon and Scotch tradition of life."

"The remarkable society" of the old South (Allen Tate's terminology) was not defeated in the Civil War. Actual defeat threatens it now. The modern invaders are a varied assortment of incompatible elements: factories, railroads, bureaucrats and civil-rights agitators. These seek to change the simplistic life of a simple people, to destroy the romantic past born of rich soil, cultured old gentlemen and docile slaves. Against this modern aggression, the twelve writers take their stand, prepared to defend "a special notion of tradition—a notion that tradition is not simply a fact but a fact that must be constantly defended."

For these twentieth-century Southern writers, tradition means what it meant for the plantation writers of the eighteenth and nineteenth: a theory of society which goes back to the founding fathers of the old South, one based on the doctrines of Plato and Aristotle, wherein man's destiny is determined by race and birth; a tradition wherein the Great Chain of Being stands as the metaphor of man's hopes and strivings, and where the aristocrat, the farmer and especially the black man know their places. "In the past," writes Robert Penn Warren, "the Southern Negro has always been a creature of the small town and farm. That is where he still chiefly belongs by temperament and capacity; there he has less the character of a 'problem' and more the status of a human being who is likely to find in agricultural and domestic pursuits the happiness that his good nature and easy ways incline him to as an ordinary function of his being."

How then, Allen Tate asks the rhetorical question, can this tradition which survives in Southern letters be resurrected again in actuality? His answer is definitive: "The answer is by violence . . . Since he [the Southerner] cannot bore from within, he has left the sole alternative of boring from without. This method is political, active, and in the nature of the case, violent and revolutionary. Reaction is the most radical of programs; it aims at cutting away the overgrowth and getting back to the roots."

Like the novels of Thomas Dixon which sanctioned the activities of the Ku Klux Klan when other men believed with Dixon that tradition should be defended to the death, the contributors to *I'll Take My Stand* provided the rationale for the violence enacted against Auteurine Lucy and James Meredith, for the murders of Emmett Till, Jimmy Lee Jackson and Medgar Evers, for the bombing of four black children in a Birmingham church, and for the elevation of the Bull Connors and George Wallaces to a national eminence approaching sainthood.

Tate and his fellow Southerners misjudged the

American temper. The book was written as a defense of the Southern way of life and directed at a supposedly hostile audience in the rest of the nation. However, Americans, to paraphrase William Blake, were not only of the Devil's party but, with the exception of a few misguided liberals, recognized their close affiliation. America is most Southern in her inclination to favor Aristotle over Immanuel Kant, to opt for the simplistic life instead of the complex one, and to believe as passionately in the concept of the Great Chain of Being as the most rabid Southern aristocrat.

The true character of white America was difficult to analyze during the period of continual wars and migration from country to city and from city to suburbs. The case is quite different today. Supplied with a life of affluence and leisure surpassed in American history only by that of the plantation owner and the managerial capitalist, today Americans look forward to peace, comfort and security. Few would be shocked by the philosophy displayed in *I'll Take My Stand*; a great many would accept these fascist myths of the thirties as the truths for the seventies. The republic imagined in writing stands a chance today of being established in fact by the administration of Richard Nixon, whose architects seem determined to transform America into a shadow image of the plantation system of yesteryear, replete with lords, ladies and darky servants.

The nation was thirty years late in recognizing its true character. However, the university, quick to move on reactionary principles, fell sway to the sophistry of the agrarians in less than two years. The teachers of English were the most culpable. Guardians of the national taste, these men of letters determine what cultured Americans will or will not read, what work of art deserves or does not deserve the National Book Award or the Pulitzer Prize, what writer will or will not receive a fellowship to work in leisure or obtain a seat at a renowned university. The control of the nation's cultural apparatus rests in the hands of English professors and critics who, more often than not, peer out upon the American society with a condescension reserved for idiots and half-wits.

Such men welcomed the attempt of the New Critics to establish an aristocracy in American letters equal to that which they envisioned in the social sphere. The days of Hippolyte Taine and Charles Augustin Sainte-Beuve were no more. Literature which dealt with man in terms of "race, moment and milieu," which considered the life of the author as important as the work itself, which argued that literature should not only mean but have a moral function as well, was denounced as irrelevant in a society wherein the artist sought not the elevation of mankind but the cultivation of his art.

A poem or novel, like a well-wrought urn, was an "autotelic structure," governed by inner rules and conforming to verbal structures which only the chosen few could analyze or interpret. The function of the writer was not, as Henry Fielding had believed, to instruct, but to produce masterpieces which would satisfy the aesthetic tastes of the cultured elite—tastes conditioned by four years of English courses in the best colleges and universities.

If America is again to become the legendary Athens, a literature which serves the demands of the aristocracy is a necessity. Still dreaming of the past, still enamored of the theories of the utopian society propounded by John C. Calhoun, the agrarians seized the psychological criticism of I. A. Richards and the ambiguous criticism of T. S. Eliot, imbued them with their own biases, and formulated a theory of art for art's sake with the concomitant denial of the democratic spirit and disdain for the masses that such a formula entailed.

When the English departments accepted the *ars poetica* of the Southern agrarians, they chose to deal with literature in terms applicable to the plastic arts;

moreover, they substantiated the Southern myth and gave authenticity to a society constructed along class lines. Their hypnotic attraction to the Greek ideal led them to accept the agrarian formula of a master class for whose personal comfort a literature is created. In so doing, they championed the worst of the plantation tradition and preceded the nation at large in succumbing to the philosophy of the descendants of John C. Calhoun.

The influence of the plantation tradition transmitted through the literary criticism of the agrarians predominates American cultural thought. Nowhere is this influence more pronounced than in criticism of literature which deals with blacks. Afro-Americans are the descendants of those whose presence in America made the plantation system possible; and the literary tradition based upon it owes as much to their presence as to the works of Plato and Sir Walter Scott.

Assigned the lowest position on the Great Chain of Being, blacks, in attempting to extricate themselves, have evoked repercussions from white Americans in social, political, economic and cultural areas. After the Emancipation Proclamation, in order to preserve the legacy left by the Plantation School of writers, white writers and critics instituted cultural slavery to replace the chattel slavery ended by the guns of war.

In 1925, in the preface to *The New Negro*, Alain Locke noted the cultural servitude under which blacks labored, and attributed it to the efforts of teachers and critics to deal with them in stereotypic terms: "Of all the voluminous literature on the Negro so much is mere external view and commentary that we may warrantably say that nine-tenths of it is about the Negro rather than of him . . . .

Locke's solution was to have the Negro speak for himself. However, Americans turned to oracles outside of the race. They preferred to listen to voices more attuned to their own, to those who spoke of peace and tranquility instead of war, who sought to assuage their fears with romance and make-believe instead of presenting the true story of America in all of its "hideous fullness."

No two oracles were more soothing in this respect than William Faulkner and William Styron. Nowhere in America literature does the plantation tradition reach greater heights than in the portraits of black characters drawn by these two writers. White critics of William Faulkner and their black fellow travelers —Ralph Ellison and Albert Murray are the best known—have praised him for his "realistic portrayal of Negro people." However, his Negro characters, whose function is to satisfy the demand of white Americans for racial peace, are remnants of the plantation tradition.

Dilsey of *The Sound and the Fury* is one example. Like the "mammies" of Paul Laurence Dunbar's *Strength of Gideon*, her literary lineage goes back to Thomas Nelson Page: she attempts to hold the white family together, she is the foundation of a dying institution. While suffering insult and abuse, she survives by virtue of patience and submissiveness. The Greek ideal is safe with the Dilseys of the earth. Knowing and accepting their places, they face each tomorrow with a Bible under their arms, not with Molotov cocktails under their skirts. They are, to be sure, far different from the Harriet Tubmans and Sojourner Truths of true American history.

Faulkner displayed great enthusiasm for the Dilseys of the race who became his metaphor for those whom other blacks should emulate: "The Negro . . . must learn to cease forever thinking like a Negro and acting like a Negro . . . What he must learn are the hard things—self-restraint, honesty, dependability, purity; to act not even as well as just any white man, but to act as well as the best of white men." The closer one comes to assimilating the characteristics of aristocratic man, the closer one moves toward paradise.

No black should emulate Joe Christmas of *Light in*

August. One cannot exist in Faulkner's world half-white or half-black, and the mulatto, a man with no discernible place, is doomed to an ignominious existence and a tragic end. Dilsey is the prototype of the good nigger, the darling of the earlier followers of the plantation tradition. No threat to the institution of slavery, she accepts her position in the hierarchy as having been ordained by God, and she will never bring chaos into the republic.

Joe Christmas, without roots in either the black society or the white, is an outcast. He is the tragic mulatto of the plantation tradition who comes to prominence after the Civil War. The bad nigger of Southern fiction, he survives in Faulkner as a reminder of the evils of miscegenation—that act for which John C. Calhoun made no provisions and which may eventually bring about the destruction of the existing social order.

A reassurance and a warning: this is the sum total of Faulkner's contribution to American letters; and Americans are more likely to remember the reassurance (Dilsey) than the warning (Joe Christmas). This is due, in part, to *The Confessions of Nat Turner,* the novel by William Styron. Coming in the midst of the Black Revolution, Styron's novel reassures white Americans who had begun to believe that Malcolm X, Stokely Carmichael and H. Rap Brown posed a threat to the maintenance of the great society. These men who chose the philosophy of Sparta over that of Athens were, it was believed, prepared to lead the Spartan hordes from the ghettos on an adventure designed to destroy the caste and class system upon which the republic stands.

Like the famed *deus ex machina* of Greek mythology, Nat Turner was thrust upon the national consciousness to remind white Americans that, historically, all black revolutionaries have had Achilles heels. What they desire in actuality is not the master's life, but his daughter, and they are so confused about their relationship vis-à-vis white society that any determined assault upon white America, if it comes at all, is many years distant. Therefore these modern-day Nat Turners pose no real threat, for not only are they half-men, but they are sexually disturbed as well, seeking to wage war not in the streets or behind the barricades, but in the bedrooms of white women.

Nat Turner in the hands of Richard Wright, LeRoi Jones or John Williams would have been altogether different. And those who condemn Styron for his portrait, who demand that he portray Nat Turner with any semblance of reality, demand the impossible. To demand a realistic portrayal of blacks by whites is to demand the impossible, for whites are neither mentally nor culturally equipped for the task. The plantation sentiments are too strong in white America, the influence of the New Critics too pervasive. Their approach to black people can only travel the gamut from crude distortion to condescension, occasioned by racism either unconscious or overt.

This is readily apparent in the area of literary criticism. Theodore Gross, the new Robert Bone of black literature, lauds Joel Chandler Harris for being "able to share the fears, laughter, and anger of the Negro; he contributed the most popular Negro characters to American fiction—Uncle Remus, Balam, Ananias, and Mingo." Richard Wright, according to the same critic, when writing of his life and experiences in *Black Boy*, is found to depict "mundane actualities."

The assumptions upon which Gross' critical thesis rests are stated in an essay, "Our Mutual Estates": whites, he argues, due to their training in "America's best universities," are better equipped to deal with black literature than blacks. His thesis is supported by, among others, Fred Ehrenfeld who, in reviewing the anthology *How We Live: Contemporary Life in Contemporary Fiction*, finds that: "Of the seven selections devoted to the Negro, two are by Jews and one by a southern white writer. The editor feels the need to justify this by contending that there are few good black writers."

These are the disciples of the New Critics, the academic architects of a new aristocracy, and their arguments are cogently summed up by Selden Rodman in a review of Melvin Tolson's *Libretto for the Republic of Liberia*. After noting that black literature has been "praised for its moral intentions and excused for its formal shortcomings," Rodman writes ". . . most of this poetry has been second rate, and critics, partaking of the general responsibility for the Negro's unreadiness to take the 'Negro Problem' in his stride, have hesitated to say so. The Negro poet's attitude of resigned pathos was followed by one of tragic aggressiveness, and both, as Allen Tate says in his preface to 'Libretto for the Republic of Liberia' limited him 'to a provincial mediocrity in which feelings about one's difficulties become more important than poetry itself.' "

To end with a quotation from the dean of Southern literary criticism is a measure of the extent of the influence of the Southern writer upon American letters; and it is no misstatement to say that American culture today is little more than a fiefdom of Southerners who exercise more despotic control over the national literature than their forefathers exercised over their plantations. Against this cultural dominance stands a small band of black intellectuals and writers whose history has been one of continual struggle against the Greek ideal. More Kantian than Aristotelian, their vision is grounded in the ideals of democracy; they believe in art for people's sake, as one of their most respected poets, Don L. Lee, has so aptly put it; and they argue for cultural freedom as opposed to cultural imperialism.

Nothing could be farther from their minds than saving America from despotism of any kind; yet, in propounding the thesis of a Black Aesthetic, they offer an instrument as potent as that of the early American

writers who sought to break the domination of their
culture by Frenchmen, Englishmen and Germans. In
freeing American letters from Southern tyranny, in
advocating critical rules opposed to the antihuman-
istic ones of the disciples of the New Critics, in postu-
lating a literature which functions in the interest of all
mankind, this group of black writers may bring about
a revolution in American letters designed to usher in
a new freedom for all writers—white and black alike.

MY MAN HIMES

An Interview with Chester Himes

by John A. Williams

NEW YORK was chilly that Friday, disappointing after a couple of days of hot weather. Then spring had beat a hasty retreat. London the next day was London: chilly, gray and somber at Heathrow. Then we boarded a Trident, as tight and crowded a plane as the Caravelle, and split with a full passenger list, mostly all British except us, to Spain and Chester Himes.

Lori brightened considerably when we crossed the Pyrenees. (Once we had driven through them, back and forth from the Spanish to the French borders, pausing now and again to picnic in the hot green areas between the snow-filled slopes.) Not long after, the Mediterranean flowed out beneath us as the coast of eastern Spain bent to the west, and we prepared to land in Alicante.

It was clear, bright and warm there, and going down the ramp I was conscious once more of the strange sweetness that lingers in the Spanish air, as though the entire nation had been freshly dipped in sherry or cognac. Down on the tarmac we saw Chester and Lesley waving, and I felt great relief. For

Himes is sixty-one now and is not well, although he takes extremely good care of himself, mostly under Lesley's guidance. He smokes a great deal less, drinks mostly wine and adheres to a strict diet. Himes' life has been filled with so many disasters, large and small, that I lived in dread that one of these would carry him away so that I would no longer have the chance to see or talk to him.

I suppose it is known that I admire the man and his work. This began late in 1945, when I was a boy of twenty. I was then on Guam in the Mariana Islands with my outfit, the 17th Special Naval Construction Battalion, waiting to be shipped home. There was not much to do. The war was over; we were all waiting.

I was a hospital corpsman and we held two sick calls a day; otherwise we slept, swam or read. Mostly I read and tried to write the kind of jive poetry a twenty-year-old will write. I don't remember how the novel came into my hands, but I never forgot it. It was *If He Hollers Let Him Go*. The author was Chester B. Himes. Years later, long after it was published, I read *Third Generation*. Until 1962 that was the extent of my Himes.

That year I met Himes in Carl Van Vechten's apartment in the San Remo on Central Park West. I had met "Carlo" when *Night Song* was published in 1961. Van Vechten met, photographed, knew and corresponded with every black writer who ever came down the pike; now that I look back, perhaps he anticipated their importance in and to American letters fifty years before anyone else.

If anything, Himes was even more handsome than his photographs. Not terribly big, about five-nine or ten. One remembers his eyes mostly; they sit in that incredible face upon which ravages show—but which they have been unable to destroy—and at certain angles the long-lashed eyes are soft, *soft*, as though clinging to some teen-aged dream of love and goodness and justice. The eyes have remained that way, although today, at certain other angles they clearly reveal the pain of life as a black man and artist.

Himes is perhaps the single greatest naturalistic American writer living today. Of course, no one in the literary establishment is going to admit that; they haven't and they won't. Reviews of his books generally wind up in the last half of the Sunday *New York Times Book Review*, if they are reviewed at all. Himes will tell you that he doesn't care; that all his career he has been shuffled under the table. Perhaps this is, after all, the smallest of hurts he has suffered. He is a fiercely independent man and has been known to terminate friendships and conversations alike with two well-chosen, one syllable words. Worse than the words is his silence. I swear I have felt him glowering at me across the Atlantic from Paris at times.

Soon after I met Himes for the first time, Van Vechten told me: "Chester doesn't like many people. He likes you."

Well, I liked him. We corresponded regularly after our meeting; we exchanged books and he gave me a quote for *Sissie*; as I recall, it wasn't used. Himes was still publishing in France in the Gallimard *Série Noire*. Although he had won the Grand Prix for detective novels for *La Reine des Pommes* (*For Love of Immabelle*, it was called here) he was still living pretty much from hand to mouth. I managed to see him once in Paris, but most often I saw him here after he arrived on the *France*. He stays at the Hotel Albert on 10th Street and University Place when he comes. In Europe I missed him often enough, for he would move frequently to avoid having his work disturbed by other expatriate Brothers. Then he would undergo periodic fits of disgust with the Parisians and go to Scandinavia or Holland. Sometimes, through Daniel Guérin ("The French expert on the Brother," Himes says), he went to La Ciotat near the Riviera to be isolated and to work. (La Ciotat, Himes says with the pride of association, is where André Schwarz-Bart wrote *The Last of the Just.*)

Chester Himes finally got a piece of what he deserves through the American publication of *Pinktoes.* He was back with an American publisher after almost a decade away from them. His detectives, Grave Digger Jones and Coffin Ed Smith, came back to America in hardcover after titillating (one of Himes' favorite words in describing the effect black people have on white people) the French for several years. The early novels of their adventures had been spirited away, more or less, by softcover publishers—often without Himes' knowing they were being published in America. He would write and ask me to confirm their presence, for word would have been brought to him by visitors to the Continent. That he was being paid little or no money for these rights only supported his contention that publishing was a brutal business and brutal businesses always take advantage of black people.

In both 1965 and 1966 we missed Himes in Europe; he had reserved a hotel for us in Paris and we were to have dinner, but he had fled France, leaving his flat to Melvin Van Peebles, the film-maker. We were to visit him in La Ciotat, but he'd packed up and taken off again. The next time we saw him was in 1967 when he and Lesley and their Siamese cat, Griot, flew to New York. That was when he started working on a film treatment of *Cotton Comes to Harlem* for Sam Goldwyn, Jr. (I read the screenplay by Ossie Davis and Arnold Perl while in Alicante and thought that if Davis as director could put on film what he has put on paper, the movie would be a very special thing.)

So, it was almost two years to the date when we saw them again in Alicante. Lesley had reserved for us around the corner from their small apartment. Lori and I unpacked, grabbed a couple hours of sleep,

then went around the corner to pick them up for dinner. Chester and Lesley lived on the ninth floor of
number 2 Calle Duque du Zaragoza, a step off Rambla
Mendez Muñoz, four short blocks from the Promenade
and the port.

With some writers you get the feeling that you are
interrupting their work; that they wish you to be gone,
out of their homes, out of their lives. I've never had
that feeling with Himes; he has always made me feel
welcome whether it was in the Albert, in the Quarter
in Paris (I repaid the hospitality that time by falling
asleep in front of the fire and holding up dinner) or in
Alicante. Besides, Himes deserved a break away from
his typewriter. He is always at it. If not books, then
letters; he has always been a compulsive letter writer.
(He once wrote a letter to President Roosevelt.) So I
was, I think, a welcome interruption.

While Lori and Lesley shopped (Lori has a thing
about Spanish eyeglasses, that never fit once we are
back home) Himes and I talked endlessly in the room
he uses as a study, in the living room with its balcony
that overlooks the city and the port, and on walks
down to and along the Promenade. There was never
a time when I dared to be without the recorder, for
out of Himes pours so much, at any time and at any
place.

He's slower getting about than he used to be, but
intellectually he is as sharp as ever and his opinions
as blunt and honest as always. I am always impressed by how well he has kept up with what's going
on in the United States. Most expatriate blacks I know
tend not to care. Not so Chester Himes; his information is as fresh as the morning paper. Another thing:
over the years he has repeated many anecdotes to
me. What amazes me is that they are always the
same. They are never embroidered or exaggerated.
They are exactly the same. Most of us, with the passage of time, tend to embellish.

Last fall Chester and Lesley moved into their new

home near Javea, still in Spain, still in the province of Alicante. We were to have seen it one day, but something came up so we were unable to make the trip.

It gave me the greatest pleasure to be able to see Himes again, to see him at a time when a kind of physical comfort was coming his way at last; to see him still producing long, articulate and sensitive works. He let me read the first volume of his auto-biography, *The Quality of Hurt* (394 pages, ending in 1955). It is a fantastic, masculine work whose pages are haunted by vistas of France and Spain, of family life in the United States, of his first marriage, of Richard Wright and Robert Graves and others. American male writers don't produce manly books. Himes' autobiography is that of a man. So we talked, and the sound of bronze churchbells filled the background, and the sweet smell of Spain blocked up our nostrils and my man Himes rapped . . .

THIS PUBLISHING BUSINESS

Williams: How do you feel about the double standard of payment, say, advances—this amount for black writers and that amount for white writers?

Himes: It's pitiful, you know, it's really pitiful, pitiful. You know, the double standard of advances is so pitiful. Even friends took advantage. . . . I got a thousand dollar advance for each of my last three books.

Williams: Really?

Himes: Yes. And they resold them to Dell for $15,000 reprint.

Williams: Each?

Himes: Yeah, and then in the end they didn't want *Blind Man* [*Blind Man with a Pistol*] and I thought—

Williams: Goddamn! Are you kidding me?

Himes: I'm telling you the truth. You know, I have never been paid anything in advance. I'm the lowest-paid writer on the face of the earth. So . . .

Williams: Now wait a minute, Chester, people have known you since the forties. They know everything that you produced and they offered you a thousand-dollar advance for each of these three books?

Himes: Oh, yes, that's what they paid, a thousand-dollar advance.

Williams: Goddamn!

Himes: You talk about double standards. I find this quite annoying. Y'know, I have been in desperate circumstances financially, which everybody has known and they've just taken advantage of this—friends and enemies and everybody alike. I remember in *The Third Generation*; I was paid a two thousand-dollar advance and they resold the reprint rights to Victor Weybright of NAL for ten thousand dollars, and that's the money I came to Europe on. But then when I got broke in Europe and I had to spend a year's time helping ——, the woman I was living with at the time, write a book of her own which never made a cent . . .

Williams: That was the book you said was much better than the Caldwell-type books—*The Silver Chalice?*

Himes: *The Silver Altar.* I have it in my autobiography. You can read it if you like.

Williams: Can I take it and read it tonight?

Himes: Sure, you can read it tonight or you can take it back to New York as far as I'm concerned. [Laughter.] I have two copies. I think if you want to do any background on me, some of the things you should know you'll find in it. But going back to the payment, you see. Now, I couldn't find a publisher for *The Primitive.* I was very broke and desperate for some money, and I finally thought that I would send it to Weybright because they had begun to publish originals. So I sent it to Weybright, and Weybright wrote me this long letter about how we'll pay you a thousand-dollar advance on this because we feel it's best for the author to have a small advance and have substantial accruals [laughter]. I'll never forget that phrase. I never got any accruals, substantial or otherwise, from that book [laughter], until five or six years later they brought out a new edition for which they paid a fifteen-hundred-dollar advance. That's why I began writing these detective stories, as a matter of fact. Marcel Duhamel, the editor of the *Série Noire*, had translated *If He Hollers Let Him Go*. The *Série Noire* was the best-paid series in France. So they started off paying me a thousand-dollar advance, which was the same as the Americans were paying, and they went up to fifteen hundred dollars, which was more.

Double standards are so pitiful. Well, as I said, the American system toward the Negro writer is to take great advantage of the fact that the black writer in America is always in a state of need, and they take great advantage of that need. They take advantage just willy-nilly. Then one or two will get through. Not one or two—I mean, the American system works like this: *Time* magazine and a few other sources and the *New York Times* and all feel that they'd like to be king-makers of a writer and they put him in a position so that he can earn some money, like Baldwin. Now Baldwin got into a position where he could command sizeable advances and royalties. But the average black writer is never paid in comparison to the white writer.

Williams: What is the most you ever made on an advance of a book?

Himes: Morrow, I suppose. Morrow paid four thousand five hundred advance, which was just for *Blind Man with a Pistol* . . . No—that's right, Putnam paid a ten thousand-dollar advance for *Pinktoes*. Walter Minton was buying up Girodias' [Olympia

Press] books. He had been successful with *Lolita* and *Candy* and he was anxious to get *Pinktoes*. Stein & Day had offered me seventy-five hundred, so Minton upped it twenty-five hundred. And then Stein & Day and Putnam started a lawsuit against one another, and that's why they published it jointly. They figured it'd be more expensive to go to court so they just decided that they would work out a system, a very elaborate one, so elaborate that I ran into difficulties with Stein & Day because—Putnam kept the trade book edition, they were responsible for that and for collecting my royalties—Stein & Day were responsible for the subsidiary rights and the reprint and foreign rights and so forth. And finally Stein & Day began rejecting various offers from foreign countries. The last one—the one that really made me angry—was that they had an offer from a German publisher to bring out a German edition of *Pinktoes* and Stein & Day rejected that, and I went to the Author's Guild and to the lawyers to see what I could do. And they said that that was the most complicated contract they had ever seen. Even now, even a couple of weeks ago I wrote to Walter Minton to find out what happened to my royalties because Corgi Books brought out a paperback edition in England which has seemingly been very successful. I know that they have reprinted the jacket design so I figure they must have sold quite a number in the first design to have brought out a different one.

Williams: Well, you know the younger black writers back home always say that Chester Himes has given away more books than most people have ever written.

Himes: Yeah, that's right. I must tell you the truth. You know that the younger generation of black writers are getting paid far more than I'm getting paid, even now. Even now I get paid so little. I just got disgusted with the whole business.

Actually, I have a good agent now. Rosalyn [Targ] for me is a very good agent because she will fight for whatever she can get, you know. And she tries everything she can.

Williams: How about some of the experiences, other than royalties, that you've had with publishers? You once wrote me something about an award you were supposed to get at Doubleday when Buck Moon was your editor.

Himes: Yes, well you know, *If He Hollers* sold I think it was eight thousand copies before publication. That was Doubleday. Well, then *If He Hollers* hit the best-seller list. Then I received a number of letters from all over the country. I'd been in Los Angeles and San Francisco—one brother was living in Cincinnati, one was down in Durham, North Carolina, teaching at the North Carolina College—and I received letters from all of these people and other people whom I'd forgotten, that they'd been in stores to buy copies of *If He Hollers* and they had been told that book stores had sold out, and had ordered copies, and the orders were not being filled.

Williams: That's something that happens to me all the time, too.

Himes: So I went to Doubleday and complained and said the same thing and showed them the letters, and at that time Doubleday was being run by five vice-presidents. I think about a month afterward Ken Mc-Cormick was promoted to editor-in-chief, and he was in control of Doubleday. He became the top vice-president, or maybe he was the president. So I talked to him. He said my complaint didn't make any sense because if they published a book they were going to sell it. I couldn't argue with this. But it got to be rather dirty. Doubleday was in the *Time* and *Life* building on 49th Street at that time and I was going up in the elevator with Hilda Simms and her husband and a joker who was doing free-lance promoting for Doubleday, and I was telling them that the book orders weren't being filled and this joker rushed in and told Ken McCormick that I was complaining about Doubleday. So I got in Ken's office and we had some bad words, you know. I said to Ken McCormick, "You know that you got this black corner here . . ." He said, "No, we haven't. It's not a black corner," and I said, "You got Bucklin Moon, he's the head of the black department in Doubleday." So then I didn't get any more information from Doubleday concerning anything. So, I think seven years later when I was living with Vandi [Haygood], Buck stopped by one day and Vandi was in the kitchen making some drinks, and Buck said that I was right about the whole thing, but he had felt it would do me more harm to tell me the truth than to let me remain in ignorance. That what had happened was Doubleday was giving an award called the George Washington Carver Memorial Award of twenty-five hundred dollars each year for the best book. And that year Doubleday had *If He Hollers*, the outstanding book on the black theme that they had published. But there was one white woman editor whose name was never told to me, who said that *If He Hollers* made her disgusted and it made her sick and nauseated, and if *If He Hollers* was selected for this memorial award that she would resign. They gave the award to a book called *Mrs. Palmer's Honey*, written by some white woman. It was about a Negro maid in St. Louis.

When Doubleday advertised *Mrs. Palmer's Honey* in the *Saturday Review*, they said this book has a nice story that will appeal to a lot of people and it was not like some other books that they had published, and they referred, but not by actual name, to *If He Hollers Let Him Go*, and called it a "series of epithets punctuated by spit." This was their own advertisement. I complained about this, too. But what had actually happened to *If He Hollers* was that this woman editor—Doubleday was printing their own books in Garden City—had telephoned to their printing department in Garden City and ordered them to stop the printing. So they just arbitrarily stopped the printing of *If He Hollers* for a couple of weeks or so during the time when it would have been a solid best-seller.

Williams: You were at Knopf too, for a while. *Lonely Crusade* was a Knopf book, wasn't it?

Himes: Yes, well, that's why I went to Knopf. I went to Knopf because of this. I was talking to Van Vechten, whom I had met, and . . .

Williams: You met Van Vechten after *If He Hollers* came out, which would be late '45 or '46.

Himes: That's right. Richard Wright had taken me over to meet him. Dick was going over to get his picture taken. And when Van Vechten was taking his picture he acted so pompous I got hysterical and I was sitting there laughing away and Van Vechten was peeping at me and . . . So he was intrigued with me and we became quite good friends because of that. But Dick was a real friend despite his eccentricities. He had reviewed *If He Hollers Let Him Go* in *PM*, a good review, and took me over to the Book-of-the-Month Club. Well, *If He Hollers* was being distributed by the Book-of-the-Month Club. So when I told Van Vechten that I was unhappy at Doubleday he said that he would talk to Blanche Knopf and she would buy my contract from Doubleday. So she bought the contract ultimately. It wasn't a very large sum because Doubleday had only given me a thousand-dollar advance for my next book, and then I went on and wrote *Lonely Crusade*, which she liked very much indeed. I'd say she liked that book as much as any book she ever published. She gave it a very good printing, very nice—you've seen copies of the book, haven't you?

Williams: Oh, sure, sure.

Himes: Very nice book, and she lined up a lot of radio appearances for me. I don't remember all of them now—Mary Margaret McBride, CBS book shows —and I was to talk to the book department at Macy's and Bloomingdale's on the day of publication. So I

sent for my father to come to New York from Cleveland and I went out early that morning to go to
Macy's and this joker down at Macy's—the head of
the book department—was looking guilty and said,
"Well, we're going to stop this procedure of having
authors speak to the book sellers because they would
show favoritism since we couldn't do it for all the
authors." So they canceled the whole thing. So then
I went over to Bloomingdale's and at Bloomingdale's
there were no books, no *Lonely Crusade* on display
whatsoever. So I realized that something had happened. The director of Bloomingdale's book department didn't want to talk to me at all. So then I rushed
home to get my wife and go to the Mary McBride
radio program but she said she'd been trying to get
in touch with me because they had received a telegram from the radio that I'd been canceled off that
program. And then before the day was over, they
canceled me off the CBS program. Then I learned that
the Communist Party had launched a real assault on
the book.

It had some of the most terrible reviews, one of the
most vicious reviews I ever read. The *Daily Worker*
had a picture of a black man walking across the page
carrying a white flag—catch the caption: "Himes Carries a White Flag." In some of the passages they had
they compared the book to the "foul words that came
from the cankerous mouth of Bilbo" [Sen., D., Miss.],
and so forth.
Williams: Didn't you tell me once that Jimmy Baldwin
did a review too?
Himes: Jimmy Baldwin did a review for the Socialist
newspaper, *New Leader* I believe, under the heading
"History as a Nightmare." I don't remember the gist
of the review. But all of the reviews I remember seeing were extremely critical, each for a different reason: *Atlantic Monthly, Newsweek, Commentary, New
Masses*—the white press, the black press, the Jewish
press, reactionary press—*all*. Willard Motley, whom

I had met at a party given for the publication of *Knock on Any Door* at Carl Van Vechten's house, wrote an extremely spiteful review for the Marshall Field newspaper in Chicago.

Williams: Was that the only book that Knopf did for you?

Himes: Yes. Knopf had given me an advance for another book, but then they . . . I had trouble with Knopf too. I tried to have some kind of dialogue with Blanche to discuss some of these reactions. I said, "Now, you have all of these reviews from *Atlantic Monthly, Commentary, New Masses,* the *New York Times,* the *Herald Tribune,* and *Ebony,* the black press. All of these reviews have different complaints about this book, different ways of condemning it. Well, this doesn't make any sense, and these reviews should all be published in an advertisement showing that all of these people from the left, the right, the blacks, the whites, that if all of these people dislike the book there must be some reason. It would stimulate interest; people would want to know why. Because I never found out why everybody disliked this book."

But I know why the black people disliked the book —because they're doing the same thing now that I said at that time was necessary. I had the black protagonist, Lee Gordon, a CIO organizer, say that the black man in America needed more than just a superficial state of equality; he needed special consideration because he was so far behind. That you can't just throw him out there and say, "Give Negroes rights," because it wouldn't work that way. And so this is what most of the black writers had against it; in saying that, of course, by pleading for special privileges for the black people I was calling them inferior.

Williams: And now that's the route that everyone is going.

Himes: Yes.

Williams: Except that they're not saying it. I think a few years ago they were saying it, but now it seems to me that what the kids are saying on the campuses is . . .

Himes: Yes, that's what they're saying, that's what I'm saying. It's the same theme because it's obvious, you know, that the black man in America must have, for an interim period of time, special consideration.

Williams: What about your experiences with editors?

Himes: Well, as a rule, the whole of my experiences has been bad. Over a long period of years the editor whom I got along with best as an editor was Marcel Duhamel, the editor of *Série Noire,* because he was a friend, but more than being a friend he was an honest man, which is very rare among editors. He was honest and straightforward, although he was surrounded by a bunch of dubious people at Gallimard. But he did as much as he could. A journalist from *Combat* once said, "You know, Marcel is a good man, but Marcel is a three-legged duck as far as Gallimard is concerned." I always remembered that. They never really included him until later years. *Série Noire* became so successful that he became a capitalist.

Williams: You know, over the years in many conversations we've had I get the impression that, well, it's more than an impression now, you never found much difference between American and French publishers and editors.

Himes: No, no, I didn't, because the only difference— it goes like this: the French don't have the difficulty that Americans do because most black people that come to France realize that they are from the undeveloped countries and they keep their place. And very few of them feel any injustice when they're not given the same accord as the French writer. They don't feel that this is unjust.

The American black man is very different from all

those black men in the history of the world because the American black has even an unconscious feeling that he wants equality. Whereas most of the blacks of the world don't particularly insist on having equality in the white community. But the American black doesn't have any other community. America, which wants to be a white community, is their community, and there is not the fact that they can go home to their own community and be the chief and sons of chiefs or what not.

Williams: That old lie again, huh?

Himes: [Laughter.] Yeah. The American black man has to make it or lose it in America; he has no choice. That's why I wrote *Cotton Comes to Harlem*. In Garvey's time the "Back to Africa" movement had an appeal and probably made some sense. But it doesn't make any sense now. It probably didn't make sense even then, but it's even *less* logical now, because the black people of America aren't Africans anymore, and the Africans don't want them.

Williams: Yes, I found this to be true.

Himes: Yes, they wouldn't have him in their world, so he has to make it in America.

Williams: You were saying that New American Library once gave you a contract with sixteen pages.

Himes: Yes. Well, I was in Paris, and like George Orwell's book I was down and out in Paris and I had submitted this book, *The Primitive*, to Gallimard. But I was in a hurry and Gallimard was taking their time, so I sent it to NAL. So NAL took it and at the same time they took all of the rights, took every right worth considering, and they sent me a sixteen-page contract to sign. So Gallimard had to buy the book from NAL. What they paid for it I never discovered. I don't remember if anyone ever paid me for that. So at that time I realized that contracts were getting much more intricate than they had been previously, much more detailed. Publishers stipulated their rights. Of course, then publishing was getting to be a big business. The artists who could command a lot of money—and who could command a lot of attention, I should say, from publishers—were also getting more rights, so they could keep their subsidiary rights, even their paper-back rights.

Williams: I think there's a move in the direction to recapture these rights for the writers once more. It's going kind of slowly. There're some writers whom I've heard about who manage to keep their subsidiary rights, or most of them, like the reprint rights. I understand Robbins is one of these guys.

Himes: Yes, that's right. The first one who I heard of who was able to keep his subsidiary rights (I heard about but probably a lot of them did before) was Wouk, when he wrote *Marjorie Morningstar*. Well, you see, that's a considerable amount of money. You take a writer like Jean Le Carré. I don't know what Putnam paid him for the advance for the book rights, although Putnam did very well with the book, but Putnam sold the reprint rights for I think twenty-five or thirty thousand dollars, and then Dell, on the first three months of publication of *The Spy Who Came in from the Cold* made three million dollars. So that's a considerable amount of money involved.

Williams: I recall that Lillian Ross story about Ernest Hemingway that appeared in *The New Yorker*, where he got a twenty-five-thousand-dollar advance from Scribner's. And now these guys are getting like a quarter of a million. What do you think about that? People like Roth and . . .

Himes: Yes, I read that piece. Well, the industry has gotten to the place where they make considerably more money out of, say, Roth's book [*Portnoy's Complaint*]. They'll make more money out of Roth's book probably than the American publishers have out of all of Hemingway, because the industry is so much bigger. The whole process of circulation of books.

There's so much advance. You know, America is a very big book market, and I wonder if these people read these books. I suppose they do. But anyway, as long as they get something that will titillate them, they will read them.

I remember when the book industry was very much afraid of television. They thought that television would do damage to the book industry. It didn't make any difference whatsoever. As a matter of fact, the book industry is very healthy now from the point of view of profit systems.

Williams: Well, I think it's healthier now than it was ten years ago.

Himes: Yes, it's healthier now than it ever was.

Williams: Who's your favorite American publisher in terms of what it does for blacks, producing good books?

Himes: Well, I couldn't say. I don't know enough about American publishers to have an opinion. As far as publishers are concerned, in talking to other people, all publishers, Morrow has a very good reputation as a publisher with other publishers. Has a better reputation I think than Putnam. But as far as publishers are concerned, that is very difficult to say.

Williams: What was the print order for *Blind Man with a Pistol?*

Himes: I don't know. Once upon a time you could get the figures. I couldn't get these from Morrow. As a matter of fact, I haven't been in close contact with them at all.

PERSONAL WORKSHEET

Williams: Well, how would you place yourself in American letters? [Himes laughs.] You're sixty-one years old now, you've been writing long before *If He Hollers* came out— You've been writing now for thirty-four years.

Himes: Yes, I've been writing since 1934. Let's see, how long is that? My first story in a national magazine was published in *Esquire* in 1934. That's thirty-five years. Well, I don't know where to place myself actually on the American scene of letters because America has a highly organized system of reputation-making which I'm afraid would place me in the bottom echelon. The American communications media are very well organized about what they intend to do and how they intend to show that this person is of great importance and that person is chickenshit. So they work this out and they make reputations. Not only do they make reputations of writers, which is insignificant, but they take people like Roosevelt and they will set out systematically to break his place in history. They'll spend millions of dollars to do so if they wish. And the same thing happens with the literary scene. That's why I never contemplate it, because I realize the Americans will sit down and they will take a white writer—he will be one that appeals to their fancy, one that has been abroad and clowned around, like Hemingway—and they will set him up and they will make him one of the most famous writers on the face of the earth. And not because of anything he has written, because his work is not that important, but because they wish to have an American up there at the top of the world literature. Anyone reading him will realize that Hemingway is a great imitator of the styles of Ford Madox Ford, James Joyce and D. H. Lawrence. As a matter of fact, if you have read the works of these four writers, you can see the lines, you can see the exact imitation. So there's nothing creative about even Hemingway's form. This was borrowed, as Gertrude Stein says.

But the Americans set out and they made him a legend. Now, it's very difficult for me to evaluate any of the people on the American scene, because if I take my information from the American white communications media then, of course, it is slanted to whatever way they wish to slant it to. So one can't form any opinion, unfortunately.

Williams: Do you foresee the time when you'll ever quit writing?

Himes: Well, no, no I don't foresee it. I mean writing is like . . . I remember I have a line in a book—I've forgotten now what book it was—where I quote [Max] Schmeling. He said a fighter fights, and I went on to say ". . . and a writer writes." That's what I do, that's all I do, and I don't foresee that I will quit, as long as I'm able to write. No. I do foresee the fact that age will deteriorate my writing, as it does everyone else's writing. I don't foresee the fact that because age will deteriorate my writing, and that I will realize that I can't do what I could do when I was young (I know damn well that I can't do what I could do when I was young), that I am going to blow out my brains like Hemingway did when he discovered that.

Williams: It seemed to me when I started reading the first couple of pages of your autobiography, *The Quality of Hurt,* that you were sort of preparing yourself for the time when you wouldn't write any more. But then I also noticed that this is Volume I, the carbon that I have. How many volumes do you foresee in this autobiography?

Himes: I imagine there will just be another volume in which I will write about the change in my writing habits or change in my attitudes toward the entire American scene, and my change from pessimism to optimism. I became much less subject to the inroads of the various attitudes of people that I didn't particularly respect. I know that I will write another volume that will concern my beginning to write detective stories, and then my beginning to write the last ten or twelve books that I have written.

Williams: In one of your letters you said—and you've mentioned it since I've been here—that you were working on the bloodiest book that you have ever worked on, that you'd ever conceived, but you didn't expect (you said in this letter) to have it published in America, that it would be difficult to have published. Do you remember that?

Himes: Well, yes, because I can see what a black revolution would be like. Now, first of all, in order for a revolution to be effective, one of the things that it has to be, is violent, it has to be massively violent; it has to be as violent as the war in Vietnam. Of course, in any form of uprising, the major objective is to kill as many people as you can, by whatever means you can kill them, because the very fact of killing them and killing them in sufficient number is supposed to help you gain your objectives. It's the only reason why you do so.

Now, when you have resorted to these means, this is the last resort. Well, then, all dialogue ceases, all forms of petitions and other goddamned things are finished. All you do then is you kill as many people as you can, the black people kill as many of the people of the white community as they can kill. That means children, women, grown men, industrialists, street sweepers or whatever they are, as long as they're white. And this is the fact that gains its objective—there's no discussion—no point in doing anything else and no reason to give it any thought.

Now a soldier, if he would have to think about the morality of going out and killing the enemy, or if he had to consider his feelings about killing people, he would be finished. To do so, he would get court-martialed or shot on the scene. A soldier just goes out and kills; no one thinks anything about it; that's his objective. The objective for a foot soldier is to kill the enemy, and that's all. It's very simple. There's nothing else to be added to it or subtracted from it.

Well, that's what a revolution by the black people in America will be; that's their only objective. Their objective is not to stand up and talk to the white man and to stand him in front of a gun and say, "Now you did so and so to me"; the only objective is to blow out his brains without a word, you see. So I am trying to show how this follows, how the violence would be if the blacks resorted to this. Even individually, if you give one black one high-powered repeating rifle and he wanted to shoot it into a mob of twenty thousand or more white people, there are a number of people he could destroy. Now, in my book all of these blacks who shoot are destroyed. They not only are destroyed, they're blown apart; even the buildings they're shooting from are destroyed, and quite often the white community suffers fifty or more deaths itself by destroying this one black man. What I'm trying to do is depict the violence that is necessary so that the white community will also give it a little thought, because you know, they're going around playing these games. They haven't given any thought to what would happen if the black people would *seriously* uprise.

The white community gets very much upset about the riots, while the black people haven't seriously undertaken in advance to commit any great amount of violence; it's just been forced on them. What little violence they have done has actually been for protection; it's been defensive, you know. So what I would hope is to call to mind what *would* happen, what *should* happen, when the black people have an armed uprising, what white people should expect. It seems that the whites don't understand this.

Because one thing is sure—I have said this and I keep on saying it over and over again—the black man can bring America down, he can destroy America. The black man can destroy the United States. Now, there are sensible people in America who realize this, regardless of what they might think about the black man. The black man can destroy America completely, destroy it as a nation of any consequence. It can just fritter away in the world. It can be destroyed completely. Now I realize of course that the black man has no money, he has very little equipment to do this, he has very little fire power, he has lots of things against him, he hasn't been trained particularly. Even a Southern white cracker colonel . . . I remember a Southern white cracker colonel in the army in the Second World War got up and he made this famous speech about the black people, saying, "You have never been taught to use violence and you have never been taught to be courageous, but war calls for these things and you must learn them." Well, he's right. That's the most right thing he ever said.

Williams: Do you think the publishers will be . . .

Himes: I don't think . . . I don't know what the American publishers will do about this book. But one thing I do know, Johnny, they will hesitate, and it will cause them a great amount of revulsion, because the scenes that I have described will be revolting scenes. There are very few war books written that have ever described actual scenes of war, 'cause in war people are killed and blown to pieces, and all. Even when they just say "blown to pieces" that doesn't describe what they *look* like blown to pieces. When a shell hits a man in a war, bits of him fly around, half of his liver is flying through the air, and his brains are dribbling off. These are actual scenes, no one states these outright.

Williams: How do you think the majority of white readers react to your books and other books by black writers?

Himes: The white readers read into a book what they wish, and in any book concerning the black people in the world, the majority of white readers are just looking for the exotic episodes. They're looking for things that will amuse or titillate them. The rest of it they skip over and pay no attention to. That was one of the remarkable things about Richard Wright's autobiography—that the white community was willing to read his suffering and poverty as a black man. But it didn't move them, didn't move them one bit. They just read it and said, "Tsk, tsk, isn't it awful?"

Williams: Well, you know, I sometimes have the feeling that when they read books like that, they say to themselves, "Boy, ain't we a bitch! Look what we're doing to them people."

Himes: [Laughs.] Yeah, something like that. They're thinking along those lines; certainly they're not thinking in the ways you'd like for them to think. That's one of the saddest parts about the black man in America—that he is being used to titillate the emotions of the white community in various aspects. Now I couldn't say exactly how he titillates them, but in any case it's titillation in a way that's not serious. America is a masochistic society anyway, so they probably just like being given a little whipping, enough to get a feeling out of it, a sensation, but not enough for them to be moved. I want these people just to take me seriously. I don't care if they think I'm a barbarian, a savage, or what they think; just think I'm a serious savage.

Williams: There's a rash of books, I hear (I haven't read them)—detective books—in which there are black detectives, and of course one of these books was made into a movie with Poitier, *In the Heat of the Night.* Do you feel that these people are sort of swiping your ideas?

Himes: No, no. It's a wonder to me why they haven't written about black detectives many years ago. It's a form, you know, and it's a particularly American form. My French editor says, the Americans have a style of writing detective stories that no one has been able to imitate, and that's why he has made his *Série Noire* successful, by using American detective story writers. There's no reason why the black American, who is also an American, like all other Americans, and brought up in this sphere of violence which is the main sphere of American detective stories, there's no reason why he shouldn't write them. It's just plain and simple violence in narrative form, you know. 'Cause no one, *no one*, writes about violence the way that Americans do.

As a matter of fact, for the simple reason that no one understands violence or experiences violence like the American civilians do. The only other people in the white community who are violent enough for it are the armed forces of all the countries. But of course they don't write about it because if the atrocities were written about the armies of the English and the French in Africa, they would make among the most grisly stories in the history of the world. But they're not going to write about them. These things are secret; they'll never state them.

American violence is public life, it's a public way of life, it became a form, a detective story form. So I would think that any number of black writers should go into the detective story form. As a matter of fact, I feel that they could be very competent. Anyway, I would like to see a lot of them do so. They would not be imitating me because when I went into it, into the detective story field, I was just imitating all the other American detective story writers, other than the fact that I introduced various new angles which were my own. But on the whole, I mean the detective story originally in the plain narrative form—straightforward violence—is an American product. So I haven't created anything whatsoever; I just made the faces black, that's all.

Williams: You know, I'm always amazed when I read your books. Here you've been out of the country for twenty years, but I'm always amazed at your memory of things and how accurate you are in details, like the guns that the cops use. In rereading the screenplay last night, there was the business of the drop slot in the car. How do you come by all this knowledge?

Himes: Well, some of it comes from memory; and then I began writing these series because I realized that I was a black American, and there's no way of escaping forty some odd years of experience, so I would put it to use in writing, which I have been doing anyway. I had always thought that the major mistake in Richard Wright's life was to become a world writer on world events. I thought that he should have stuck to the black scene in America because he wouldn't have had to live there—he had the memory, so he was still there, but it was subconsciously, which he discovered when he went back to write *The Long Dream* and the sequel (which was never published, I don't think).

Well, then, I went back—as a matter of fact, it's like a sort of pure homesickness—I went back, I was very happy, I was living there, and it's true. I began creating also all the black scenes of my memory and my actual knowledge. I was very happy writing these detective stories, especially the first one, when I began it. I wrote those stories with more pleasure than I wrote any of the other stories. And then when I got to the end and started my detective shooting at some white people, I was the happiest.

HARLEM RENAISSANCE

Williams: Chester, how about the Harlem Renaissance? You were just arriving in New York when it was . . .

Himes: It was on the wane when I got there. I knew a lot of people involved in it. There was Bud Fisher . . .

Williams: He was a doctor or a radiologist, wasn't he?

Himes: I don't know what Bud Fisher was. I only know he was a writer. And there was a young man whose name I should know, I think he wrote *The Blacker the Berry, the Sweeter the Juice.*

Williams: Was that Braithwaite?

Himes: No, Wallace Thurman, I think. He went to Hollywood and he was one of the most successful black people writing out in Hollywood. He did very well on the Hollywood scene at that time.

Williams: How would you evaluate the Harlem Renaissance?

Himes: Well, I think it was one of the greatest movements among black writers that existed up to then.

Williams: But then Hollywood wasn't interested.

Himes: No, Hollywood had no interest in the black writer, but the black writers like Claude McKay and Countee Cullen and all, produced things of substantial consequence, and so as a group, the writers of the Black Renaissance produced works that were encouraging; it encouraged all black writers.

Now, the way I look at it, the next movement of any consequence was when Richard Wright hit the scene. Nothing happened between the end of the Renaissance and the time Richard Wright came on the scene. I always had a great respect for Richard Wright because of the fact that I believe that his first works, *Uncle Tom's Children, Native Son* and *Black Boy*, opened up certain fields in the publishing industry for the black writer, more so than anything else that had happened. The Black Renaissance was an inward movement; it encouraged people who were familiar with it, who knew about it and were in contact with it, but the legend of Richard Wright reached people all over.

Williams: Well, he hit it about the same time you did.

Himes: Yes, that's quite true, but his name was taken to the masses, and that is what is important.

Williams: I somehow had got the impression from something that you had said that they didn't think that much of him.

Himes: No, I didn't say they didn't think much of him. I said that Wright's works themselves did not make any great impression on the white community, although they read them. As a writer, he made an impression on the publishing world. Although the white community read his works and gave a per-

formance of being moved and touched and so forth,
it didn't mean a damn thing to them—they just shed
it. It's unfortunate but it's quite true.

A few white people around were considerably
shocked by some of it, but I remember in Cleveland
—I think it was with *Uncle Tom's Children*; no, it was
Native Son, which was published about 1939 or early
1940—I remember various white people expressing
amazement at being told that black people hated
them. But these people were people of no consequence. I'd like to talk a little bit about Langston
Hughes. When I came out of prison I met Langston.
He was in Cleveland; he didn't live too far from
where I was; he was living with his aunt. He was
writing plays for Karamou House. As a matter of fact,
it was through Langston that I met the Jellifes; through
the Jellifes I met Louis Bromfield, and that's how I
went to Hollywood. But most of his plays were produced first at Karamou before they were produced
in New York. And Langston stayed there a great deal.
He lived there, as a matter of fact, and only visited
New York. It was some time before he moved to
New York.

Williams: Well, he's gone now. Tell me, when did you
first meet Carl Van Vechten?

Himes: The year that *If He Hollers* was published. I
knew very little about him, other than the legend. He
was only connected in my mind (until I met him) with
Nigger Heaven, which I think was his most successful
book. Although when he published *Nigger Heaven*
he was on very good terms with most of the writers
of the Black Renaissance, but after he wrote it they
practically never spoke to him again. He told me,
"Countee Cullen never said another word to me."

George Schuyler was also in this group. I knew him,
and Philippa Schuyler [killed in a helicopter crash in
Vietnam in 1967] when she was a little girl. She used
to go down to Van Vechten's.

Williams: But Schuyler became terribly, terribly right-wing.

Himes: Yes, well Schuyler was a man whose life was plotted like Pegler's. He is a man who wants to say strong things, individual things and all, and he makes some statements which are contradictory, which Pegler did all his life. Pegler contradicted himself so much that he wound up, I suppose in an insane asylum, or wherever he is now . . . [Editor's note: Westbrook Pegler died in June 1969.]

HOLLYWOOD

Williams: Hoyt Fuller [Editor, *Negro Digest*] mentioned your *Cotton Comes to Harlem.* How do you feel about that? With Ossie Davis directing the film and all. Are you pleased with it?

Himes: Well, I was talking with Sam Goldwyn, Jr. and he agreed with me that he wanted Ossie Davis in it whether he directed it or not. He had this Arnold Perl, a Hollywood screenwriter, write the first version of it. First he had a young man, whose name I've forgotten, who did a version. Then I wrote a version, a quickie, about a hundred and thirty pages, which he paid me practically nothing for. Sam Goldwyn, Jr. is a nice man to talk to, but he doesn't say anything about money.

Williams: You were working on it, then, the last time we saw you in New York.

Himes: Yes, that's right. Then Goldwyn couldn't use it, which I knew would be the case, because I'm not a screenwriter. But I told him that in advance. I said, "Now listen, you need to get a professional." He said he had sounded out LeRoi Jones, for whom he had great admiration as a playwright. As a matter of fact, he had extreme admiration for him as an artist, for his sharp scenes. He said that he had taken many screen-writers and producers to see LeRoi's plays when they

were showing in Los Angeles, and he contacted LeRoi.
LeRoi said it was a matter of money; what LeRoi
wanted was for Goldwyn to pay him in advance (I
don't know how much it was). Anyway, he would
undertake to write the screenplay and he would do
as many revisions as were required, and then he
would get a second payment. And Goldwyn said it
didn't work that way—which was a damned lie.

Williams: Of course it is.

Himes: Anyway, the reason he didn't get along with
LeRoi was because LeRoi wanted to be paid like the
Hollywood writers—

Williams: Like the white writers.

Himes: —and Goldwyn didn't want to do that, so that
was that.

Williams: Are you pleased with the present screenplay of *Cotton Comes to Harlem*?

Himes: Well, no one could be pleased with that. But
I don't know enough about screenplays to know what
it'll be like when it's finished.

Williams: That's true. But in terms of what you see on
the paper . . .

Himes: Well, it's not as bad as it was. It's much improved. Ossie Davis improved it considerably over
the Perl version . . . And he has some good things
in it.

Williams: He's updated it a little, with the militants
and . . .

Himes: Yes, he has a black orientation, which I like.
That's what I told Sam Goldwyn, Jr. That's what I
like best about Ossie Davis' treatment of it. He took
the Perl treatment, which had some stuff in there that
was really offensive. The treatment of the blacks in
there was so offensive . . . You know, some of the
Jewish writers, because of the fact that they belong
to a minority too, can get more offensive than other
writers do.

Williams: They mistake closeness for familiarity.

Himes: What I dislike most about the screenplay—

and I told Goldwyn—it's a good story, but it's a story about Deke, and the main purpose of Goldwyn is to make a series of movies of Coffin Ed Smith and Grave-digger Jones; he wants to keep them alive. But if this is the purpose of the first movie, they are dead because they are of no consequence in the movie. He has to bring them out stronger if he wants to keep them. What you have now is a movie of a swindler, which is a good movie. But it's about Deke; Deke is the character in this movie. As a matter of fact, in Ossie Davis' treatment he comes through very fine; he comes through as a real solid character.

Williams: I started reading it. I got about a quarter of the way through just since we left you, and it recalled the book for me, which I guess is good. As you say, the difference between the printed page and what they put on the film can be—

Himes: Oh, yes, I will give them credit; they have stayed closer to the book than the usual Hollywood treatment of a book, because as a rule Hollywood lets it go altogether. It was to Hollywood's advantage to keep the story in this book because they couldn't improve on it. If they're going to depart from the story altogether, then it would deteriorate and I'm not a big enough name to carry it. Like Hollywood buys a lot of name writers and they do what they want to because the name of the writer is sufficient. The treatment of the book doesn't make any difference. But Hollywood is a strange business; don't get me talking about Hollywood.

Williams: Well, talk about it.

Himes: I went out to Hollywood because I had been working on Louis Bromfield's farm in Malabar, and he read my first version of my prison story. He became excited about it and said he'd like to see it get submitted to the movies. So Bromfield was going to Hollywood to work on a screen adaptation of Hemingway's *For Whom the Bell Tolls.* They paid him five thousand dollars a week, but finally they just threw

his version away and they got a screenwriter to write
the movie version. But he took my book out there and
he gave it to some producers and I followed him. I
was trying to get work. And then I went to the shipyards in San Francisco.

Williams: Were you aware at this time—or did you
have the feeling—that your work would probably out-
last Bromfield's?

Himes: No, it never occurred to me at all. But I didn't
think that Bromfield's work was substantial enough to
last. It didn't occur to me that Bromfield had been
very successful then with *The Rains Came.* He was
making quite a bit of money at that time. This was in
the late thirties or 1940, and writers like Bromfield
were getting that large money from the serialization
in magazines. They were not so much concerned
with things like book clubs or reprints and so forth.
But the magazine serializations: *Cosmopolitan* was
paying Bromfield seventy-five thousand dollars for
the serialization of the book. Anyway, I went out to
Hollywood—Los Angeles—where I met Hall Johnson
and a number of other black people on the fringes
of the movie industry. As a matter of fact, Langston
Hughes gave me a list of names of people to see when
I went out there. Most of them were connected with
the Communist Party. I saw these people and then I
got involved also with the communists out there. Politically I was never intrigued by communism. Communism was very strong in the States, in Hollywood
particularly. —— was out there; he was the dean of
the communists. Great numbers of stars and producers
and directors were fellow travelers, at least. There
were two young men, black men, who had been in
the Abraham Lincoln Brigade in Spain. —— was
the one I knew. I forgot the other's name, but his
brother had been wounded and he was quite a celebrity among the Communist Party there. But anyway,
the Communist Party was collecting old clothes, which

they sold and then sent the proceeds to a refugee camp for Spaniards from the Spanish Civil War in Mexico. I would go around with——in his truck to pick up these clothes and various stuff. And we would drive up to many, many big Hollywood estates, of producers and various people (I wish I could recall the names) and they'd come out and set us up a few drinks in the kitchen.

Williams: In the kitchen! But you were supposed to be a part of them, right?

Himes: Yes, but this was their home; it didn't mean we got out of the kitchen! [Laughter.] I swear to God, my material for writing *Lonely Crusade* came from these experiences. I met these people. And the CIO union there was beginning to print a newspaper. At the same time I had been considered for a place on the staff. But, you see, the communists were also playing a game. They wanted people like me to help break the color line. I was a tool; they wanted to send me to thousands of places that had no intention of employing blacks at that time because Los Angeles was a very prejudiced place and the only jobs black people had were in the kitchens in Hollywood and Beverly Hills.

Williams: But they liked them; that was a status job.

Himes: Yes, but the point of it was the Negro ghetto at that time was not Watts but Central Avenue from 12th to about 40th, I guess. And you know, they didn't open those night clubs and restaurants on Central Avenue until Thursday.

Williams: Maid's day off.

Himes: Yeah, they were closed. Because, you know, some of Raymond Chandler's crap out there, he writes in *Farewell, My Lovely*, he has this joker ride about in the Central Avenue section. Some of that's very authentic—it was like that. A black man in Los Angeles, he was a servant. So there was nothing I could do out there and that's why I went to work in the shipyards. And then someone told me to come back to Los Angeles because they were filming *Cabin in the Sky*.

Williams: Oh, yes, the great all-Negro epic. [Laughter.]

Himes: That's right. And Hall Johnson was the technical director, getting twenty-five thousand dollars. They used his music, anyway. I don't know what he was—musical consultant or something. Anyway, he was being paid quite well. And I went back to Los Angeles, to MGM, because I had been told (I don't remember who had told me) to go out there and see a joker named Wheelwright, who was head of the publicity department, and I could probably get an assignment doing publicity. So I went out to get a job doing publicity for the Negro press, but they had already hired a young black man named Phil Carter. Well, when you go into MGM, just to the right of the entrance was the publicity department. And then you go in a little more and you come to what they called "Old Dressing Room Row"—a long string of old dressing rooms. Well, they had this young man named Carter to do the publicity for the black press in America. They gave him, for an office, one of the old dressing rooms, at the very end, as far as they could get from the publicity office.

I got on fairly good terms with the editors of *Collier's*. I felt I could get an assignment from them to do a *Collier's* profile on Lena Horne. But then one of *Collier's*' white writers, Kyle Crichton, decided he would do the story. It was one of Lena's first big publicity breaks.

Williams: You'd said something once about the black people in the cast—no matter how high up they were —and the extras . . .

Himes: Being jim-crowed in the "commissary"—the public diner. Yes, what had happened was that I had been out to MGM several times. But first, let me tell you this: One time Marc Connelly, who wrote *Green Pastures*, had a number of screenwriters, so-called intellectuals, and various others whom he had invited to a conference to discuss a film on George Washington Carver—along with two black faces for color, me and Arna Bontemps, I think.

Williams: The story of Stepin Fetchit. [Laughter.]

Himes: Marc Connelly was sitting at the head of the table with about twenty people sitting around, and he said, "Well, now I know how we're going to start this film; I know that much about it, and then we can go on from there. Well, you see, Dr. Carver was a very humble man and he always ironed his own shirts. So when we start this film on Dr. Carver, he goes into the kitchen and irons his shirt." So at that point I left.

At that time, they had black people out there for décor. They almost always had some black face out there. I was reading something recently in the paper about black technicians and various people who are beginning to break through out there, making it seem like a real advance, when actually so few, if any, technicians are employed by studios. But to get back to my story, later I made my efforts to get work in Hollywood. I met the head of the reading department, I suppose they call it, you know, where they have people read the novels and write a one-page synopsis, which is all producers ever read; they don't have time to read a book. So I was tried out by the young man who was head of this department at Warner Brothers. It was a job of no consequence. They were only offering something like forty-seven dollars a week to start, whereas you could make eighty-seven a week as a laborer. Anyway, he offered me the job and I was going to take it. I wrote the synopsis for *The Magic Bow*, a well-known book about Paganini, and submitted it. He said it was a good job and that they would employ me. And then—this is what *he* said: he was walking across the lot one day and he ran into Jack Warner and told him, "I have a new man, Mr. Warner, and I think he's going to work out very well indeed." Warner said, "That's fine, boy," and so forth. "Who is he?" And he said, "He's a young black man." And Warner said, "I don't want no niggers on this lot." [Laughter.]

But what I was going to tell you about *Cabin in the Sky* ... Well, in the commissary they had a sort of reserved section for people like producers and the like. Everybody ate at the commissary, and if people had a guest they would just bring them to the commissary. When they were making *Cabin in the Sky* they had this entire black personnel, and they wouldn't serve the blacks in the commissary at all. They couldn't go in there and get a piece of *bread*. And so, Lena Horne stopped Louis B. Mayer on the lot one day and told him that none of the cast of *Cabin in the Sky* were permitted to eat in the commissary; they had to bring their lunch. And then he made out like he was amazed. [Laughter.]

When you think about how things happen, then you get very discouraged about what the white community is doing.

BLACK ON WHITE

Williams: What about today's racial scene?

Himes: Nowadays, since twenty-five years have passed, my opinions have changed; because I don't believe the whites have any desire, any intention whatsoever, of accepting the Negro as an equal. I think the only way a Negro will ever get accepted as an equal is if he kills whites; to launch a violent uprising to the point where the people will become absolutely sickened, disgusted; to the place where they will realize that they have to do something. It's a calculated risk, you know, whether they would turn and try to exterminate the black man, which I don't think that they could do.

Williams: You don't think so?

Himes: I don't think the Americans have the capability, like the Germans, of exterminating six million. I don't think the American white man could. Morally, I don't think that he could do this; I don't think he has the capacity. Even to kill a hundred thousand blacks I think would disrupt America, actually ruin the country.

Williams: You're saying that *morally* the white man in America is unable to do what the Germans did?

Himes: Yes, he's unable to do it because it would destroy America. He doesn't want America to be destroyed, you see. I think that if he has to take the choice between giving the black man his rights or destroying the entire economic system in America, he'll give the black man equality. But that's the *only* reason he would do it now. Appeal to him—doesn't mean a thing. I think that he just has to be given a choice, because America is very vulnerable, you know. Armed uprisings by millions of blacks will destroy America. There's no question about it. There's not any question in the fact that the Americans can release enough power to destroy the blacks. Obviously the Americans could destroy North Vietnam and the whole people physically. It's not a question of whether they could destroy the blacks physically; it's the fact that they can't do it *morally*—and exist in the world. Because America exists in the world by a certain balance . . .

Williams: A sort of jive morality.

Himes: Yeah, a certain balance in more than just morality. It's just a certain balance in its relationship with other nations in the world, so that it cannot do this. It cannot destroy the black man. The black man in America doesn't realize this, or probably he doesn't act because he doesn't want to get killed; of course, life is precious. I can see why no one wants to get killed. But other countries realize the fact that the blacks have the power to destroy this necessary balance. When Israel first got its independence, you realized that Britain couldn't kill all the Jews that were in Israel, and the Jews were damn few in number compared to the blacks. Israel realized they couldn't kill them all, so Britain gave them independence.

Williams: Yes, but weren't those different times, though? Everyone was feeling guilty because of what had happened to the Jews in the camps?

Himes: Different times but the conditions now are the same—even more sensitive. Even America cannot afford to fall out, not only on account of the economic balance of the world, which is so sensitive; it cannot even afford to form any enmity with all the nations with whom it collaborates, even the small nations in South America. It's just an absolute fact that if the blacks in America were to mount a revolution in force, with organized violence to the saturation point, that the entire black problem would be solved. But that is the only way the black man can solve it. So the point is, that the white people are jiving the blacks in America by putting on this pretense of wanting the blacks to suggest how *they* can do this without submitting the white race to violence; whites want the blacks to find a solution where the blacks will keep themselves in a secondary state, which would satisfy the whites perfectly, because the whites themselves haven't been able to devise any way acceptable to the blacks.

Williams: It's quite a theory, and it's one I've not heard anyone discuss. I find that younger kids are all for insurrection and rebellion and rioting on an indiscriminate, unplanned, unorganized kind of thing. I discourage it.

Himes: Yes, well, I discourage that too because what that does—by means of the white communication media, the press and television and radio—is divide one group of the black race against the other group, and thus damage the progress the blacks are making.

Williams: How big a role do you think that book publishing has in all of this?

Himes: Well, the book publishers, first of all, are trying to exploit the black consciousness to sell books. As long as it titilates the whites, they will do so to sell books.

Williams: Except that there are some books that frighten them, like your book [*Lonely Crusade*] that they pulled off the stands.

Himes: Very few. And when they do, the white press kills them. White people in America, it seems to me, are titillated by the problem of the black people, more than taking it seriously. I want to see them take it seriously, good and goddamn seriously, and the only way that I think of to make them take it seriously is with violence. I don't think there's any other way. I see it on the faces of the whites around the world— the smirks, the sneaking grins and all this stuff; I realize they're not taking the blacks seriously. There are certain segments that are beginning to take them seriously, but they are so isolated and so unrelated to the entire problem. Like the uprisings in the colleges and the elementary schools. Of course, the white people realized the uprisings in the elementary schools [school decentralization] in New York created an extraordinary amount of resistance and enmity and animosity. But since that was in one small section they felt that they could contain it, put it down with force. But if the conflict had been enlarged to the place where every black man was out on the street popping down white people right and left, this might have achieved the black goals, as in the African countries. Africans killed the colonials and burned their flags. I remember the time in London when they thought of Kenyatta as being a black murderer of the most depraved kind. Well, then the Mau Mau killed enough of these Englishmen over there so that there was nothing else they could do but give Kenya independence.

Williams: That's kind of remarkable, because I think in total the Mau Mau killed maybe fifty-four or a hundred fifty-four whites and just hundreds of blacks, so that if you can kill a small number of whites, then the effect is . . .

Himes: Yes, now in black uprisings in America, blacks would have to kill considerable numbers of other blacks in order for it to move, because the whites will employ some of those blacks to speak up against uprisings. In addition to this, the white press will find enough blacks to publicize. When they do, they *know*, of course, that they are weakening the position of the black leaders. Take Stokely Carmichael, for instance. They give him enough publicity to realize that they are weakening his position so that in a period of time that will make him absolutely valueless.

Williams: In the black community.

Himes: Yes, in the black community. So they give him publicity to the saturation point, where his value in the black community is just dissipated. They devised that technique from handling Malcolm X. They figured that they would give Malcolm X the saturation of publicity so that eventually his effectiveness in the black community would be weakened. Of course, when you sit and look at it from a distance you realize exactly what they're doing, and I think part of the reason my relationship with the white community in America is so bad is the fact that they know that I know this. My relationship with the white community in America is as bad as a black man's could be. But what saves me is I'm not important.

Williams: Would you then agree that the amount of publicity that they gave Martin Luther King created the same reaction?

Himes: Yes, yes. Of course, absolutely.

Williams: Now, you knew Malcolm pretty well.

Himes: Well, I knew him, not very well. I met him in 1962, I guess. He told me he had read *If He Hollers Let Him Go.*

Williams: He used to visit you when you were on rue

Bourbon; well, how do you feel about his death? Most people feel that the government killed him.

Himes: Yes, well, personally I believe—and I will always believe this—that the CIA organized it and black gunmen shot him. Because it would take an organization, the way it was so perfectly planned and executed with certain methods that blacks don't generally use. It's the first time that I ever read of black gunmen employing gangster techniques from Chicago of the 1920's. And we know the CIA has employed these techniques before. So the way that it was so perfectly organized—that with all of the bodyguards that he had they were able to rise up there in that place and shoot, gun him down—it had their trademark on it. And then the fact that the Black Muslims had already threatened him gave the CIA a perfect, ready-made alibi. They were doing this in many countries until lately. They were doing this in the East, in Morocco and North Africa, all over. If one studied their techniques, one would realize that this very easily could have been done by the CIA. And since I'm the type of person who believes it *was* done by them, I *do* believe it was done by them. Nothing will change that. They can say what they want to; I believe it.

Williams: How do you feel about the kind of mythology that has grown up around Malcolm? Last night we were talking about the movie that they're making now.

Himes: Yes, well, I think the reason why they became frightened about Malcolm X is, as I've always said, as long as the white press and the white community keep throwing it out that the black man hates white people, he's safe. It doesn't do a damn thing to him; he can walk around wherever he wishes to. Look at LeRoi Jones, who stands up there and tells those white people whatever he wants to tell them. Stokely Carmichael, Rap Brown, anybody—they're

safe. They might find something to put them away,
but most of the time they don't do a damn thing to
them. But then, you know, when the black man en-
larges this philosophy and includes a greater scope
of people in it who will understand . . .

Williams: He'd opened his own mind.

Himes: Malcolm X had developed a philosophy in
which he included all the people of the world, and
people were listening to him. And then he became
dangerous. Now as long as he was staying in America and just hating the white man he wasn't dangerous. But then when he involved others, they figured
that if he kept on—since they themselves had brought
him to the attention of the world—that he could use
this; that they had set up for him to bring in masses
of other people, masses of whites, masses of North
Africans, masses of yellow people, all that would
make him dangerous. So the only thing to do with him
was kill him. Because that's the way white Americans
solve every problem. You know, I have never even
thought for a moment that the Black Muslims organized his assassination on their own. It never even occurred to me. First of all, there are a few Black
Muslims who are rehabilitated from prisons and drug
addiction and various things; there are a few that are
personally dangerous to each other. But when a person gets the stature of Malcolm X at the time that he
was executed, I think that he is absolutely safe from
the Black Muslims. It would take an organization
which is used to toppling kings and heads of states
and big politicians to organize his assassination. I
think he was absolutely untouchable by the Black
Muslims.

Anyway, you know, there is no way that one can
evaluate the American scene and avoid violence,
because any country that was born in violence and
has lived in violence always knows about violence.
Anything can be initiated, enforced, contained or destroyed on the American scene through violence.

That's the only thing that's ever made any change, because they have an inheritance of violence; it comes right straight from the days of slavery, from the first colonialists who landed on the American shores, the first slaves, through the Revolutionary War, the Civil War, the Indian wars, and gunslingers killing one another over fences and sheep and one goddamned thing or another; they grew up on violence. And not only that, it's gotten to be so much a part of the country that they are at the place where they are refining the history of their violence. They don't refer to the massacres of the Chinese during the last century out on the West Coast in California.

Williams: But not until they'd helped put the railroads in.

Himes: Yeah, that's right. They got all the labor that they could out of them before they killed them. Yes, they grew up on violence, and this is the only thing that they're going to listen to, the only thing that will move them. The only people that the white community in America has tried to teach that it is Christian to turn the other cheek and to live peacefully are the black people. They're the only people they have said bounce back. They have never even suggested it to anyone else. That is why the whole legend of Martin Luther King is such a powerful legend—because his was the teaching of nonviolence.

Williams: Right. He was a godsend to the American white people.

Himes: Absolutely. There's no question about it.

BLACK WRITERS

Williams: What happens, Chester, to young black writers who go over to Europe? It seems to me they're not producing like you and Wright and Harrington and Gardner produced. You were talking about Lomax [S. P.], who started out to be a writer. William Melvin Kelley was in Paris for a while and I think he

got disgusted with it and now he's in Jamaica. What's happening to these younger guys who go over there?
Himes: Well, I don't know. I never met Kelley. Some of them continue to write, you know; some of them work very hard at it. But it's just the fact that there is a great resistance among American publishers against expatriate blacks, so that they have a much better opportunity of getting their work published in America if they're living there. Because if they are living abroad the American publisher, as a rule, will just reject their works out of hand. Now this I know for a fact because I sent a number of manuscripts, recommended them, to American publishers myself, which have been turned down flat. Now the American publishers feel that the blacks should live in America and they have a sort of spiteful attitude toward blacks who escape from getting a head-beating in America.
Williams: They don't want them to get away.
Himes: Yes, that's another thing. That's part of the scene that makes magazines like *Time* have such a great and hard and relentless fury against Richard Wright, because Wright got away and *Time* never forgave him for that. And they continued to pick at him in one way or another. They thought, "Now, we helped this black man to become famous and so forth, and here he is escaping us." So they set out to punish him. Well, Dick was suffering under these various things—being the black writer who was best known in the world—he was the one that the white communications media could pick on. He was the only one who was vulnerable enough, being famous as he was. They could conceivably pick on me, but there wasn't any point 'cause nobody knew me [laughs]. When people began finding out who I was, they did begin picking. Until then they just left me alone entirely.
Williams: So your advice would be for them to stay in the States?
Himes: My advice to the black American writer would

not be to stay in America, but just to continue to write. Not to be concerned about the attitudes in any place they are because one thing is for sure: there are great segments of the world who will be opposed to them, and this opposition, if they let it hurt them, will destroy them. That will happen anywhere they are. But there's no particular reason why—if they are young, have great vitality and a great love of life—why they just simply shouldn't stay in the States and write there. There's nothing they can learn here, that's for sure. There's nothing they can learn about their craft or anything else from going to places like Paris. The only reason for going to Paris is just to have a certain amount of freedom of movement for a limited period of time. But they won't even get any inspiration from being in France. *I* don't think they will.

Williams: Let me ask you kind of a cliché question. Two questions, really. What is the function of the American black writer now, and what do you think his role will be in another ten years?

Himes: Well, I think the *only* function of the black writer in America now is just to produce works of literature about whatever he wants to write about, without any form of repression or any hesitation about what he wishes to write about, without any restraint whatever. He should just produce his work as best he can, as long as it comes out, and put it on the American market to be published, and I believe now it will be (which it wouldn't have been ten years ago). All right, now, what will come out of this ten years from now? No one knows. But at least the world will be more informed about the black Americans' subconscious. And it is conceivable, since black people are creative people, that they might form on the strength of these creations an entirely new literature that will be more valuable than the output of the white community. Because we are a creative people, as everyone knows, and if we lend ourselves to the creation of literature like we did to the creation of jazz and dancing and so forth, there's no telling what the impact will be.

Williams: Can we do this? Can we make this impact without owning our own publishing companies?

Himes: I suppose so. Look, I have talked to black sharecroppers and convicts and various black people who could tell, without stopping, better stories than Faulkner could write. And they would have the same alliteration, the same wording. Some of them couldn't even read and write, but they had the same genius for telling stories that Faulkner had, and they could tell continuous stories, too. The narrative would go on and on, and they would never lose it. But then these people couldn't write, you see. So I believe that the black man certainly has a creativity that is comparable to the highest type of creativity in America because he has the same background. And probably even greater. And then the blacks of the Northern ghetto have an absolutely unlimited source to draw their material from. Somebody else comes up—like Upton Sinclair—and draws a little from this material, and builds a great reputation. Well, look at the black man now in the slums in Chicago; look what he can do. If Richard Wright had kept writing about Chicago he could have written forever.

Williams: But isn't there a kind of censorship that goes on if you don't have your own publishing outfit?

Himes: Yes, that is very true. You say "censorship"; the American publishers have what is called a conspiracy of censorship where they don't even need to be in contact with one another to know what they are going to censor; there are certain things that they just automatically know they are going to censor, and they all will work in the same way. Yes, it's true that this automatic and unspoken conspiracy of censorship among white publishers works against the black man. He has an absolute wall against him, but in the course of time this will break down. In literature, it seems as if it's already breaking down, and it will if black writers particularly find that they need their own publishers very badly. Then white publishers, faced with competition, will have to change. That is one of the unfortunate parts of the entire American scene, that the black—well, I wouldn't say industrialists—but the black heads of firms who have sufficient money to do these things won't do them. And one doesn't know why, because it's possible for everybody else. One doesn't know why a black publisher wouldn't come up and tap this source of wealth of the black community of writers, because it seems to me it would be unlimited wealth. One wonders why one of them doesn't do so, since the white publishers realize it is rich and they are tapping it as best they can, even with their standards of censorship.

Williams: There's another young black writer on the scene. His name is James Alan McPherson. He's just published a collection of short stories called *Hue and Cry*, and most of the stories are pretty damn good. Ralph Ellison has a blurb on the back of the book in which he says that this kid is great, this is real writing. The implication is that a lot of black writers whom he considers "obscenely second-rate" use their blackness as a crutch, as an excuse for not learning their craft. What do you say?

Himes: Well, I don't know what to say about that. If Ralph means that the black writers are writing about their experiences of being black in the world— what else can they write about? Now, that reminds me of this famous conversation between James Baldwin and Richard Wright that various people have written about, this confrontation they had in Paris. Baldwin said to him, "You have written my story." He meant, of course, that when Dick wrote *Black Boy* he had written the story of all black boys. Anyway, the point I'm trying to make is what else can a black writer write about but being black? And it's very diffi-

cult to hide. It's not insurmountable, but it's difficult.
And then, any beginning writer will always write
about his experiences.

Well, you know, I think that Ralph is rather a little
bit hipped on the business of learning his craft. I remember when he was imitating Richard Wright to the
point where there was a confrontation and Wright
accused him of it. Dick told me that Ralph said to him,
"Who else can I imitate if I don't imitate you, Dick?"
So I think he's gotten a little bit pompous in making
the statements about the craftsmanship of the young
black writers of the world. *Invisible Man* was a very
good book, but that didn't make Ralph an authority.
It didn't mean to me that Ralph was a particularly
outstanding craftsman in relationship to other black
writers. I think that particular remark is uncalled for;
it's not a particularly beneficial type of criticism. It
seems that a remark like that appeals more to the
white community than the black community.

Williams: What advice do you have for all these
young black writers who are growing up and getting
on the scene?

Himes: Well, I was reading that book *Yellow Back
Radio Broke-Down* by Ishmael Reed out there, and I
agree that there's no reason why every black writer
shouldn't produce a style of his own. If he has the
talent. No particular purpose is served by imitation in
writing, you know. You take a writer like Joyce. He
had to produce his own narrative style, which any
black writer can—I don't say that they can produce
what Joyce produced, but they can produce a style of
their own whatever it might be. Like Ishmael Reed.
And I think that's what they should do. And then in
the course of time this will make an impact. They will
have their style. I find that hard to do myself. I can
give that advice, but people are creatures of habit. I
would like to produce a definite style. Of course,
I won't be able to do that now, that's for sure. But I

have always wanted to produce an entirely different approach to the novel form.

Williams: Than what you now use?

Himes: Yes.

Williams: What do you find lacking in the form you now use?

Himes: Well, I would like to see produced a novel that just drains a person's subconscious of all his attitudes and reactions to everything. Because, obviously, if one person has a number of thoughts concerning anything, there is a cohesion. There has to be because they belong to one man. Just let it come out as it is, let it come out as the words generate in the mind, let it come out in the phrasing of the subconscious and let it become a novel in that form. Of course this has been done, but not purely; there's always been an artificial strain. Since the black American is subject to having millions of thoughts concerning everything, millions of reactions, and his reactions and thoughts will obviously be different from that of the white community, this should create an entirely different structure of the novel. Of course, that requires youth ... I remember when I used to be able to write creatively thirty-five or forty pages a day. When I first began writing I was doing much better in introducing a story than I was doing in later years, because I would put down anything. I would be going along in a narrative form and listening to jazz and then a trumpet solo, say, would take my mind off for a second, I would follow it and write about it, and then go back to the narrative, and that would become part of the narrative. But of course this was always rejected by the editor.

Williams: You know, we once had a conversation about *The Primitive* and I told you I'd been reading it on the subway and I missed my stop. Remember? And I told you I thought it was a brutal book, I think a great book, and I remember that you apologized for its being a brutal book. But I hadn't said that it was brutal in the sense that an apology was necessary. If you're talking about attacking the sensitivities on all levels, this is what I mean; this is what *The Primitive* did.

Himes: Yes, but that was what I was able to achieve in Mallorca because I didn't have any distractions with *The Primitive.* I wrote that out of a completely free state of mind from beginning to end; where I saw all the nuances of every word I put down, so *The Primitive* is my favorite book.

Williams: Yeah, that's a fantastic book. It's my favorite, too. But you once said *The Third Generation* was your most dishonest book. Do you remember?

Himes: Yes, yes. I had read a number of pages of a manuscript that my mother had written about her family. Her family was one of these slave families that had been interbred into the Southern white slaveowners until the time of the Civil War. My mother's grandfather (I think it was) was the half-brother of his master; they were about the same age and they looked a great deal alike. When his master went away to the war, this half-white slave of his went with him as his body servant.

Well, she had produced this novel in detail and I thought that that should have been part of the book. The reason I didn't use it was that—I needed for it to be published and I thought that would be offensive to the publishers and would make it difficult for publication at that time. That was some time ago. Nowadays, the black man has got over that thinking. They do have the freedom to write, more or less, what they want. Many books I read now by black writers would not have been published fifteen years ago under any circumstances. And there are a number of themes that won't be published now, and that's why I want to write a book and break through a certain reticence on the part of the publishers.

I read *The Godfather* [Mario Puzo] and the author

has experienced a certain hesitation on the part of the publishers to publish a book that relates all the gruesomeness and the power of assassination, of ruling by this power; that relates the effect that a group of people can have by controlling—by simply shooting other people in the head. Shooting people in the head generates power. This is what I think black writers should write about. I remember Sartre made a statement which was recorded in the French press (I never had any use for Sartre since) that in writing his play *The Respectful Prostitute* he recognized the fact that a black man could not assault a white person in America. That's one of the reasons I began writing the detective stories. I wanted to introduce the idea of violence. After all, Americans live by violence, and violence achieves—regardless of what anyone says, regardless of the distaste of the white community —its own ends. *The Godfather* is not only a successful book, but it's a successful book about a successful organization that rules by violence. And not only do they rule by violence, but the American community has never been able to do anything about them.

Williams: Well, I think this is largely because people who control the American community are in cahoots either directly or indirectly with the Mafia.

Himes: Yes, that was the same thing during all the days of prohibition, when everybody realized that the gangsters and the politicians worked side by side, close together. As a matter of fact, the gangsters were only servants of the politicians, the servants of the rich. That's why the gangsters in America were almost an untouchable breed during that time.

WHITE WRITERS

Williams: What about your experiences with white expatriate writers?

Himes: I don't have any experiences with white expatriate writers.

Williams: Remember once you told me a story about how James Jones used to hold this soirée every Sunday at his place, and he said he'd like to meet you and you should come over, and you said, "What the hell do I want to see James Jones for?"

Himes: Yeah, that's probably true. I never met James Jones all the time I was in Paris. I actually don't know if I'd know him if I saw him. Lesley's pointed him out once or twice, but I don't remember what he looks like. I have nothing to say to James Jones, absolutely nothing to say to him whatsoever. And from what I've heard about his career and so forth, I don't *want* to know anything about him.

The thing about white writers ... it's very pitiful you know. Take white writers like Hemingway, for instance. Now Hemingway became one of the great writers of the world, but as far as I know Hemingway never, one time, in one book or one story, had any message or statement to make about anything other than what he called courage or bravery and so forth, which I think is simpleminded. And that is all. But then, you see, to a black writer they say, "Well, what statement is he making?" He could write a book, one of the most fabulous stories in the world, and they'll say, "That's a good book, but what is the statement? What is he saying about the conditions of the black people in America?" Well, most black writers have something to say about this because most black writers from America—what else can they say, what else can they write about, what else do they think about? So that is why it becomes an absolute part of their writing, because it's part of their thinking. But I don't think that it's all done deliberately—just to sit down and make a statement; it's subconscious. Of course, most writers of any consequence are against various forms of social injustice. Take them all—even go back to old Russian writers like Dostoyevsky, old English writers, Dickens and so forth, and the new English writers, Joyce and all. Because this is part of the human emotion, you know, to protest against various forms of social injustice. And all the rest of them who are famous throughout the world. So the black writer does so because as a writer this is part of his trade. But to sit down and deliberately do so, results in a tract which quite often gets away from the author.

Williams: Are there any white writers that you admire? Not necessarily contemporary. You mentioned Dostoyevsky ...

Himes: Yes, I mention Dostoyevsky so much because I've always admired him to a great degree because by reading him I understand his process of writing. There was a man who wrote very rapidly and very brilliantly all the time, and the reason that he did so was that he needed money all the time. He'd need it all the time, and as soon as he'd get money he'd throw it away. Also, being epileptic he had this extraordinary perception that most epileptics have.

But then I also like Faulkner because when Faulkner was writing his stories, his imaginative stories about the South, he was inventing the situations on sound ground—but still inventive. He was inventing them so fast that if you breeze through Faulkner you can find any number of mistakes. Faulkner would forget characters. You can read certain books, especially *Light in August,* and Faulkner has forgotten the names that he attaches to certain characters, then he goes on and he gives them other names.

Williams: I've noticed this, but I always figured it was something I had misread.

Himes: No, no, he was writing so fast he forgot. I do that myself. I remember years ago when I was starting to write short stories I had a joker shot in the arm but later I forgot he was shot in the arm. [Laughter.] Yes, you know this happens quite often, especially in the movies. Not that they forget it; they just pass it over.

Williams: You know, Chester, there seem to be more white guys who are writing about black people today than ever before. There have always been some, but now they seem to be crawling out of the woodwork.

Himes: Oh, yes, everywhere, everywhere. This has been happening about the past five or six or seven years. And you know why this is? Because at the beginning of the black uprisings in America, when the blacks were seemingly going to use violence to the point where it would have some meaning, well then they had world coverage. They had the greatest coverage of any story—more than even the assassination of Kennedy or the politics in Russia. Total saturation in the world press made the white writers eager to cash in on what they figure will have the greatest appeal, so as you said before they came up with the idea. On the whole, the white writers are better trained than the black writers, because they've had more facilities for education in many of the techniques and crafts of the trade. So a white writer can sit down and he can write some of the goddamnedest, most extraordinary bullshit about the blacks, but he will successfully project his story since he's not interested in having any authenticity. All he's concerned about is reaching the largest audience and what he can do with it. Like this joker who wrote the book, *The Man.*

Williams: Oh, Irving Wallace, yeah.

Himes: He didn't give a damn about whether this story was possible or whether it had plausibility; the main thing was to write a story that would titillate the greatest number of whites and make them buy the book. It wouldn't even make them think; it would be a diversion. It is true that the white writers of the world have a much better chance of learning their craft.

Then, the white writers in America conduct writing as a major business, which it is. Harold Robbins has more writers working for him than Shakespeare had. All he has to do is just sketch out the plot and put his writers to work and knock out his books.

Williams: I didn't know he used other writers.

Himes: The way I found out, I was in New York talking to Bucklin Moon, who had become, after some hard times, the editor-in-chief of Pocket Books. And I found that in addition to working as editor-in-chief, he was also working on Harold Robbins' *The Adventurers.* Yes, he was a competent writer, so he was writing some of the passages. Harold Robbins didn't have time to write. [Laughter.] After all, it was a million-dollar project. He could afford to pay Bucklin Moon probably better than Pocket Books was paying him as editor-in-chief.

Williams: Did you read the Styron book, *The Confessions of Nat Turner?* You know the big stink about it.

Himes: I didn't read very much of it, just off and on. I read in an English paper that Styron was employing a gimmick there. He figured that he could write about Nat Turner as long as he made him a homosexual, lusting after white women. That was the only way the story of Nat Turner could be acceptable, because Nat Turner was one of the only black slaves who had the right idea: the only thing to do with a white slave-owner was to kill him. But Styron couldn't have him just kill him outright because he wanted to be free; he had to make him a homicidal homosexual lusting after white women. Which I find very . . . [laughter] funny. It was a cute gimmick, you know, and it went down very well.

Williams: Yes, it was an immediate best-seller.

Himes: Yeah, obviously. Black homosexuals and black eunuchs have always been profitable in white literature. The profit incentive has corrupted American writing, but that's what writers write for anyway— white writers as well as black writers; they write for profit. The only thing is black writers get such very little profit. In the last ten or fifteen years it's become very big business. Now, whether this is true or not, I heard that when Martin Luther King was assassinated, no serious money-making publisher was particularly interested until they realized the world was

not only incensed but extremely interested in the life
of a black Christian who had been assassinated, and
that it was a very big story, a tremendous story. So
the publishers began bidding for the biography of
Martin Luther King which was to be written by his
widow. I don't know who told me this, but probably
my editor, that the publishers bid for this book, unwritten of course, but it didn't make any difference whether
she could write or not because they would supply any
number of writers to write it. But anyway, McGraw-
Hill won it on a bid of a contract to pay her $500,000
advance.

Williams: I heard it was $450,000, but who the hell is
going to quibble about $50,000 when you're talking
about that kind of money.

Himes: Yeah, well, there you are—half a million
dollars.

Williams: That's a lot of money involved in that book.

Himes: Yes, because anything which will hold the
public interest, for the next ten years anyway, will
be popular. King was a much greater man in the
world and a much more significant personality in the
world and touched more people in the world after he
was killed than before. That's when most of the people in the world even got to know who he was. But
everybody knows who he is now—even the people
walking down the street here, and most of the people
who live in Spain.

Williams: So you say that for the next ten years he'll
be a viable subject?

Himes: Yes, that's the way I feel. It might be longer
than that, but I think certainly ten years.

Williams: The piece that you have in here [*Beyond
the Angry Black*, 1966] I see quoted pretty frequently:
"Chester Himes says . . ." And you told me that you
did that piece in nineteen-forty . . .

Himes: I guess I must have done that when I was at
Yaddo [a writer's colony] and that was in 1948. Horace Cayton, who was the director of the South Park-

way Community Center, and the woman who was teaching creative writing out at the University of Chicago got together and decided that they would bring me to Chicago to read a paper on The Dilemma of the Negro Writer. When I finished reading that paper nobody moved, nobody applauded, nobody ever said anything else to me. I was shocked. I stayed in Chicago a few days drinking, and then I was half-drunk all the rest of the time I was in Yaddo. That was the time I started getting blackouts, I was drinking so much. I would get up in the morning and go into town, which you weren't supposed to do, and by eleven o'clock, I was dead drunk.

Williams: Into Saratoga . . .

Himes: Yes. I lived across the hall from Patricia Haysmiths who wrote *Strangers on a Train* which Hitchcock bought for practically nothing but made a classic out of. He bought the full movie rights for five thousand dollars. Hitchcock doesn't believe in paying writers either, you know.

Williams: Who else was up there in Yaddo when you were there?

Himes: Well, part of the time, there was Truman Capote. I think he had already published *Other Voices, Other Rooms*.

Williams: He's done very well.

Himes: Yeah. I don't remember any other people who were there. I think Katherine Anne Porter, who wrote *Ship of Fools*, was also there most of the time, but I didn't see her. She spent almost all her days when she was in America up at Yaddo. She had a special room up there in the big house in a tower.

Williams: What did you think of *Ship of Fools* as an example of an American book that's supposed to be long-awaited, with the great writer?

Himes: I found it innocent enough but I didn't think it was a serious book that had any particular meaning other than the fact that I could see her up there typing away. It wasn't worth waiting twenty years for it.

I would think that the book that —— and I wrote, called *The Silver Altar*, was certainly as good as *Ship of Fools*.

"BLACK ANTI-SEMITISM"

Williams: What does the "B" in your name stand for?

Himes: That was my mother's family name, Bomar.

Williams: Because when I first read *If He Hollers* . . .

Himes: Yes, I was using the "B" then.

Williams: Chester, let me ask you, do you know what your name "Himes" is derived from? Is it English or . . .

Himes: It's Jewish, like "Chaim," "Jaime" . . .

Williams: Spanish Jewish?

Himes: I don't know. It came down from "Heinz." Anyway, my father's grandfather's owner was "Himes." I don't know, maybe it was his father's—my grandfather's—owner. He was a slave blacksmith, that's how my father got into that. It was a trade that came down from father to son. My father was able to go to college and learn a few other things, like wheelwrighting and various skills. But the trade of blacksmithing was a hereditary business. It came out of slavery and the owner of our family was named in a certain variety of "Heinz," but it was a Jewish name. My forebears just took the name "Himes"—that's the way it was pronounced by the slaves. It was a literal translation, whether it was "Chaim" or "Jaime" or "Heinz." I don't know. But the "Bomar" of my mother's family's slave name is Irish, of course. I should call myself Chester X.

Williams: That's interesting. That's interesting. Let me ask you one final question and we'll quit for the day. I see you sitting there getting kind of wilted. I'm getting pretty tired myself. I don't know whether you've been reading about it or not, but there appears to be growing animosity, at least in New York City, between blacks and Jews (though one can't really trust the press). Do you think this is a result of the closeness, as I said earlier, whereby familiarity breeds contempt?

Himes: No. You know, I have a very long discussion of this in *Lonely Crusade*. That whole business between the black people and the Jews in America is part of the book, and that's the part the Jews disliked so much. As a matter of fact, I have a copy of the French Jewish magazine which has a photo of me on the cover. They ran an eighteen-page interview on my discussion of the relationship of blacks and Jews in *Lonely Crusade*. It was obvious, even when I was a little boy in the South that the only stores black people could go to, like hardware and department stores, were owned by Jews. When you went to non-Jewish stores you couldn't get in the door. So, where the black man and the Jew are concerned, the Jew has always taken the black man as a customer. Because the Jew has always been in business, and he found out that in a basically anti-Semitic country like America the most available market for a poor Jew on the lower rung of business was the black man. That was his market. He could rent them houses and he could sell them food.

Well, because the blacks were ignorant and the descendants of slaves, the Jewish merchants and landlords misused them. Where blacks might have been creative in other ways, in the ways of the commercial world they were babes in the woods. They were pigeons; anyone could take advantage of them who wanted to, so the Jewish merchants did—and the Jewish landowners (the ghettos were owned by Jews). It's very seldom any other name than a Jewish one appears as a landlord or proprietor in any ghetto in any city of America. All businesses in the ghettos were owned by Jews, and then a few of the blacks were eventually able to buy some of them. Then, of course, the black majority developed an unspoken anti-Semitism, even though they were doing business every day with the Jew around the corner. The black had an ingrown suspicion and resentment of the Jew. He realized that he was being used in certain ways by all Jewish landlords and merchants. Even today a Jew will make a fortune out of the race problem, and this builds up a subconscious resentment—although most of the white people I do business with, who help me, whom I love and respect, are Jews. But that doesn't negate the fact that the Jews are the ones who had contact with the blacks and took advantage of them. Now the gentiles had enslaved the blacks and worked them as beasts, but when they were freed, the gentiles didn't want to have a damn thing to do with them. They left the blacks without food or shelter. They worked them for a pittance and that was all. Whereas the Jew realized that to house and feed the freed black man was a business, a business that paid off. This paid off better than any other business because where else could Jews, who were in a ghetto themselves, open up any kind of a business and have customers, other than in the black ghetto?

Williams: Well then, why is there such a great reaction—as in New York—to the fact that, particularly in the school system, the black teachers want their thing, the black people in the community want their thing? The Jews are saying this is anti-Semitism—which to a large degree it is—but it's also, as you seem to imply, an awakening to the fact that they have been used.

Himes: Yes, that's right. You see, the way it is in the city school system in New York, a quarter of a century ago the only white teachers who would teach in black communities were Jews.

Williams: That's where the Irish sent them.

Himes: Yes, they're the only ones who would go there. So, over a period of time they got entrenched, and now that the black people are rising up, they're resentful of the kind of uncommitted teachers, more so than the fact that they're Jewish teachers. It just so happens that most of them are Jewish teachers and that they are guilty. The blacks claim they're guilty of: giving kids bad education, ignoring them on certain points. These teachers on the whole are Jewish, but they have been entrenched in the school system because this is where the gentiles sent them. It's an unfortunate situation but it's inevitable, because as the blacks begin to have any kind of protest, it's a spontaneous protest against the first individuals whom they have had direct contact with—who they know are guilty. They have not looked back far enough to realize that the Jewish schoolteachers are no more guilty of actually misusing black students than the white gentiles who exiled them there in the first place. No one is looking at it that way, because no one ever does. The younger Jews, I read, seriously are trying to get the older Jews, who are people of great habit too, to see that there is a different side . . .

Williams: Yeah, this is something that I've noticed too.

Himes: Well, this whole problem in America, as I see it, developed from the fact that the slaves were freed and that there was no legislation of any sort to make it possible for them to live. So this is what has built up to such a tremendous problem that now . . .

Williams: Right. They felt that freedom was enough by itself.

Himes: Yeah, what is it that they have in heaven—milk and honey? That some poor nigger could go and live on nothing. Just to proclaim emancipation was not enough. You can't eat it; it doesn't keep the cold weather out.

WRIGHT

Williams: What was Paris like, with you and Wright, Harrington, William Gardner Smith and Melvin Van Peebles? It must have been a pretty great scene.

Himes: Well, we always met at the Café Tournon. In fact Dick Wright wasn't in it as much as Ollie Harrington, who was actually the center; and Melvin wasn't there then. Ollie was the center of the American community on the Left Bank in Paris, white and black, and he was the greatest Lothario in the history of the whole Latin Quarter. And he was a fabulous raconteur, too. He used to keep people spellbound for hours. So they collected there because of Ollie. Then the rest of us came. Dick was a good friend of Ollie's; as a matter of fact, he used to telephone Ollie every morning. Dick was a compulsive conversationalist in the early hours of the morning. When he woke up he had to telephone somebody and have a long conversation. When Ollie wasn't there he had to find someone else—Daniel Guérin or even Jean-Paul Sartre. But they got tired of these conversations, so he chose Ollie. As long as Ollie was in town Dick would telephone him as soon as he woke up in the morning, whether Ollie was awake or not (it didn't make any difference) and have long conversations about the CIA and the race problem and all. You know, that kind of conversation doesn't go down too well at seven-thirty in the morning.

Williams: What did you decide about the CIA in Paris? I know that Wright had some pretty positive ideas about what they were doing.

Himes: I don't know really. You see, I can't make any definite statement about the CIA in Paris because I didn't have any knowledge or even any thoughts about their operation. I realized that the FBI had a dossier on me going back to my childhood anyway, so it didn't make any difference to me one way or the other. And when I got my passport from the State Department I had to go and send my certificate for the restoration of my citizenship.

Williams: What's the restoration certificate?

Himes: Well, you know, when you've been to prison they take your citizenship away. And then the governor of the state returns your citizenship after a period of time. And my citizenship had been returned to me by a governor named Burton, who later became a Supreme Court Justice. He was a Supreme Court Justice at the time I applied for my passport. So I realized that the CIA knew everything they wanted to know about me already. They weren't interested in me anyway. The CIA was only interested in Richard Wright, and only because of the fact that they thought that he might have had information concerning the communist affiliations of people in high places in government, and that he might conceivably be having a dialogue, not a conspiracy or anything, but just a dialogue with people that they considered dangerous such as Nkrumah or Frantz Fanon. The only other person I know they were seriously interested in was Malcolm X. And of course everyone knows the CIA was interested in Fanon. They went to Fanon's assistance in the last years of his life to show that they had good will. Took him over to America and put him under medical treatment. By the way, he wrote a long article on my "Treatment of Violence" which his wife still has, and which I've thought I might get and have published. Because he had the same feeling, of course, that I have.

Williams: How long is the piece?

Himes: I don't know. Julia Wright told me that she had read it and that his wife has it.

Williams: You know, Julia is in New York. No . . . it's Rachel.

Himes: Yes, Rachel. Well, Rachel never got along with her mother. Rachel was Papa's daughter all her life. 'Cause she was a little blond daughter, you know, and Dick was devoted to her. But Julia looks just like her father.

When Dick died Ellen was in London and then she didn't know what to do. When she came back she wanted to have a private funeral. Ellen and I personally had a furious argument about this. I told her she couldn't do that. When Dick died Lesley and I were spending the winter in St. Tropez and our landlady asked us if we knew a man named Richard

Wright. And she said he had died; it had just come over the radio. So we got into our little car and rushed up to Paris and when we got up there we found that Ellen had said that she was going to have a closed funeral, and that no one was going to be admitted, and that Dick's body was going to be cremated.

Well, we were staying with Ollie Harrington. As a matter of fact, he had just moved into this apartment, so we were sleeping on a mattress on the floor. So Ollie didn't say anything—he didn't want to cross Ellen. Ollie was a great diplomat. But anyway, I telephoned Ellen and told her she couldn't possibly have a closed funeral for Dick. So she decided after Dick had been dead three or four days and the funeral was rapidly approaching that she would open it. Which meant that a great number of people were not there who would have been if they had known earlier that it was to be an open funeral. But as it was, Dick had been on the outs with great numbers of people by that time. The head of *Présence Africaine*, Alioune Diop, was one of the people who gave the funeral oration. But at that time, before Dick's death, Dick and Diop weren't speaking. It was a relatively small funeral and he was suddenly cremated. After his cremation a very strong rumor started in Paris that he had been poisoned.

Williams: I remember hearing about it at the time.

Himes: Yes. Now, Ollie was supposed to have more testimony; he had more evidence than anyone because Dick had sent Ollie a telegram, which I saw when I was in Ollie's house, which said something like "Come to see me right away." And Ollie hadn't gone because, as I said, Dick was always telephoning him early every morning and he was sort of pissed off with him, so he didn't go. Well, the next Ollie heard of Dick, he was dead. He *did* die suddenly. Everyone knows the circumstances of his death —the fact that he was being released and was in supposedly good health. And then supposedly a mysterious woman had come to see him. Whether this is true or not, I couldn't say; this is the essence of the rumor. And the rumor still persists. Personally, that is one death I do not connect with the CIA, although of course with these things one never knows because the CIA was interested in many, many things . . . And Dick realized that he was a sick man and he might have had some revelation to make and decided to make it, and people might have decided he was better off dead. This is all guesswork on my part.

Williams: Had he made a public talk in the American Church two or three weeks before this, in which he was running down the CIA activities of people connected with the arts? Connie mentions it in her book.

Himes: Yes, well, everyone was doing that too, you know. And whether that has any relation to his death or not I couldn't say. I wasn't there anyway. I had been away from Paris for some time, moving around. I wasn't close enough to the scene to have any definite information until I arrived back and talked to Ellen, mostly just about the funeral.

Ellen and I never got along, as you already know. We got along very well once upon a time, but then we fell out just around the time Richard Wright was writing *The Long Dream,* because she didn't want him to write it. She didn't want him to go back into his Mississippi childhood and write about the black oppression in America, because he had written a number of books on the world scene. And I felt just the opposite. I felt that he should go back to the roots, the sources of his information, and write about the American scene. As a matter of fact, I was doing the same thing myself at the time. And Dick had come and talked to me at great lengths before he began writing this book.

Then Ellen stopped me on the street one day and said that I shouldn't encourage Dick. And I said, "Well, you know, I can't encourage Dick to do anything." And she said, "Yes, you're encouraging him to go back and write this book, and he's a big man now and he should not do this." So that made me so angry that I said some very impolite things, and we were shouting at one another on the Boulevard St. Germain. After that Ellen and I never got along. I see her now, I kiss her and embrace her because we've known one another many years. But it's just the fact that I know without a doubt that she wants certain information about Richard Wright's life not to be revealed. If Dick hadn't had his sexual relationships, if he hadn't seen the people that he had, if he hadn't had that certain type of curiosity that he had, he wouldn't have been Richard Wright. So there's no point in trying to hide the character of a man. But Richard Wright also reached a point, after he had been in France for four or five years, where he was well entrenched, had a really splendid apartment equipped in the American fashion, was a real celebrity to the press and everybody else. As my translator said, he was such a celebrity that if he had called a press conference at the foot of the stairs leading up to the Sacré Coeur and said, "Gentlemen, I want you to run up these stairs," they would have done so. But anyway, after a time, Dick became ashamed of his own image. The French continued to think of Dick as "Black Boy," and Dick was beginning to think of himself as a world figure, which he was. But at the same time, he was still Black Boy. The French were subject to thinking of him as Black Boy exclusively and excluded the fact that he was a world personality. Also, the French liked to believe that he belonged to them.

Williams: Why did they turn on him?

Himes: Well, they turned on him primarily because just that—the fact that he began writing on the world political scene. The French are very sensitive to any world figure in France who writes on the world political scene, especially if he's a black man. They are very sensitive about it. And then what the French do, they just take him out of the press. And to take Dick out of the press, since he had been such an extraordinary celebrity . . . He was plagued by it—this sort of comedown bothered him. So eventually this sort of corroded him and he decided he was going to move from France and go and live in England. But then he discovered England wouldn't give him the—racism in England had tightened up to the point where they wouldn't even consider having Dick living there.

Williams: I remember Ollie's description about when Wright went in to see about his passport, his permanent visa. He wanted an explanation from this official, who threw his passport at his feet and said, "I don't have to explain a goddamned thing to you."

Himes: Horace [Cayton] actually knew quite a bit about Richard Wright from the time of the publication of *Native Son* until Dick left for France. He was quite close to him. He'd have Dick up to the South Side Community House in Chicago, where he was director. Dick was very naive, you know, and Horace used to get embarrassed because he was such a slick cat himself, and he'd have some of these white chicks over from the University of Chicago, and Dick would get excited and wouldn't know how to behave. Dick was a strange man anyway. He was not only a genius but an astute political tactician—but in some ways he was very naive, too.

I was released from prison in May 1936. The first short stories I remember writing were published in 1932–33 in *Abbott's Monthly*, a monthly magazine published by old man Abbott, the founder and publisher of *The Chicago Defender*.

—Chester Himes

THE WORKS OF CHESTER HIMES

1932　SHORT STORIES (about prison life), *Abbott's Monthly*.

1933　SHORT STORY (domestic), *The Bronzeman*.

1933　SHORT STORIES, the *Atlanta Daily World* and the *Pittsburgh Courier*.

1934–　SHORT STORIES ("Crazy in the Stir"; "To What Red Hell";
1937　"Marijuana and a Pistol"; "The Visiting Hour"; "Every Opportunity"; "Strictly Business" and others), *Esquire*.

1939　*This Cleveland* (Forty-odd prose poems), the *Cleveland Daily News*, editorial page.

1940–　SHORT STORIES AND ARTICLES (SHORT STORIES: "Mama's
1947　Missionary Money"; "Two Soldiers"; "So Softly Smiling"; "All He Needs Is Feet" and others. ARTICLES: "Zoot Suit Riots"; "The Quest for Equality"; "The Time Is Now" and others), "The Crisis," Journal of the NAACP.

1940–　SHORT STORIES AND ARTICLES, *Opportunity*, Journal of the
1947　National Urban League.

1945　ARTICLE: "Equality for 125,000 Dead," *The Chicago Defender*.

NOVELS:

1945　*If He Hollers Let Him Go*, Doubleday, Doran, & Co.; 1950: reprinted by NAL; 1955: reprinted by Berkley Books.

1947　*Lonely Crusade*, Alfred A. Knopf, Inc.

1952　*Cast the First Stone*, Coward-McCann.

1954　*The Third Generation*, World Publishing Company; 1956: reprinted by NAL.

1955　*The Primitive*, New American Library (original).

1960　*A Case of Rape/Une Affaire de Viol* (published only in France), Editions les Yeux Ouverts.

1961　*Pinktoes*, Olympia Press, Paris; 1965: G. P. Putnam's Sons, New York. 1967: reprinted by Dell Publishing Company.

HARLEM DOMESTIC DETECTIVE STORIES:
[THE COFFIN ED SMITH/GRAVEDIGGER JONES NOVELS]

(The following stories, with the exception of the last one, were all originally published in France. The Paris publisher and French title are therefore listed first.)

1957   *La Reine des Pommes*, winner of "le Prix du Roman Policier" for France in 1958, Série Noire-Gallimard; 1959: *For Love of Imabelle*, Gold Medal Books; 1964: *A Rage in Harlem*, Avon Books.

1958   *Il Pleut des Cours Durs*, Série Noire-Gallimard; 1959: *The Real Cool Killers*, Avon Books; 1966: Berkley Books.

1958   *Couche dans le Pain*, Şérie Noire-Gallimard; 1960: *The Crazy Kill*, Avon Books; 1966: Berkley Books.

1959   *Dare Dare*, Série Noire-Gallimard; 1968: *Run Man Run*, G. P. Putnam's Sons; 1969: reprinted by Dell Publishing Company.

1959   *Tout pour Plaire*, Série Noire-Gallimard; 1960: *The Big Gold Dream*, Avon Books; 1966: Berkley Books.

1960   *Imbroglio Négro*, Série Noire-Gallimard; 1962: *All Shot Up*, Avon Books; 1966: Berkley Books.

1961   *Ne Nous Everons Pas*, Série Noire-Gallimard; 1967: *The Heat's On*, G. P. Putnam's Sons; 1968: reprinted by Dell Publishing Company.

1963   *Retour en Afrique*, Librairie Plon; 1966: *Cotton Comes to Harlem*, G. P. Putnam's Sons; 1967: reprinted by Dell Publishing Company.

1969   *Blind Man with a Pistol*, William Morrow & Company, Inc.

COMING HOME

by George Davis

STACY

I COME INTO the red wooden shower house. It is up on piles to keep snakes—cobras, vipers—from crawling up the drains.

Childress is there already with the water coming down over his head. Above the roar of the water, he says: "I'm not going to let a Harvard-trained nigger inherit the best whore in Thailand."

I repeat it: "So you're not . . ." I say. I do not want to say nigger because I don't know if he'd like hearing a white person say it. I drop my shower clogs out the door into the sand.

"Nope," he says. The water is coming down over him, beating the top of his head, pulling the curls out of his slightly Negroid hair. He opens his mouth and lets water flow into it.

"Why?"

"I don't know," he says as he stops soaping himself and stares for a moment. "I don't know."

I watch him and say to myself: why, if you're back in America and don't give a damn about Thailand or Asia or the Vietnam War?

He gets out of the shower and starts to dry himself
on a large green towel. I come out and down the
stairs too. His brown skin is a little grayish from all
the water that has run over it. He must have been
in the shower a long time before I woke up. Grayish
like his mouth is sometimes when he comes down
from flying and takes his oxygen mask off. Gray and
greaseless.

"She's been with me six months," he says. "For
some reason it just wouldn't feel right, him having
her."

"So you got a way to stop him?" I ask.

"No. But I'll think of something before I go."

"You'd better hurry and dry off. We only got fifteen
minutes."

"What time is briefing?"

"Thirteen past. You wouldn't want to be late for
your last run."

"Yea. I got to go kill my last Gook."

I stare at him as he continues to dry himself. He is
heavy but muscular. His toes are curled up to keep
them out of the sand.

"Either you or Ben in my flight?" he asks.

"No, Ben's earlier and I'm about a half-hour later."

"Too bad, I'd like for one of you to see-me-do-it
this one, last time."

I start across the sand, walking along a path which
separates the beach from the reedy jungle. The towel
hangs around my waist. Dozens of pilots come out of
their tents and out of the other small raised shower
houses. Childress follows me along the path.

BEN

A DUMP TRUCK wakes me. Noisily the truck plows along the dusty road beside the tent, groaning. Another truck follows. I open one eye and watch them through the screen at the side of the tent. The wheels pick up dust and throw it off like water off the prow of a boat. Soon they will finish the new runways they are building down near the gulf, I think.

Stacy's and Childress' cots are empty. I think about Childress singing in the shower. I think about this being his last mission, and about me getting to know his girl, Damg, after he goes back to the States. For a moment I wonder how it would work out if I took her back with me. Marry her. I would marry her. I push myself deep into the mattress on my cot. Twenty more missions for me. Eighty gone. I wonder how many people I have killed. I never think about killing unless I consciously decide to think about killing. Childress must never think about it. I must be more lost than he is, more self-divided, or maybe he is more self-divided than me, less aware of his other human self. Rhyme. No.

I pull myself out of the bed and smother my face in my hands, trying to seal my nose from some of the dust that the sun seems to beat out of the canvas tent top. Already the day is hot. I don't feel like taking a shower. I have sweated in my bed and I feel funky in my pits and groin. I feel the sweat, perspiration,

a Harvard man would say, along the side of my body
and along the inside of both arms so that my arms
stick to my body when I press them against me. I feel
myself funky. I feel funky. As if funky. Through the
door I see a bulldozer pushing down a section of the
jungle where they are going to build the oil storage
tanks. Past that I see treetops wavering and then falling and I think of the barefooted Thais at the bases
of the trees chopping away, clearing a site for the
permanent quarters near the barbwire fence. To me
the barbwire is as much to lock us in as it is to keep
the Asians out.

I take a still-damp towel and wipe my face. I wonder what it will be like having a whore who can
speak English. I wonder what it will be like getting
to know Asia through her. In a way I will be glad to
see Childress leave. I would marry her, yes.

My boots are scuffed. I look down at them and try
to think about napalm because I want to think about
dropping napalm. The floor of the tent is rough. I jam
my feet into the hollowed-out innersole of my boots.
Time for briefing. I stand and visualize myself standing naked in my boots. Then I slip dirty undershorts
over my boots and pull them up. Then I slip on my
flight fatigues. No one can see that I am flying with
no socks on. If I get shot down over the mountains,
my feet will freeze. I never think about getting shot
down.

I leave the tent.

CHILDRESS

THE WAR is changing Stacy, or was he that way when he came into the war. I sit on the side of my cot and dry my feet. Maybe he always was a silly-ass white boy. Otherwise why would he want to room with the only two niggerflyers in the outfit. Hippie-type motherfucker. One of these times I'm going to catch him in the tent singing folk songs.

Ben's gone. Stacy's gone. I look at my watch and laugh. My last motherfucker. Boots untied, I run across to the briefing room.

STACY

THE BENCH IS HARD against my haunches. The Air
Force has enough money to put backs on the benches.
They don't want people to get comfortable enough to
sleep, I think. I am not sleepy.

Captain Peterson is briefing. He briefs the primary
targets. Weather is always bad over primary. We
always go first alternate because the weather over
primary will not be good until April. Peterson leans
forward. His face is bathed in the fluorescent light
from the podium lamp. I hate the briefing because I
have heard it sixty to seventy times. Peterson has
given it two hundred times, but he seems not to
notice.

"One-quarter mile visibility with thunder bumpers
over primary," Peterson says.

I squirm on my bench. Childress stiffens against me
after I rock into him. "We ain't going primary," he
whispers out of the side of his mouth.

"I know," I say.

"Tell Peterson, the ass."

"Let the bastard do his duty," I say. I think Peterson lives by rote. I watch his dumb lower jaw move.
He has a round, reddish face that looks redder yet in
the fluorescent light. The red EXIT bulb is the only
other light in the room.

I am better-looking than Peterson. He has blond
hair. Most girls would think that he is better-looking

because he has blond hair. He looks like he dyes his hair.

He turns on the squawk-box and the weatherman's voice booms into the darkened room. "Weather over primary: one hundred foot overcast, one-quarter mile visibility with towering cumulus . . ." Peterson snaps on a little light above a weather chart. He moves his pointer robot-like across an area just north of Hanoi.

The weatherman's voice is so loud it is distorted. "Any questions?"

No one asks. Peterson comes back into the podium light. The weatherman gives the weather over alternate. Peterson does not point to this area, Pleiku, but I watch it. "Any questions?"

No one speaks. Peterson's head moves out of the light as he puts his pointer down. His wife probably makes him dye his hair. His stupid, little, tight-titted, faithful wife who probably wants blond children.

Childress rocks against me. "No anti-aircraft guns," he whispers.

"Is that what he said?"

"Sure, you know they don't have any in the Pleiku area." Childress laughs.

There is something that I've never really liked about Childress, and it's not a color thing either because I like Ben; but deep down I don't think Ben likes white people.

Peterson's jaw looks dead and heavy as if he has just gotten out of the dentist's chair. "You are executed alternate mission," he says.

My spine is tired from sitting on the backless bench. I stiffen and concave my spine, hoping to put some of my weight on my stomach muscles. I know my back will get sorer yet when I put my parachute on. If I never see an F-105 after this war I'll be happy.

"Any questions?" Peterson asks. We are already out of our seats, milling toward the door.

CHILDRESS

I SAY: "Red Dog 2 is ready for takeoff." I watch to
see when Red Dog 1 releases brakes. His nose gear
tire is a little flat on the runway. I begin to sweat
almost as if I had not taken a shower. Heat from the
sun and the jet engines of the planes—F-105's and
tankers—that have taken off before us bounces up
from the slab of concrete. Number 1 fires his after-
burners sending flames out in back of him. Smoke
drifts across my windshield.

I feel almost guilty having an easy one for my last.
But there is always a chance that some lucky son-of-
a-bitch will get me with ground-fire.

Red Dog 1 releases brakes. I release. We roll.

I break ground and climb fast to catch Red Dog 1
as he levels his wings to climb straight out. I can see
Red Dog 3 closing on me from the left. Red Dog 4 is
sliding into position beside him. Sunshine flashes off
number 1's wings and he looks like a silver bullet in
the empty blue sky.

My radio is garbled. If there is a MIG warning I
wouldn't hear it, but there are no MIG's down where
we are going. Only some lucky son-of-a-bitch on the
ground has a chance of getting me. I nudge my
throttles.

"Red Dog 1 changing frequencies," number 1 says.

"Red Dog 2, changing," I say.

"3, changing," number 3 says.

"4."

After we change frequencies I can hear better. We start eastward along the Cambodian border. There is a light haze across the landscape. For a moment I almost wish that I would see a MIG so I could get me one before I go home. Win another medal. Take it back to Baltimore and wave it in the man's face.

When he says: "Boy . . ." I'll say: "Boy, my ass," and slap him across the nose with one of my medals.

"Turning," Red Dog 1 says.

"Turning," I say and tuck in close in the turn. I look down through the haze and try to locate the large lake north of Phnom Penh, but it is too far away and a little behind us. I strain to look back over my shoulder then I turn around to keep number 1 in sight. The Mekong River is barely visible ahead of us, and I watch it as it seems to slide in our direction until it is directly below us, and I think that after today I will never see the river again. We fly south where the river spreads out like a giant swamp. I rock my wings and look down.

"Turning," number 1 says.

"Turning."

"Turning."

"Turning."

The forward air controller is southeast of us and we take up a course to the southeast toward him. His radio is good.

I see him below us, flying slow just above the tree-tops. The trees lie like a hedge field beneath him, and he seems to hang blue-silver and motionless above the hedges.

"Do you have enough fuel to work with me a half-hour?" he asks.

Red Dog 1 says: "We can stay for a half-hour."

"That should be enough. Do you have four birds?"

"Roger, four chicks," Red Dog 1 says.

Forward air controller directs us south toward our target. Mare's-tail clouds lay between us and a flat

narrow road which zigzags out of the mountains off
to our right and runs straight toward the river before
it disappears into a swamp.

We make a low pass to take a look, then pull up
to wait for forward air controller to drop a smoke
marker where he wants us to hit. We come back
across flying northeast and see bright orange smoke
from the marker drifting up out of the forest.

Forward air controller says some Gooks in trucks
pulled off the road northeast of the smoke. We come
back across flying southeast. The lush foliage is thick
enough to hide something as large as a group of
trucks. I try to spy the path that they made getting
off the road, but the jungle has enveloped everything.
We streak across too fast for me to see much, but I
wonder if there is some lucky son-of-a-bitch down
there in the trees waiting for me.

Red Dog 1 and I come in first. Number 1 lays his
bomb close to the road. I come across. My stomach is
knotted, tensed for the first burst of machine-gun fire.
I put mine closer to the smoke and pull up too soon
to see if we have knocked anything loose. Three more
to go. No machine-gun fire, yet.

Number 1 and I climb and circle back while 3 and
4 come across. I think that the Gooks must be trying
to make us think that they are not down there.

I watch my instruments as I come down again,
lower, and I wait for some unseen hole in the treetops
to begin cracking with machine-gun fire. Red Dog 1
has hit on the road. I oblique to him, pull level and
let the hedge-green trees shoot under me. Then all of
a sudden I pitch up and crash my bomb into the trees
directly on the smoke. Then I pull straight up, spinning. Not that time.

For a moment I feel giddy and am aware of my
hands sweating on the stick. For some strange reason
I want to see the trucks. But then I think it would be
stupid for me to get shot down on my last one. I think
about Ben and my moon-faced, yellow-brown whore

which I risked a court-martial to take away from a
stupid-assed white colonel . . .

I look at my toggles and my fuel gauge. Because
she thought I was a confused and fucked-up black
motherfucker like Ben. But I wanted her pussy not
her sympathy. "Soul-brudder, soul-brudder. I am
same-same you."

She came with me and then she found I did not
need her love. I just wanted her to walk with me. The
finest whore south of Bangkok . . .

I am down almost to the top of the trees and I have
forgotten to flip my toggles. I tell Red Dog 1 my toggles stuck and I break away from him and roll over
and come across upside down, screaming, then pull
up just enough to turn over and let my bomb fly into
the orange smoke, and pull up, spinning.

Ben might fall in love with the bitch, and she would
fall in love with him. Marry her and take her back to
the States and settle down near some nice liberal
college and be happy for life. If I wasn't married I
would marry her and take her back and have her
mess up the mind of anyone I wanted her to mess up
the mind of. Give him some pussy if necessary. Pretty
bitch. Soft. Loyal. Smooth-skinned. Ah . . .

We cloverleaf and come back across target for the
last time and I think if they don't get me now they
never will. If the trees don't open up now they'll
never get me.

Forward air controller says: "Number 2, you're too
low."

I go lower. Fuck him. I lean forward and look but
cannot see, then I tilt to the side and let the last one
go and convince myself that I hear metal crash
against metal as it explodes, and I climb straight up,
past number 1, and the pressure locks me to my seat.
It is over. It is over. I laugh until I almost cry.

BEN

THIS WAR is like Harvard. Nothing in it is real. Everything seems abstract.

I should have joined the infantry, been splattered with the blood, then it would have been real. This is like Harvard, like death in the twentieth century. The killers never see the killed.

Maum lights another reefer. "I've never seen a person die in this war," I say, but I know she does not speak English. She smiles. Then she frowns playfully because she does not like marijuana herself, but she never complains about lighting one for me. Oriental women never complain about anything, I think. I dry my right hand on a towel on the floor, and take the reefer from her and take a heavy drag. I hold my breath to allow the stuff to soak into my lungs. In the abstract situation I'm in, I can only hate whitey for the smaller symptoms of the disease that he is spreading around the world, like segregating the whorehouses and bath houses over here in Thailand.

Maum lifts my left leg out of the tub and soaps it. Like trying to get the Thai girls to hate Negroes by telling them niggers have tails and niggers have big dicks and will hurt them. Maum drops my leg back into the water. She walks around to the other side of the tub and picks my right leg out of the water and soaps it. She hums a little and smiles. I watch her soft, round, smooth, completely hairless, brown-yellow face, so inward-seeming as if she could teach me things that the narrow gnomic bastards at Harvard could never teach in a million years. If she could only speak my language, or I hers. I shiver for a moment knowing that I must not go back to America with all this hatred in me.

I should never have come into the war, but I came like a sheep. During all my life in America I have been led to loving the wrong things and hating the wrong things like I was nothing more than a goddamn sheep.

I lean forward for Maum to soap my back. I keep on letting myself be led the wrong way because our survival has always depended on our lying to ourselves about . . . But our survival does not depend on that any more. Like I could get shot down, and even the lying will not have saved me.

Maum soaps my chest. "Mass-sagee, mass-sagee," she says while helping me out of the tub onto the massage table. I lie on my stomach. She begins to knead my flesh like black bread dough. I keep my head hanging off the table so I can smoke the fifth reefer that Maum has lit for me.

She has smooth legs and small feet. She pulls herself up on her toes as she kneads the flesh on my rib cage. I watch her little toes grabbing the floor. Then she gets on my back and walks around breaking all the stiffness in my body. Her toes grab my back like they did the floor. I moan a little because it hurts and feels good at the same time. She snaps my arms and legs, then she slides to the floor again while I turn over on my back. She puts a towel over my erected penis. I take the towel off. She blushes. I do not smile back at her. She stops smiling. "Mass-sagee, mass-sagee," she says and takes it in her small yellow hand. I shake my head, no. Then I pull her up on the table with me.

CHILDRESS

THE BLUE SKY BAR is crowded and loud. My whore and I come into the main room which looks like nothing so much as a long lean-to with a concrete floor and crepe paper streamers hanging from the ceiling. A row of whores sit near the bar. A single light bulb illuminates them as they talk to each other. The juke box, playing Aretha Franklin, glows in the dark near the door. It makes me think of a red-hot, pot-bellied stove. All the corners of the room are dark.

Another small light bulb hangs from a cord near the center of the dance floor. A few black GI's are dancing with whores.

Ben and some friends are sitting at a long table talking shit. I sit down next to Ben. My whore sits across the table.

"Hey," I say.

My whore says, "Hi." She smiles. Her teeth are perfect.

"Lieutenant Childress, Damg. What's happening?" Ben makes a slight bow toward both of us. "So you're finish?" he says to me.

"Yeah."

"I bet you glad."

"That would be a damn good bet," I say. Ben slides his glass across the oilcloth table. I sip. Damg sips. "Scotch. Nice," I say. Ben signals for the waiter to bring two more glasses.

My whore listens to Ben's friends. Ben and I talk, but I listen to what my whore is listening to. A fat darkskin GI says: "That's how the Chucks got ahead of everybody else in the world. Because the average motherfucking Chuck doesn't *feel* anything. He acts like his emotions are dead. I told this white boy the other day: 'At least I have a heart. You don't have one. You've got icewater in your veins. You would kill your own father if the price was right.' "

Another smaller GI added: "I really don't think the white man can feel anything. He acts like his feelings are numb until he gets scared. Then one of them come crying to me: 'You think they coming back?' Talking about the VC. I say: 'Shut up, motherfucker.' We were up near the DMZ. I think that the only time a Chuck cries is when he's scared."

"That's one thing: a brother will cry when he's sad or when he's happy or when he's fucking," one GI says. They laugh.

The GI continues, "A Chuck never stops thinking. He can't even fuck for thinking. He can't dance for thinking. Here he is walking down the street in Bangkok. The nigger is looking at the Thai women, finest women in the world. You hear me: in the world. And he thinks the Chuck is doing the same thing until all of a sudden the Chuck says: 'When the war is over I'd like to buy up some of this cheap property and hold it until the price goes sky high.' " They laugh. "Damn."

My whore says: "Chuck have no love."

Ben looks at my whore. The others keep talking. "Like most of the antiwar motherfuckers. They ain't really antiwar, they're anti-getting-killed-their-damn-selves. A few of them care. But the vast majority of them don't give a damn about these Vietnamese people."

Ben and my whore glance back and forth at each other. I am afraid. I could never live it down if Ben took my whore right from under my nose. Peaches

& Herb are singing from the juke box. Ben's legs are moving under the table. I am afraid that he is going to ask her to dance, and they are going to get to talking about that wet-eyed shit, and she will choose to go to the bungalow with him instead of me.

The slow song ends. I relax. The juke box plays:

> I just want to testify
> That you sure look good to me.

I think about the money I have saved during my eleven months in Thailand. In the dim light the Thai girls look like little yella colored girls.

A group of GI's are dancing in a line.

> I just want to testify
> That you sure look good to me.

I feel like I want to join in, but I sit still. Every third beat they stomp and the line slides in the opposite direction. Slide. Slide. Stomp.

Two Thai girls are shoving a huge black sergeant, trying to make him lose the beat. He laughs whenever he double-times and falls back in step. His forearms are like giant smoked ham hocks. He double-times. Stomp. The girls try to pull him off balance. He half-times. Stomp.

> I just want to testify
> That you sure look good to me.

He grins and looks at the ceiling, confident now that he is so into the music that he can stay in step without looking at the feet ahead of him. Half-slide. Long-stride. Stomp. "A-a-a-ah!" He wiggles his ass, spins and slides. Stomp. The two girls continue pushing at him. I look around at the dirty place, at the mismatched chairs and tables. I think about the matched-up white whorehouses up the row.

Ben is saying something about flying. I am ready to leave. A slow record starts. Ben asks my whore to dance. I grab her hand. "We got to go. I hadn't planned to stay this long."

"Okay. Childress. Damg." He stands up and bows a little toward each one of us and smiles. Some of the others say: "So long." "Peace." "Later."

I hold her hand and rush, almost run outside. The night is cool. I stop a baht-bus.

The boy says: "One man, two baht."

I say: "One man, one baht."

"One man, two baht," he says.

My whore tells him something in Thai. He pouts and accepts the two baht for the two of us.

The air is peaceful as we ride along. Night air blows into the open sides of the baht-bus. The small boy hangs on the rear running board and jumps down whenever the baht-bus stops to pick up other passengers. Each time we have to slide further forward until we are sitting directly against the cab, Damg on one side and me on the other. The breeze is not so strong. I can lean down and look through the rear window into the cab, past the driver and out the front windshield. I decide to take Damg to the luxury hotel that the Americans have built up past the base.

Through the windshield I can see other baht-buses racing toward us down the narrow road between garish little whorehouses with neon signs. They look like all-night, three- or four-lane bowling alleys with tin or thatch roofs. The Hong Kong-made signs: red, blue, green, blinking FLYBOY, THAI HEAVEN, SWEET HOME, YELLOW ROSE, BOOM BOOM ROOM, HONEY BEE, DREAM-LAND, THUNDERBIRD.

Further up the road where the Americans are tearing down a mountain to get dirt to build a runway on the sand, the air is full of dust. We are near the base. Three white GI's get off the baht-bus. Dump trucks clog the road. Jet engines whine like wounded animals in the Siamese night.

BEN

THE BLUE SKY is almost empty. I walk to the rear and ask Papa-san to fix some fried rice for me. Then I walk over and sit on the concrete floor near the well. The other GI's have gone to the bungalows to sleep with their girls, or back to the air base. I do not want to sleep with anyone. My head hurts from too much scotch.

Papa-san watches me while he cooks, but I do not want to pretend that I am cheerful in order to prevent him from feeling sad that I am alone.

He cooks over a small blazing fire in a pan which he never sets down unless to add more ingredients. The food sizzles, and he lets the smoke come up into his face as the small flames lick up from a bed of rocks and touch the bottom of the pan. He serves the fried rice in a wooden bowl. I pay him a quarter. There are large reddish shrimp in the mixture but I do not feel like eating.

"Lieutenant," he says, "Lieutenant."

I smile.

He goes back to the fire, whispers something in the ear of his youngest son and sends the boy off on an errand. I hear the boy running barefoot on the stones outside the rear compound fence. The old man is plum. The faces of his family are lit by the light of the flames. They sit without eating, without talking, for no apparent reason, they are simply there.

The son returns with a thin, youngish girl. Her clothing is wet in spots, which makes it apparent that she
has been working in a bath house. Papa-san pushes
her toward me, saying: "You sleep with her tonight,
Lieutenant."

She takes the last few steps toward me as if she
has not lost the momentum from his push. She is a
dainty, seventy- or eighty-pound girl with shoulder-
length hair and a small mannish shirt covering her
pointed teen-age breasts. She tucks her head and
blushes. Her shorts are white like the shirt and she
has a scotch-plaid belt holding them up. She would
look tinier yet if she did not have on high-heel shoes
over her white bobby sox. She is amusingly beautiful.
Papa-san and his family are happy that I have someone for the night.

"No, Papa-san," I say.

"She no have VD," he says, his voice quickens and
rises to assure me. He shows me her card which has
a blue circle on it to show that she has passed her
last VD inspection. He takes my hand and places it to
my ear. I know I am supposed to take wax out of my
ear and rub it in her pussy to see if it burns her, but I
do not. "I don't want to pom-pom," I say.

The family laughs at the way I say pom-pom. The
youngest son urges me by slapping his hands together to make the sound that two bodies make slapping together.

The entire family has turned to look at me—four
children, a wife and a mother. I hear a transistor radio
playing from one of the bungalows.

The girl is embarrassed. "We walk," I say.

"Chi," she says, and the old toothless woman sitting on the other side of the flames shakes her head,
yes.

"Yes, poo ying," I say.

We leave along the back path in front of the dark
wooden bungalows where several GI's are sitting out
with their girls.

The bungalows are in a row like a series of out-houses in back of an old Southern church. A wooden platform runs along in front of them and a naked shiny-skinned GI runs down the platform to where the vat of water is. He squats and washes his privates, then tiptoes back past us into his bungalow.

For a stretch the narrow path leads into the jungle before it turns toward the main road. The girl and I hold hands as we walk along the ditch that carries waste from the tapioca mill down to the ocean. The girl laughs and holds her nose at the wet-dog odor of the ditch. I laugh.

For a moment I wonder what would happen if I disappeared forever into the human and bamboo jungles of Asia.

We reach the road and walk along the stony shoulder. She takes off her high-heels and walks in her sox for a while, then she takes them off too. In some places the air is chilly, and in others we walk through warm air. Walking through ghost, we used to call it down South, before Harvard, before everything became literal and scientific, and then became more unreal than ever it was before, leading straight to Vietnam. Before a million explanations came down between me and what I wanted to feel, and then all the explanations proved to be lies.

As I walk I feel strangely free, and I dread the thought of going back to America. I do not know how I can ever feel right about America again, after what they got weak-assed me to do over here.

I want to go to graduate school, but I know I will never sit in a class and learn from a white man. And who will I work for, and where will I go.

The road turns out of the trees and runs along the beach. The Gulf is empty and the black morning is peppered with stars. The air on the beach is cool. I feel the presence of billions of people around me whose lives are menaced in the same way that my life is menaced. Like the millions of Chinese who were slaves in their own country for centuries.

I think of Damg. I know she understands this, and I know that here, in this small place beside the ocean she is lonely with that knowledge. But just as I could give her an account of the treachery and ambition of the West, she could lead me into Asia so full of endurance like the earth itself. Into Bangkok, Rangoon, Kuala Lumpur, Djakarta, Calcutta and across the Indian Ocean to Africa.

We walk down toward the water's edge. There is nothing man-made in sight except for a puny wooden dock where the trucks come down to pick up the ammunition and jet fuel as it is loaded off the ships anchored in deep water.

"Pom-pom?" the girl says in a weak voice and sits down and begins to undo her shorts.

"No," I say and take out my wallet and give her five dollars anyway. Tomorrow I want to bring Damg on this same walk. We could sit on the edge of this continent which has been kept under the foot of white men, until finally China had to get an H-bomb and say: no more. And the people I am fighting, me, in Vietnam had to say: you can kill me but you can't enslave me any more. And me fighting them. As if my own fate and the fate of American blacks is not linked to the fate of nonwhite people all over the earth.

STACY

THE WATER IS COLD. I try to turn hot water on but none comes. I get wet gradually and then I do not shiver as the cold water comes down across me. I look through the door down toward where they are building the new runway. Then I see Childress walking toward the showerhouse. He is almost a silhouette against the clear blue sky. I can see that he has civilian clothes on, and that he must be just getting back from town.

He walks slower than usual. But, I think, there is no reason for him to hurry since he does not have to fly this morning.

"Just back from town?" I ask.

"Wheew! Yeah. Walked all the way for a change." He sits down on the shower-house stairs and takes off his shoes.

"Having your last big fling?"

"Yeah. I feel sweaty, funky and drunk." He stands up. "Tonight I'll be in Bangkok. Friday, Hawaii. Sunday, San Francisco. How about that shit?"

"Shit, I wish I was leaving too."

"It takes time, my boy." Naked, he walks up the stairs, turns on a shower and slides slowly under the water. I watch his toes curl up until he gets used to the cold water then his feet relax and flatten out on the wooden floor.

"What about your whore?" I ask.

He laughs slightly. He takes water into his mouth and gargles briefly. He spits. "She's fine. Beautiful as ever with her Chinese-looking self."

"I mean about Ben," I say. "You said you wasn't going to let a Harvard-trained dude inherit the best whore in Thailand."

"I know," he says.

"But there's no way you can stop it from back in the United States, is it?"

The water seems to freshen his appearance. He spits again. There is something frightening about his naked, muscular cleanliness. I step out of the shower and stand on the steps drying myself.

"I hid some communistic papers in her room," he says.

"So?" I stop drying.

"Now all I have to do is call the Office of Special Investigation." He is out from under the water standing in the shower-house door. "When they find the literature, they'll swear that she's a communist. See. And no red-blooded Amurrican, including Ben, will be allowed within a mile of her."

I look at him.

He steps out of the shower onto the top of the stairs. I feel empty inside.

"It is as simple as that."

"I bet."

"Really," he says.

All I can think of to say is: "You didn't bring a towel to dry yourself."

"I can use yours when you are finished," he says. "I'm not afraid of catching white folk's germs," he says.

The Atlantic Slave Trade and Slavery

*Some Interpretations of
Their Significance in the
Development of the United States
and the Western World*

by C. L. R. James

EVERY PEOPLE, every race, has passed through a stage of slavery. That which ought to be a commonplace of history has been obscured, corrupted and ignored by the injection of slavery into a modern and advanced society like the United States. It would be not only inextricably confusing but impossible to attempt any summary of the infinite varieties of slavery in past ages. However, it is useful to bear in mind two of these varieties. The first is the systematic breeding and selling of their own children into slavery by the backward peoples of Northern Europe. They traded with the highly developed civilization of Rome, even when Rome was ruled by the papacy. The second is the oft-repeated sneer that the magnificent civilization of ancient Greece was based on slavery. Slavery did not help to build the social order of the Greece that laid the foundations of Western civilization in so many spheres. Rather, it was the growth of slavery which ruined ancient Greece. Furthermore, the term "slave" did not then have the meaning it has had since the

African slave-trade to the Americas. The slaves in
the mines of Greece were cruelly exploited, but in
Athens itself slaves could become educated and officials in the city administration, and could attend the
ritual performances of the dramatic festivals. As late
as the fourth century B.C., when the democracy was
on the decline, Plato complained that the concept and
practices of democracy were so deeply engrained in
Athenian society that not only the slaves, but the very
horses and dogs walked about in the streets of Athens
in a manner that proclaimed their democratic rights.

Today it would be impossible to examine the most
important of all phases of slavery, African slavery in
the American continents, without having some view
of the slavery in Africa itself before the Europeans
established the Atlantic slave-trade, and the African
slavery which was the result of that trade. African
slavery before the European slave-trade was internal.
For the most part it was also patriarchal. Thirty years
ago, I summarized African civilization and the effects
of the European slave-trade as follows:

> . . . In the sixteenth century, Central Africa was a
> territory of peace and happy civilisation. Traders
> travelled thousands of miles from one side of the con-
> tinent to another without molestation. The tribal wars
> from which the European pirates claimed to deliver the
> people were mere sham fights; it was a great battle
> when half-a-dozen men were killed. It was on a peas-
> antry in many respects superior to the serfs in large
> areas of Europe, that the slave-trade fell. Tribal life
> was broken up and millions of detribalised Africans
> were let loose upon each other. The unceasing destruc-
> tion of crops led to cannibalism; the captive women
> became concubines and degraded the status of the
> wife. Tribes had to supply slaves or be sold as slaves
> themselves. Violence and ferocity became the necessi-
> ties for survival. The stockades of grinning skulls, the
> human sacrifices, the selling of their own children as
> slaves, these horrors were the product of an intolerable
> pressure on the African peoples, which became fiercer

through the centuries as the demands of industry increased and the methods of coercion were perfected . . .

Within recent decades an immense amount of research has been done on pre-European Africa. Not only does that analysis still hold its ground, but there has been added to it a conception of pre-European African history, which stresses the intellectual achievements of the postwar world. In a study done for UNESCO on *Race and History*, Claude Lévi-Strauss, after a recognition of the "richness and audacity of the aesthetic invention" of primitive peoples turns to Africa:

> The contribution of Africa is more complex, but also more obscure, for it is only at a recent period that we have begun to suspect the importance of its role as a cultural melting pot of the ancient world: a place where all influences have merged to take new forms or to remain in reserve, but always transformed into new shapes. The Egyptian civilisation, of which one knows the importance for humanity, is intelligible only as a common product of Asia and of Africa and the great political systems of ancient Africa, its juridical creations, its philosophical doctrines for a long time hidden from the West, its plastic arts and its music which explored methodically all possibilities offered by each means of expression are equally indications of an extraordinarily fertile past. The latter besides is directly attested to by the perfections of the ancient techniques of bronze and of ivory which surpass by far all that the West was practising in those spheres in the same period.

Neolithic man tilled the soil, domesticated animals, invented and used tools, and lived a family life subject to certain social regulations. Claude Lévi-Strauss believed that this was the decisive moment in the history of human civilization. However, he is prepared to admit that there has been one other fundamental change in the life of civilized man. The Industrial Rev-

olution, bringing mechanical power into use, altered
the conditions of life and created a new type of society.

We can see this most dramatically in the two most
important concerns of civilized man, war and revolution. Alexander the Great, Hannibal, Julius Caesar,
and Napoleon each would have understood what the
others were trying to accomplish on the field of battle;
their strategy and tactics would have been much the
same. But the moment we examine the American
Civil War, military conflict breaks entirely out of the
limits in which it had remained for thousands of years.
The reason was the introduction of mechanical power
—in the form of the railway—into war. Armies could
now be five times as large as before. This larger
army, with its rapidity of movement, upset the industrial and the social structure of the nation. Today, a
little more than a hundred years later, the development of industrial power imperils the very continua-
tion of civilized life.

It is the move to large-scale industry and the accumulation of great numbers of men in factories which
is the starting point and the basis of Marx's theory of
socialist revolution, and the contemporary nightmare
of social destruction. There is no question today that
the resources which initiated and established this
epoch-making change in human life resulted from the
Atlantic slave-trade and the enslavement of Africans
in the Americas. Jean Léon Jaurès, in his history of
the French Revolution, a work which is a landmark
not only in the history of the Revolution, but in the
writing of modern history, comments wistfully: "Sad
irony of human history ... The fortunes created at
Bordeaux, at Nantes, by the slave-trade, gave the
bourgeoisie that pride which needed liberty and contributed to human emancipation." But Jaurès, whose
thought represented the quintessence of Social Democracy, was here limited by his preoccupation with
parliamentary politics. Gaston-Martin, in his *L'Ere des*

Négriers, makes it clear that nearly all the industries which developed in France during the eighteenth century had their origin in goods or commodities destined either for the Coast of Guinea or for America. It was the capital gained from the slave trade which fertilized what became the Industrial Revolution. Though the bourgeoisie traded in many things, everything depended on the success or failure of the traffic in slaves. In *Capitalism and Slavery*, Eric Williams has demonstrated that it was in slavery and the slave trade that the power originated which created modern industry in England, making it the workshop of the world.

The overwhelming majority of historians show a curious disinclination to deal with the seminal role played by the slave trade and slavery in the creation of what distinguishes Western civilization from all other civilizations. As far back as 1847, Karl Marx stated in very aggressive terms what modern civilization, and in particular the United States, owed to the enslavement of black people from Africa. Karl Marx, in 1846 in his polemical work *The Poverty of Philosophy*, made slavery in the United States the center of his comprehensive uncovering of the fires which stoked Western civilization.

> Direct slavery is just as much the pivot of bourgeois industry as machinery, credits, etc. Without slavery you have not cotton; without cotton you have no modern industry. It is slavery . . . and it is world trade that is the pre-condition of large-scale industry. Thus slavery is an economic category of the greatest importance.
>
> Without slavery North America, the most progressive of countries, would be transformed into a patriarchal country. Wipe North America off the map of the world, and you will have anarchy—the complete decay of modern commerce and civilization. Cause slavery to disappear and you will have wiped America off the map of nations.
>
> Thus slavery, because it is an economic category,

has always existed among the institutions of the peoples. Modern nations have been able only to disguise
slavery in their own countries, but they have imposed
it without disguise upon the New World.

Fifty years after Marx's statement, an American historian, a young man twenty-four years of age, tackled
the question. In 1954, looking again at his doctoral
dissertation written for Harvard University in 1896,
*The Suppression of the African Slave Trade to the
United States of America, 1638–1870,* Dr. W. E. B.
Du Bois, in an apologia of two and a half pages, three
times expressed his regret that when he was doing the
work he had not had the benefit of any acquaintance
with the works or theories of Karl Marx. Yet with his
own independent, if youthful, judgment Dr. Du Bois
here showed himself as far in advance of American
historiography as he was to show himself in other
spheres of American life.

First of all, the title of the book could be misleading.
The actual attempt at suppression (1807–1825) is
treated as late as Chapter Eight. What we have here
is a history of the slave trade and slavery in the
United States. It is true that the very first sentence of
the monograph, as he calls it (197 pages of text and
98 pages of appendices), declares that he proposes to
set forth the efforts from early colonial times until the
present to limit and suppress the trade in slaves between Africa and America.

He first separates the Planting Colonies (the South)
from the Farming Colonies (New Jersey), and then
moves into the period of the Revolution. He notes that
from about 1760 to 1787, there is a "pronounced effort
to regulate, limit, or totally prohibit the traffic." Chapter Six deals with the Federal Convention and the
spirit of compromise leading each state (i.e., in the
South) to deal with the question of slavery as it
pleased. Then comes a most interesting chapter where
we see at work the same mind which in *Black Re-*

construction in America linked the emancipation of the slaves in 1865 to the Paris Commune in 1871, and the black struggle for freedom in 1935 to the world-wide struggle against fascism and for colonial emancipation. Young Du Bois heads the chapter "Toussaint L'Ouverture and Anti-Slavery Effort, 1787–1807." The Haitian Revolt sharpens the debate for and against slavery in the U.S.A. It is "the main cause of two laws" and soon was "the direct instigation to a third." But despite the combined efforts of fear and philanthropy, the profits of trade won in the end.

Du Bois is pretty certain that it was the Haitian Revolution and its influence which was one of the main causes of the suppression of the slave trade by national law. But to the apathy of the federal government is now added "The Rise of the Cotton Kingdom, 1820–1850." He concludes with a chapter on "The Lesson for Americans." The Constitutional Convention had avoided the issue when it had been possible to do something about it. "No American can study the connection of slavery with United States history and not devoutly pray that his country will never have a similar social problem to solve, until it shows more capacity for such work than it has shown in the past." The last sentence of the text is even more clearly a product of moralistic thought. "From this we may conclude that it behooves nations, as well as men, to do things at the very moment when they ought to be done."

We can only estimate the numbers involved, but it is certain that the slave trade shifted many millions of Africans from their homeland. A conservative estimate is that 15,000,000 Africans landed after crossing the Atlantic; but some estimates give 50,000,000 and some go even higher. Further, the mortality rate on the voyage to the Americas was often high, and in addition some were killed in Africa in the raids and wars conducted to get slaves, and some died while waiting to be sold or shipped.

Effectively (and officially) the slave trade lasted three centuries, from about 1550 to 1850. Its period of greatest activity began after the middle of the seventeenth century. There have been many arguments about the effects of the trade on the African economy and population. We know it led directly to nineteenth-century colonialism in Africa and the accompanying degradation of the Africans. But an important area of research remains uninvestigated, which we can only mention here. What were the social and moral effects of slaving on the Africans who bought and sold slaves —what did they think of it themselves? What have been the long-term effects on the African peoples who remained on the continent? Our sources and scholarship are almost entirely Western, and Western thinking has governed our assessment, regardless of whether our standards have been overtly racist or antipathetic to slavery. But surely one of the most important areas of study is what Africans themselves thought of the trade, and what effect it had and perhaps lingeringly continues to have on Africa itself.

Scholars continue to argue about the effects on those taken into slavery. A plateau was reached in 1959, when Stanley Elkin examined the basis for what he called the "Sambo" stereotype of North American slave character. One of the most important bases of his argument is that the capture, voyage, sale, and adjustment to the new environment of the Africans may have created a "shock" that stripped them of their former personalities and rendered their cultural background meaningless.

Most revolts came either at the point of embarkation or between that time and actual sailing. Gaston-Martin catalogues several slave revolts on board ships, and says that he discovered fifty references to revolts, or about one every fifteen trips, in his studies of Nantes slaving. (Nantes is a French seaport.) He adds that there were almost certainly many revolts which were never recorded, and he comments that they were very likely accepted as a normal hazard of the trade. Some revolts even took place at sea, where the slaves would perish even if they overcame the crew, for they had no idea of how to steer the ships. Ships' logs record the ferocity of these revolts. Usually they failed, with only a few slaves and crew members dead; sometimes the death toll went as high as forty or fifty. Rather than be taken again some blacks drowned themselves. Many crew members died. A few revolts did succeed, in which case the crew was usually massacred, sometimes merely taken captive.

In these revolts, captains accessed the most Europeanized slaves as the leaders—for some slaves had been to Europe at one time or another. Informers among the slaves existed from time to time; but when they were discovered by their fellows, they were killed.

One writer quotes a 1788 account saying the blacks were always on the lookout to rebel or escape. "Insurrections are frequently the consequence, which are seldom suppressed without much bloodshed. Sometimes these are successful and the whole ship's company is cut off." Basil Davidson himself adds, "When they failed in revolt before they reached the Americas, they revolted there." Of the slaves, he writes, "The best and strongest took the first or second chance to resist or revolt: the rest endured. But endurance did not mean acceptance."

Revolts might also take place in coordination with attacks by Africans on the ship or shore "warehouse." Around 1760, the *Diane* was attacked by Africans while the captives revolted. The French crew was captured and ransomed by Europeans who later handed them over to a French ship. The *Diane* was lost. The

Concorde underwent two revolts. During the first, forty-five blacks disappeared; in the second a coordinated attack between revolting slaves and a party from land destroyed the ship and killed all the crew but one.

Once the ship had sailed, the danger of revolt was greatly diminished. Suicides were frequent among slaves who could not bear their misery or stand the idea of enslavement. Some slaves threw themselves overboard during the voyage, and there are many reports of slaves dying of nostalgia either en route or in the Americas. To combat nostalgia and simultaneously give the slaves an early recovery period from the first stage of the voyage, which was invariably the worst stretch for them, about one fifth of the Nantes slavers out of Guinea would stop off for four to six weeks at islands in the eastern Atlantic. Here the slaves could rest, get fresh food, and rebuild the strength they had lost during the first stage of the voyage. Sometimes a high rate of sickness would prompt a ship to make a stopover. "Already isolated from the continent, the Negroes, in spite of a few examples of revolts, seem less antagonistic than on land, returned to good physical condition, they better endure the two or three months at sea separating them from the American islands."

Epidemics were frequent and could kill up to half to two thirds of the cargo. The most common illnesses were scurvy, diarrhea, and various skin diseases. Insurrections, as we have seen, were still an occasional threat, and if the attempt failed masses of slaves might commit suicide together rather than submit to recapture. The mortality rate varied considerably from voyage to voyage and year to year. This is reflected in a list of mortality rates among slaves traded by Nantes shippers between 1715 and 1775. The rate ranged from 5 to 9 percent in sixteen years; from 10 to 19 percent in twenty-two years; 20 to 29 percent in fourteen years; and was 34 percent in 1733. In 1751, the year of the greatest slaving activity on the records, 10,003 Negroes were traded and 2,597 died, giving a mortality rate of 26 percent. For the total period from 1715 to 1775, 237,025 slaves were shipped and 35,727 died, giving a mortality rate of 15.1 percent.

After leaving the African coast and any stopovers, the "middle passage" began, lasting normally two or three months, though large ships might occasionally make the trip in forty days. The slaves could still die or commit suicide, though if there had been a stopover for "refreshment," the number of these deaths declined. But other dangers and the length of the middle passage eclipsed the earlier problems. Storms and calms were equally dangerous—the former because it could sink a ship, the latter because it could extend a voyage beyond the range of provisions. Pirates were a constant threat, and the frequent European wars put many enemy ships on the main sea lanes. As with the gathering of captives, a slaver's life, from his point of view, was not an easy one, and expenses could be disastrous. The degree of profit had to be calculated after several voyages, averaging out likely single losses against long-term gains. Whatever the problems, the trade was so extensive that it surely must have been profitable overall.

Treatment of the slaves on board depended a great deal on the captain. But if slavers were not systematically cruel, they were not at all benevolent.

A few writers emphasize that captains were normally not excessively cruel, for it was in their own interest to bring into port as large a live shipment as possible. But when we say "excessively," we are certainly speaking in relative terms. The slaves were never well treated; they were crowded into pens too small to stand up in. The slavers' basic doctrine was that the blacks would obey only in the face of force and terror. Fear of the slaves was the permanent psychological feature of slaver, slave trader, and slave owner. The captives were kept in irons throughout the voyages; the whips would be used for the most trivial purposes. And revolts were brutally punished. Normally only a few suspected ringleaders and examples were executed; but the manner of execution involved torture.

Upon arrival at his destination, the slaver first had to be cleared with health authorities. The inspectors were often bribable—indeed, they often refused clearance unless bribed. Sometimes they would demand that the captain disinfect his ship—buying the disinfectant in the colony, of course. A local governor who feared the captives might be dangerous could quarantine the ship under pretext of fearing a health problem. And genuine epidemics existed often enough to make genuine quarantine a necessity.

Next came port taxes. In the French colonies, Louis XV decreed that the island governors should receive a 2 percent ad valorem gratuity, half for themselves, half to be split by the two lieutenant governors. In fact this gratuity system was often used as the basis for extortion of much higher amounts. Captains who protested too much could find themselves in jail.

Official cheating of slaving captains was common, even when forbidden by royal edict. Large fees could be extorted for such things as anchorage, legal costs, registration of documents, and so on. And of course if the captain had to make calls at several ports, these expenses all were multiplied.

Captains normally tried to give their slaves refreshment to prepare them for sale. When they did not have time, they doped the slaves to give them as healthy an appearance as possible. Slavers would first get rid of their worst-looking slaves at a low price. Many speculators were prepared to take a chance on buying such slaves and hoping they would survive, reckoning a one-third survival rate as satisfactory. The slaver would receive about what he had originally paid for them.

Sometimes the sale might be held up until a propitious moment, especially if there was a glut on the slave market. Either the captain or the company's agent would handle the sale, sending out leaflets to announce the time and place, and the time when the "merchandise" could be inspected. The seller would divide his slaves up into lots of about three or four, grouping them in a way that would bring the highest bidding. The auction would either be done in the usual way—taking competing bids until the highest was reached; or else bidders would be allowed each to make one bid for an entire lot.

If the sales were transacted on board, there was a reasonable chance of suicide by some of the slaves; if on land, there was a reasonable chance of escape. Here, again, we have evidence that at least some of the slaves were not so shattered at this point that they had lost all sense of personality.

Payment was rarely in cash. Often it was on credit, and defaulted payments were frequent. Apparently noncash payments accounted for over half of the sales for Nantes slavers. At the start of the French and Indian War, they were owed 15,000,000 pounds. In order to stay on in the islands and collect their money, captains would frequently send their ships home under command of their first mates.

A second method of payment was either in merchandise or by deposit transfer at home. Most French planters kept bank accounts in France, and captains seem to have been good judges of which ones to trust. The most common method, certainly, was exchange of commodities. Either the buyer would give his goods to the seller directly, or else the buyer would write out I.O.U.'s which the captain would quickly spend on the island, buying up goods to bring home. The captains suffered some loss on the merchandise in this way—but presumably they more than made up for it when the commodities came to be sold in Europe, where they commanded very high prices.

This, then, was the slave trade. It was not easy on the slavers or on the slaves. It is notable that probably as many crew members as slaves died during the voyages. African leaders, if not ordinary free Africans, often willingly collaborated in the trade; and if they and the Europeans were out to get what they could from each other, and prepared to cheat each other where possible, it remains those who were actually enslaved who suffered the greatest miseries and hardships, and who died in vast numbers.

Who were the slaves? They came for the most part from West Africa, these slaves who had been stolen and taken from their homes and brought virtually nothing with them, except themselves. The slaves not only could not bring material objects with them, they could not easily bring over their older social institutions, their languages and cultures. Coming from a large area of West Africa in which dozens upon dozens of distinct peoples lived, with their own languages, social relations, cultures, and religions, these Africans were jumbled together on board the slave ships, "seasoned" by the middle passage and then seasoned again in their first years in the New World.

For the slave brought himself; he brought with him the content of his mind, his memory. He thought in the logic and the language of his people. He recognized as socially significant that which he had been taught to see and comprehend; he gestured and laughed, cried, and held his facial muscles in ways that had been taught him from childhood. He valued that which his previous life had taught him to value; he feared that which he had feared in Africa; his very motions were those of his people and he passed all of this on to his children. He faced this contradictory situation in a context into which he was thrown among people of different African backgrounds. All Africans were slaves, slaves were supposed to act in a specific way. But what was this way? There was no model to follow, only one to build.

The slave from Africa was denied the right to act out the contents of his mind and memory—and yet he *had* to do this. How was this contradiction resolved? What were the new forms created in the context of slavery?

A new community was formed; it took its form in the slave quarters of the plantations and the black sections of the cities. In the United States, this community developed its own Christian church, one designed to meet the needs of slaves and Afro-American freedmen in the New World. It had its own system of communication based on the reality of the plantation. It had its own value system, reflective of the attitudes of African peasants, but at the same time owing its allegiance to dominant American modes. It had its own language patterns, because of the isolation of the plantation system from steady European linguistic influences. West African words and speech patterns were combined with the speech of the eighteenth-century Scotch-Irish.

This black community was the center of life for the slaves; it gave them an independent basis for life. The slaves did not suffer from rootlessness—they belonged to the slave community, and even if they were sold down the river they would find themselves on new plantations. Here, people who shared a common destiny would help them find a life in the new environment.

Each plantation was a self-sufficient unit. The slaves worked at all the skills necessary to maintain the plantation in working order and keep at a minimum the expense of importing necessary items from England. Slave blacksmiths manufactured everything from nails to plowshares. Coopers made the hoops

around the tobacco barrels. The clothing they wore
was turned out by slave shoemakers, dyers, tanners,
and weavers. The slave artisan moved from one task
to another as the need arose.

Skilled labor also took the slave off the plantation.
Black pilots poled the rafts laden with tobacco from
the tributaries of the river to its mouth, where the
ship was anchored; black seamen conducted the fer-
ries across Virginia's rivers to transport new settlers.
Many planters found it more profitable to hire out
their skilled black workmen for seventy-five to two
hundred dollars a year. This black craftsman living
away from the plantation was allowed seventy-five
cents a week as his allowance for food and board.
When the colonies engaged in their war with England for independence, all imports from the mother
country ceased. Crude factories were started and
slaves were used to work them; also, out of the mines
they dug lead, a necessary ingredient in the manu-
facture of bullets.

The tedium of tobacco cultivation was worse than
the exhaustion of simple physical labor. Cotton, which
succeeded tobacco as the plantation's output, had to
be chopped with great care when the young plant had
no more than three or four leaves.

Overworked field hands would take off to the
nearby weeds or swamps where they would lay out
for a time. At night they would steal back to the slave
quarters for food and information about what the master intended to do about their absence. In the swamps
of the eastern section of North Carolina, runaways
were employed by black lumbermen or the poor
whites and could raise their own children for a time.
The master, who didn't know the hideouts as well as
the slaves did, let it be known through a word passed
on to the slave quarters that he was prepared to nego-
tiate for less work and no whippings if only his precious laborers would return.

The slaves fought to set their own tempo and rhythm of work. Says Frederick Douglass:

> There is much rivalry among slaves, at times, as to which can do the most work and masters generally seek to promote such rivalry. But some of them were too wise to race each other very long. Such racing, we had the sagacity to see, was not likely to pay. We had times out for measuring each others strength, but we knew too much to keep up the competition so long as to produce an extra-ordinary days work. We knew that if by extra-ordinary exertion, a large quantity of work was done in one day, the fact becoming known to the master, the same would be expected of us every day. This thought was enough to bring us to a dead halt whenever so much excited for the race.

There was very little of the slave's life that he could call his own. In the slave quarters at night there was a lowering of the mask that covered the day's labors. Bantering and mimicry, gossiping and laughter could be unrestrained. House servants regaled other members of the "row"—some of whom had never set foot in the big house—with tales of "master" and "missus," would "take them off" in speech and gesture so faithful that the less privileged would shake with laughter.

Besides the oppression of the master himself, his laws and his overseers, the slaves were oppressed by their limited knowledge of the world outside the plantation. Masters felt that a slave who learned how to read and write would lose his proficiency at picking worms off tobacco leaves or at chopping cotton, so thoroughly had slavery separated thought and feeling from work. But the capacities of men were always leaping out of the confinements of the system. Always with one eye cocked toward the door, the slaves learned how to read and write, thus they attained that standard—besides the accumulation of money, tobacco, cotton, and lands—by which society judged the standing of its members. The Bible was the most readily available book; its wide and varied use by the slave would have made the founders of Christianity proud. It was a course in the alphabet, a first reader, and a series of lessons in the history of mankind.

The capacities of men were always leaping out of the confinements of the system. Written passes, which slaves were required to carry on their person when away from the plantation, could be made up by those who had learned how to read and write. Deciphering the alphabet opened new avenues to the world. A primary achievement of the slaves as a class is that they fashioned a system of communication—an illegal, underground, grapevine telegraph which would stand the test of an emergency.

When hostilities broke out between the thirteen colonies and the King of England, the British field commander in the South offered freedom to every slave who would enter his army. In Virginia alone, thirty thousand fled their labors; the bitter comment of a slaveholder points up this situation: "Negroes have a wonderful art of communicating intelligence among themselves; it will run several hundred miles in a fortnight." There was such a large proportion of slaves in the state, that South Carolina did not even dare enter the War of Independence for fear of what its laboring force would do. It lost twenty-five thousand nevertheless. Across the South every fifth slave fled toward the British army.

An independent national state was being set up by an American Congress. The very air became filled with expressed passions of human rights, liberties, dignity, equality, and the pursuit of happiness. One of its effects on the slaves was seen on the night of August 30, 1800. Over one thousand slave rebels gathered some six miles from Richmond, capital city of Virginia, the state which was to produce four of the first five American Presidents. All through the spring of that year the slaves prepared their own arms, including five hundred bullets, manufactured in secret.

Each Sunday for months, Gabriel Prosser entered the city, noting its strategic points and possible sources of arms and ammunition. Their plan was to proclaim Virginia a Negro state. If the merchants of Richmond would yield their fortunes to the rebels their lives would be spared and they would be feted at a public dinner.

On the night appointed for the march a heavy rain had fallen, making the road into Richmond impassable. The delay gave the stunned authorities an opportunity to mobilize themselves. Some forty slaves were arrested and put on trial. They revealed no names of other participants. Some estimates placed the extent of the rebellion at ten thousand slaves, others put the figure as high as sixty thousand. The demeanor and remarks of the prisoners on trial— Gabriel: "I have nothing more to offer than what General Washington would have had to offer, had he been taken and put on trial by them. I have adventured my life to obtain the liberty of my countrymen . . ."

In this early period the slave who ran away was most often a skilled craftsman, a man with confidence of making his way in the world. As described by a newspaper advertisement of the day:

> Run away from the subscriber's farm, about seven miles from Anapolis, on the 8th instant; two slaves Will and Tom; they are brothers. Will, a straight tall well-made fellow, upwards of six feet high, he is generally called black, but has a rather yellowish complextion, by trade a carpenter and a cooper, and in general capable of the use of tools in almost any work; saws well at the whip saw, about thirty years of age. When he speaks quick he stammers a little in his speech. Tom, a stout well-made fellow, a bright mulatto, twenty-four years of age, and about five feet nine or ten inches high; he is a complete hand at plantation work and can handle tools pretty well . . . they have a variety of clothing, and it is supposed they will not appear abroad in what they wear at

> home. Will writes pretty well, and if he and his brother
> are not furnished with passes from others they will
> not be lost for them, but upon proper examination may
> be discovered to be forged. These people it is imagined
> are gone for Baltimore as Tom has a wife there . . .

Except in a general way he could not be sure of the
direction of his travels, guiding himself by the stars
and by the moss which grew on the shady side of the
trees. In earlier days the safest places of concealment
were the nearby swamps, the neighboring Indian
tribes and Spanish Florida. The long military arm of
the slavocracy eventually reached into all these temporary outposts of freedom and incorporated them into
slavery. Then soldiers returning from the War of 1812
brought the news that slavery was outlawed in Canada. The route of flight began to cut across the Kentucky mountain ranges and the Atlantic seacoast.

John Parker, a free black man from Ripley, Ohio,
considered it below his dignity to ask any white man
how to conduct slaves to freedom; he was responsible
for the successful passage of one thousand runaways,
but left no memoirs as to how he carried out his work.

In later years the work of the scout took him into
the Deep South rather than await the knock on the
door. On her expeditions, Harriet Tubman would take
the precaution of starting on Saturday night so that
they would be well along their journey before they
were advertised. Harriet often paid another black person to follow the man who posted the descriptions of
her companions and to tear them down. The risks of
taking along different types of people in one group
had to be considered. Babies were sometimes drugged
with paregoric. She sometimes strengthened the faint-
hearted by threatening to use her revolver and de-
claring, ". . . you go on you die . . . dead [N]egroes
tell no tales . . ."

As with practical people everywhere, everything
was done with the materials at hand. An iron manikin in front of the home of Judge Piatt marked an

interrupted station; the judge was hostile to the activity, but his wife was an enthusiastic undergrounder. A flag in the hand of the manikin signaled that the judge was not home and that his house had become a temporary station on the road. For disguise one runaway was provided simply with a gardening tool placed on his shoulder. He marched through town in a leisurely way like a man going to work somebody's garden, left the tool in a selected thicket at the edge of town, and proceeded on his way.

The Underground Railroad in the period of the 1840's grew so saucy that it advertised itself publicly as the only railroad guaranteed not to break down. Multiple routes were the key to the practical success of the railroad. It all came into being after the period of the Founding Fathers had definitively come to an end. The men of education, the leading figures of the Revolution, Washington, Jefferson, Adams, Hancock, Hamilton, Lafayette, and Kosciusko, all expressed opposition to slavery in their private conversations and correspondence. But their chief fear was that pushing antislavery to the fore might permanently divide the country into antagonistic sections.

Washington accurately described the sentiment in certain parts of the country after he himself had lost a slave in New England. "The gentleman in whose care I sent him has promised every endeavor to apprehend him; but it is not easy to do this when there are numbers who would rather facilitate the escape of slaves than apprehend them when they run away."

In the early formation of the Underground Railroad, another group whom the runaway touched with his fire was the Quakers. When they arrived in America to escape persecution, the prosperous trade in slaves corrupted even the most tender of consciences. Not being interested in politics, and prohibited by religious belief from being diverted by the theater, sports, or drink, the Quakers became highly successful businessmen and farmers. The Quakers were prominent and influential people and could afford to rely on the letter of the law which in Northern states had declared slavery illegal.

Having established the principle, effective organization for antislavery work came naturally to a group whose life had been drawn tightly together for hundreds of years as a religious sect. By 1820 there were some four thousand fugitive slaves in the Quaker stronghold of Philadelphia and all advertisements for runaways disappeared from Pennsylvania newspapers.

Free blacks, Quakers, and New Englanders, linked up to each other, conducted the Atlantic coast route of Underground Railroad operations. Men of a different stamp initiated a section of the western route. At the turn of the century the back-country farmer of Virginia and the Carolinas suffered much from the poverty of his land. The state legislatures were in the control of coastal planters and their lawyers; new government taxes and old debts magnified his poverty. He freed himself of all these burdens by migrating westward into the wilderness.

The slaves who accompanied this first great tide of migration, which depopulated Virginia of two hundred thousand people, were as scattered as their masters. On the early frontier there was less consciousness of their slave status. They helped in the household chores, building cabins and protecting them from Indian attack. Often they were the boatmen, whose arrival was as welcome in the settlement as the ringing of a postman in a modern apartment house.

The runaway slave heightened the powers of the popular imagination. Here was a figure who not only fled oppressive institutions, but successfully outwitted and defied them. And his flight was to the heart of civilization, not away from it; he was a universal figure whose life was in turn adventurous, tragic, and humorous.

The runaway, freed from the disabilities of slavery,

was in the second and third decades of the nineteenth century coming into close contact with another highly specialized group of people—the intellectuals. The thinking of intellectuals is characterized by the fact that they view matters whole and in general, however one-sidedly and abstractly. This jamming up of two diverse elements—the black man who supposedly had no civilization in the range of his existence, and the white intellectual in whom society had placed the whole heritage of civilization—produced those works that reminded people who gave thought to the slave held in bondage that they were themselves intimately bound with him for life.

The antislavery movement was produced by the specific relation of blacks and whites during the first third of the nineteenth century. It is a fantastic phenomenon climaxed by the central phenomenon of all American history, the Civil War. Writers offer various explanations, but after a certain amount of reflection it becomes clear that abolition must be seen as an absolutely necessary stage in making America a distinct civilization, rather than just one more piece of boundaried territory in the mosaic of the world's geography.

Abolition is the great indicator of parallel movements before the Civil War and after. History really moves when the traditionally most civilized section of the population—in this case New Englanders representing the longest American line of continuity with the English tradition of lawful sovereignty—joins as coequals with those without whose labor society could not exist for a day—in this case the plantation chattel. Otherwise, history stays pretty much the same, or worse yet, repeats itself. Such was the case of the independent lay preachers in the Great English Revolution, who joined with the apprentices and day laborers; the French intelligentsia in conjunction with peasants and slum proletarians of royalist France; the Russian intellectuals meeting on certain grounds with factory workers under a Czar. In all these instances history moved forward with lasting impress.

Abolition, itself an important instance of democracy, took upon itself the extension of a certain practice and mode of national behavior. Much of the mode of national behavior was based upon regional considerations—the great potential for abolition was the Southern slave in flight to freedom from plantation labor. Then there was the firmest base of abolition extant, the free black communities of Northern city and town. New York City, for a time, provided heavy financing. Garrison's Massachusetts was becoming an antislavery fortress and the rest of New England followed, in various degrees. Children of New England had settled in the fine agricultural flatlands of Ohio and upstate New York; a momentous development as "free soil" was prepared to clash with slave expansion appetites. Pennsylvania housed an antislavery diffused with Quakerized quietist feelings.

Without the self-expressive presence of the free blacks in the cities, embodying in their persons the nationally traumatic experience of bondage and freedom, antislavery would have been a sentiment only, a movement remote and genteel in a country known as impetuous and volatile. The bulk of subscribers to Garrison's *The Liberator* were blacks in New York, Boston, and Philadelphia. It was the publicity surrounding the revolt of Nat Turner which guaranteed that Garrison, the white advocate of immediate abolition, would become a household word. The independent conventions of free blacks were anterior to the rise of Garrison and his friends. The succession of slave personalities delivered by the Underground Railroad would eventually lead to black political independence from Garrison himself.

Ohio was the scene in the 1840's of the "Hundred Convention"—political life as daily fare, with regional figures turning into nationally representative ones. Douglass, the self-emancipated slave by way of Baltimore; Garrison, who hardly had left New England before except to visit neighboring New York or far-off merrie old England; these two together spoke themselves hoarse and into general exhaustion. This now-settled middle frontier, this venerable Old Northwest, was clamoring to hear about the state of the nation from true figures of national stature, since nothing more was heard from the doughfaces in Congress sitting on the hundreds of thousands of petitions pleading for justice to the slave, and discussing the role of free settlers in a democracy.

Impending war with Mexico was a spur to far-reaching conclusions. The revived National Negro Conventions listened to a proposal for a general strike by the slave laborers of the South, who would act as a human wall barring the United States Army from invading Mexican territory and turning it into a slave planting domain. The proposal lost by one vote.

Sophisticated prejudice tells us that *Uncle Tom's Cabin* by Harriet Beecher Stowe is another vast mistake! In impact and implications marking off the hour and the decade of its arrival it rang true; in universal aspect, clear. The average worker competing with the free black man for a job and a place to live, and wrestling with his prejudices all the while, went to see the play and wept upon his identification with the slave runaway. Where formal government failed on the slavery question, people reached for a government which the Greeks had introduced so very many years earlier: that of popular drama—which the city-state then made sure everyone could see for free—so that whatever they thought of politics they could see, through the form of dramatic representation, principles, conditions, and resolutions, and sense from that emotional experience where a whole society was going. Mere political representation was succeeded by a more intense social reproduction, a more popular accurate representation; in book form, *Uncle Tom's Cabin* circulated more widely through the whole of the nineteenth century than any other, with the sole exception of that book of books, the Bible.

And if it was the running debates with Stephen A. Douglas which elevated Abraham Lincoln from the legislator's semiobscurity to national star-fire, who or what besides abolition had initiated the debate, fixing free discussion of nearly obscured cruelties on a Mississippi cotton field as the nation's prime business; set forth the concrete choices, which no mere election could decide, on the future of mid-nineteenth-century America? And if the abolitionists' method had so elevated Lincoln, what shall we say of their achievement in turning each runaway slave, now threatened with kidnapping under a new and permanent sectional compromise, into a monument either to the American's love of liberty or acquiescence to captivity? Before abolition enabled Lincoln to hallow his name, it inscribed Shadrach and Anthony Burns and Dred Scott onto the heavens for the whole world to read the American future through them.

The leading charge against abolition in the 1850's was aimed at its nearly absolute trust in the uninterrupted processes of civilization. The main critique centered upon Garrison and Phillips' endorsing—before civil war broke out—the secession of the South, confident that slavery, separated from federal protection, must die.

The Civil War was a corrective of the notorious nineteenth-century optimism which trusted free speech and free press and the industriousness of unchatteled labor to push authoritarianism of every familiar type over that same cliff where the vestiges of feudal relations had been shattered or left to hang for dear life.

Confronted by preslavery compromises which were a source of infinite corruption, abolition gave obeisance to certain eternal principles: themselves corollaries of the civilizing process at a certain stage. Growing transcending morality titled "the higher law" would overwhelm all momentary deviousness, nullify all expedients and prearrangements disguising themselves as pillars of the Federal Union.

Belief in the morality of "the higher law" was hardly an empty absolute, devoid of content and barren of result. It was a driving impetus separating democracy in politics from the growing "hunkerism," mere hankering after public office and governmental seatwarmings which dulled the very sense of social accountability and paled before the historical momentousness of American existence.

The years of Civil War show what might have been done much earlier during the War for Independence itself when this nation was first born, and egalitarian feelings were at a zenith. But then there had been no antislavery organization. The unity of the young nation, monarchies all, had taken a certain turn at the Constitutional Convention and elsewhere, indicating that the semblance of national solidity could be maintained only if the slave kept his back bent to his labor; then North and South, East and West would not divide, and foreign enemies would wait in vain for internal weakness as the signal to spring upon their prey, the New World as distinguished from the old. But national unity excluded the black from independence; national prosperity was guaranteed by subordinating the laborer to his labor. The very existence of abolitionists during the next climactic phase of this very same question—Civil War—simply insured that the slave would not be lost sight of no matter how much the government tried to lose sight of him.

The destruction of the Colonizationists earlier was the main factor staying the hand of the government which wanted to colonize blacks, freed men, even in the midst of, and because of, the tensions of Civil War to avoid disputations as to their American destiny.

On the universal effect of American abolition: it helped free the Russian serf on the other side of the world—but not directly. Indirectly, it is clear enough if we go by stepping-stone geography. Harriet Beecher Stowe's book was banned in Italy as an incitement to the peasantry. But the leading Russian publication of the intellectual exiles translated the whole work as a free supplement for all subscribers. Keep in mind, too, that from the time of Peter the Great, Russia had been trying to make its way through the front door of world civilization. Add to this a fact of international power politics: When England and France threatened to join the South, Russia shifted its weight to the North. In the middle of the Civil War the Russian fleet showed up in New York harbor, a great ball was thrown and a festive time was had by all. Abolition of serfdom there and of slavery here occurred almost simultaneously.

Something should be said about the white American worker in regard to abolition. Some were antislavery, some were not. Skilled workers, proud of their craft which brought them a measure of independence, were by and large antislavery. The unskilled, fearing possible competition from the blacks, inclined toward neutrality or gave in to caste prejudice. However, skilled or unskilled, the worker in America was an ardent democrat. No matter how much he suspected another man might take his job, he could not develop a great affection for plantation life as the prototype of American life as a whole.

Abolitionists were not only concerned with the rights of blacks, free and slave, they were concerned with their education. The abolitionist created the first integrated education in the United States—including higher education. And when they did not create integrated education they conducted classes and schools for the ex-slaves, schools partially staffed by black teachers. The abolitionists were at the center of the educational reforms and changes of this period in the United States. In schools for Negro children they experimented with improved methods of education.

But more. They fought not only for the emancipation of Negroes and the improvement of the lives of freedmen. They fought for the emancipation of women, their education, and their own self-development. Oberlin College, the first college to accept Negroes in the United States, was also the first college to accept women in the United States, becoming the first co-educational institution of higher learning.

In their struggle for women's rights, a struggle that went on inside and outside of the movement, abolitionists set in motion the liberation of women—and consequently of men. What Margaret Fuller and other great female abolitionists were trying to establish was their right to create relations with men in which they were not in effect the chattel of their husbands through the marriage contract, as slaves were chattel in the grip of property holders.

The abolitionists were involved in a crucial way in the most significant struggles for human emancipation that were going on in the United States: the abolition of capital punishment, prison reform, attacks on established religion in the name of a purified religion, work for the rights of new waves of immigrants and better treatment of American Indians, and the movement to abolish war. Though they often differed among themselves, and were very often confused in the way that people are who are going forward, there is a very direct development from the Declaration of Independence to the abolitionists' efforts to Lincoln's understanding that the Civil War was about whether government of the people, by the people, and for the people would perish from the earth.

It must be said that the slave community itself was the heart of the abolitionist movement. This is a claim that must seem most extraordinarily outrageous to those who think of abolitionism as a movement which required organizations, offices, officers, financiers, printing presses and newspapers, public platforms and orators, writers and petitions. Yet the center of activity of abolitionism lay in the movement of the slaves for their own liberation. The general impact of the abolitionist movement upon the slave communities was profound. It gave the slaves that hope that enabled them to survive and to engage in the day-by-day struggles that won for them that amount of extra room in which to live that made more than mere continued existence possible.

The abolitionist movement led to a change in the climate of American life. The reaction after the American Revolution had led to a period in which a profound pessimism touched the lives of all those who lived by the ideals of the Declaration of Independence, that clarion call for a new birth of freedom for mankind. Abraham Lincoln, a son of the Declaration, had in 1837 felt that all that could be done was to defend the gains of the Revolution, and to hope that in the future gradual forward motion could be made. The work of the abolitionists, of black slaves changed all that. By the end of his life Lincoln could see the path of the Declaration, of human freedom, open once again. This was a mighty achievement for the movement.

The spontaneity and universality of feeling which accompanied the antislavery movement indelibly stamped itself on the opening days of the Civil War. The people arose. When the people arose in the North it was a self-mobilization of men and women. Of the 700,000 total Union Army, half a million were volunteers. This was, perhaps, the last great voluntary war in the history of mankind.

Savor the following words:

> . . . So large an army as the government has now on foot was never before known, without a soldier in it but who has taken his place there of his own free choice. But more than this: there are many single

regiments whose members, one and another, possess
full practical knowledge of all the arts, sciences, pro-
fessions, and whatever else, whether useful or elegant, is known in the world; and there is scarcely one
from which there could not be selected a president, a
cabinet, a congress, and perhaps a court, abundantly
competent to administer the government itself.

. . . It is worthy to note that while in this, the government's hour of trial, large numbers of those in the
army and navy who have been favored with the
offices have resigned and proved false to the hand
which had pampered them, not one common soldier or
sailor is known to have deserted . . .

. . . The greatest honor, and the most important fact
of all is the unanimous firmness of the common soldiers and sailors. To the last man, so far as known,
they have successfully resisted the traitorous efforts of
those whose commands, but an hour before, they
obeyed as absolute law.

This is from Lincoln's absolutely sober message to
Congress, July 5, 1861.

One of the great underestimations in the whole
sphere of historiography is undoubtedly the contribution of the slaves to the making of America as a
civilization. Some of the justifications for such an
underestimation are quite elementary. It is said that
all civilization rests upon city life; the bulk of slave
labor was on the countryside. The actual documen-
tary works by which much of early America lived are
those of the Anglo-Saxon heritage with some bow to
Plutarch and perhaps Rousseau, Montaigne, and De-
mosthenes. The slaves produced little of this kind of
literature. They are therefore to be left on the fringe
of the matter.

But a New World view of the old question of slavery
induces a greater wisdom. For one thing the triangular
trade in sugar, rum, and slaves in an instance of pro-
grammed accumulation of wealth such as the world
has rarely seen. "American slavery," says one author,

"was unique, in the sense that, for symmetry and precision of outline, nothing like it had ever previously been seen." The element of order in the barbarism was this: the rationalization of a labor force upon which the whole process of colonization depended had the African at its most essential point. If he had not been able to work or sustain himself or learn the language or maintain cooperation in his social life, the whole question of America as a distinct civilization could never have arisen. We might be then talking about a sort of New Zealand or perhaps Canada.

The native American Indian was migratory in his habits and a hunter in his relation with nature. But the slave had to be an African laborer, a man accustomed to social life, before he could ever become a profitable grower of cotton or tobacco—the vital element required before America could claim that it had salvaged something from the wilderness. Something which could be extended to the point where it would win recognition as a landmark in man's emergence from subservience to any laws of nature . . .

The man who made it possible, and we do not know if he knew he was making it possible, was the transported African. Rationalization of the labor supply was tied in with rationalization of production itself. Planters in Louisiana would weigh the pros and cons of working slaves to death in the hazardous work of the rice paddies as against protecting the slave from excessive labor in order to maintain the interest in him as property. The long letters George Washington wrote on the organization of labor on his plantation represent merely one side. The exchange of letters between Thomas Jefferson and Benjamin Banneker, the surveyor of what was to become Washington, D.C., about the propensities and capacities of black people enslaved and otherwise is the other side of the same phenomenon: the recognition that for reasons both clear and obscure the fate of America had depended upon the blacks as laborers. This was to be argued

out in the antislavery movement at a higher level, and
in the midst of the Civil War and Reconstruction. It is
also a seemingly inescapable fact to everybody, but
historians have managed to escape it. That is not altogether a surprise. The writing of history comes about
at a period when men think about their activity so as
to record it in a more permanent form. To give the
slave his actual historical due is to alter one's notion
about the course of civilization itself. If, for example,
each plantation had to strive to be self-sufficient as a
unit, it was the skilled and semi-skilled black who
would make it so.

The runaway slave fled to the North without com-
pass or definite point of destination, without being
blessed like Columbus by Queen Isabella selling her
jewels for the voyage, or like the pilgrims to Plymouth
Rock—members of a church soon to make a revolution affecting all of England and Ireland; or like pioneers into the wilderness, trying to set a distance
between themselves and civilization. If, as can be
later demonstrated, the flight of the runaway slave
from the South is seen as setting in motion a whole
series of forces, which no other class of people, no
mere party or political sect, no church or newspaper
could succeed in animating, then the whole configuration of America as a civilization automatically
changes before our eyes. The distinguishing feature
of the slave was not his race but the concentrated
impact of his work on the extensive cultivation of the
soil, which eventually made possible the transition to
an industrial and urban society.

The triumph of slavery, the negative recognition
that the slave received in every work sphere shows
how little the South or skilled workers themselves
sometimes could tolerate the black as an artisan. In
prebellum America he had to be driven out of trade
after trade before the assertion could be demonstrated
that the black man is fit for nothing more than brutish
labor with its inevitable consequence.

Historically one can now begin almost anywhere to show what civilization meant to the slave as a preliminary to showing what the slaves meant to civilization. The natural form of organization was the work gang during the day and the slave quarters at night. The large scale of cultivation required for a profitable export crop guaranteed social connections for the slave even if he was isolated from the centers of "civilization" by the rural surroundings.

But the first specific form of slave organization was the fraternal association which was organized to accompany to their permanent resting place those caught up in life's mortal coils. Small coins were saved for accomplishing that occasion in at least minimal style. The slave was no more afraid to die than is or was any other mortal; he was fearful of dying unaccompanied by those with whom he had associated in the fullness of his life.

Given a holiday, that is, an occasion, the slave was, like most working humans up to this day, his own person. It was for naught that the defenders of the planter's way of life feared the effect of Fourth of July oratory. They might just as well have feared the Christianity in Christmas. It was not only intellectually that everything universal in sentiment panicked the "peculiar institution." It was the concentration of people all experiencing the unbridgeable gap between their arduous daily toll and the exceptional holiday from work—with the to-ing and the fro-ing from plantation to plantation, the arrival of guests and the spreading of news—which brought about the system of slave patrollers and written passes across the South.

We are dealing with matters of individual skill and social impulse. Small equivalents of the strike action took place at work. Flight to the neighboring woods, followed by messages trailed back to the work area showed that the blacks knew above all that, even if despised for race, they were necessary—vital to a labor process geared to the agricultural season. Feigning of illness was a commonplace; indeed, one simple definition of the abolition of slavery is that a man or woman need not go to work when incapacitated. This absenteeism may seem of no great import by itself, but the diaries and records of the slavemasters show it to be a matter of grave concern. Everybody knew what was involved in the work process.

And the blacks knew what was involved in their day of rest. The growth of an autonomous black church draws up a balance sheet on historical Christianity. It is not finished yet, but if Christianity, as some assert, brought the principle of personality into a world that knew no such thing, and in the person of a simple carpenter who later recruited an equally simple fisherman and so on, the climax of that primitive church was the mass joining together of a population considered as so much flesh to be traded and hands to be worked and backs to be bent or broken under the lash. To the whites religion may have meant a buttress to conscience. To the blacks it meant a social experience out of which would come the active principle of personality: the black preacher.

In the more practical workings of the plantation, the slave owners themselves discovered that the position of foreman or driver was one which fewer and fewer whites measured up to in personal stature. So that in the decade before the Civil War there was a wholesale increase in the number of black overseers. Though it did not mean that race prejudice on the part of the slave owners had changed one whit, this problem of supervision was proof of the demoralizing effect black laborers had upon those who not only considered themselves superior to the slave's lot but had the weapons and the authority to put their superiority into momentary practice. Most white overseers went even before the slave system fell into the dust of Civil War. And by a healthy process of circularity, the fictional summations of the type, the Simon Legrees of the world, were portrayed with such effectiveness that it stimulated the movement toward that system which produced such monsters wholesale. The important point of the slave's contribution to civilization is that he recognized and did battle with the slavery system every day before, long before, white audiences would stare with horror at the representation on stage or in a book.

There is also the matter of the link-ups of the plantation to the outside world. Blacks were the boatmen and teamsters of that day in the South. They would have been the longshoremen as well, but were driven out. Simply by driving the master's coach around they learned of the outside world and brought back information to the slave community. It was known in some of the deepest haunts of the South that there was some kind of underground which would transport a runaway from one hiding place to another if he would but risk the trip.

Indeed, if by virtue of the brutishness and isolation of his situation the slave were himself a brute, how then could he make contact with such varying and even opposing sections of the population as he did? Harriet Tubman had a rapt listener in the philosopher Ralph Waldo Emerson, and Frederick Douglass in governor—and later Presidential candidate—William Seward. William Wells Brown could speak to all size groups, from two hundred to two hundred thousand people across Europe. It was not a matter of a dispute about the capacity of the Negro; it was not even the great political debates about the future of America— slave or free. It was something so concrete, so easy to overlook and yet so broad in its consequences: The black man was a social being, in some senses the most highly social product of the United States. This was not necessarily due to skin color, but to the close relation between labor and society that he experienced more than did planters, ethnic immigrants, religious societies, pioneering settlements and their human products, political parties and their candidates.

That link of labor and society took on national and even international proportions. Starting from obscure places which nobody ever heard of or even wanted to hear, it became writ large as the experience of slavery intertwined with everything else—politics, diplomacy, commerce, migration, popular culture, the relation between the sexes, the question of labor and civilization in the future of America as a whole. The black man was not in any popularity contest as to who most represented this new man—this undefined American —who so intrigued the Europeans. He was something more: a self-appointed minister with nothing but experience, social experience, to guide him toward those qualities most universally recognizable in the ordinary people—some of whom are still tied to the land in Europe; some recently incorporated into proliferating industry; some hearkening to the American experience; some settling matters with crowns and courts in their Old World countries. The black man was the supreme example not just of how to rise in the world but of how to raise the world toward his own level. He inherited the Declaration of Independence which the plantation plutocracy mocked. In politics, Frederick Douglass took the Constitution as an anti-slavery document when his own abolition colleagues, Wendell Phillips and William Lloyd Garrison, set the match to it. The runaway slave, Dred Scott, threw the Chief Justice of the Supreme Court (and the country as a whole) into confusion on whether slavery was a national or regional issue. The black man was not afraid to declare war on war, for instance the conflict with Mexico over Texas in 1846. He could link himself to movements for temperance in drink or for the right of women to divorce or to the nonpayment of rents by upper New York State farmers.

It was training in social labor which gave blacks the opportunity to increasingly affect all social questions of their day. It was their concrete ability to turn from the faculties used in physical work to the powers of speech and other forms of self-expression which made certain of the ex-slaves the astonishing figures they were. After he drew two hundred thousand people to hear him in Europe, William Wells Brown then returned to a port near the Great Lakes, between America and Canada, to help fugitive slaves across the water, unite families, violating the mere boundaries of national existence. In addition he printed a paper announcing the uniting of families, the successes and sometimes failures of the underground travelers, their adventures and misadventures; and denouncing the "peculiar institution" and all those who would compromise with it, thinking they could thereby escape compromising themselves.

The startling challenge to current notions about civilization was presented by the slaves, as soon as they won the public's ear, on the familiar matter of conscience. The contribution of the blacks was that type of social experience—whether it was lyceum, church, or Underground Railroad—which challenged one set of social institutions with a social impact of a most original kind. Doomed by slavery to impersonality, the ex-slave responded with a personality and personal force that had the most obvious social implications and conclusions. Condemned to seasonal labor, and the rhythm and routine determined thereby, the blacks carried on agitation in and out of season until the body politic came to recognize that the country could no longer survive as it was; could survive only by embarking on an uncharted course of slave confiscation and Southern reconstruction. After having been isolated by slavery in provincial fixity, the runaway traversed national boundaries and oceanic waters. Graded by the abolition movement itself as fit only to tell slavery as an atrocity tale, Frederick Douglass and others insisted on publishing their own political policies. This is a long way from the reflex response to slavery by a disturbed conscience. It is a social impact on all media that distinguishes civilization from barbarism. The impact of the slave labor system upon the South as a distinct region has a number of aspects clearly visible to this day.

The plantation was an organized community that was part of a larger regional configuration, but given the isolation concomitant with the rural character of slave society, the social stamp upon the individual, particularly the slave himself, guaranteed certain results. The internal economic principle of the plantation was self-sufficiency. To the slavemaster this meant insularity: foreign immigration mainly excluded; missionary society activity suspect (including the riding preachers who would as likely as not be antislavery); no lyceum or lecture circuit on any extensive scale; no compulsory elementary or secondary education; little exercise of the faculty of logical speculation. For a break in the routine of plantation life there were visits to the North, often no further than the river port city of Cincinnati; or politics in the state capital or in Washington, D.C., actually a Southern city.

To a large extent, certain of the above characteristics were true of America as a whole, or at least of its western part. Especially the smaller Southern planters had certain characteristics in common with the yeomanry of the American Northwest: the need to create isolated pockets of white habitation in a land belonging to the Indians, the establishment of paths into the wilderness, the harsh life for the women of the family, the back-breaking toil in wresting some socially productive result from the natural surroundings, and the independence of habit and speech that is the inevitable result in people living under these conditions.

The dialectical set of connections of the South to the old Northwest is both genuinely subtle and profound. Both were agrarian areas, with the Mississippi and other rivers serving as the turnstiles to ports and

citified places. Other similarities were the suspicious-
ness toward all those outside the isolated region where
one's house and cultivated areas and perhaps hunt-
ing grounds were located; the tightness of the family
and usually its patriarchal basis; the shortage of mon-
ies and credit, such that life frequently remained,
generally according to the season, on a subsistence
level, with only the holiday season to punctuate with
some enjoyment above the everyday standard.

Further, there is the historical connection. All of
American settlement, at its origins, proceeded in the
same manner for both inland planters and Northern
yeomanry, and their pioneering ways continued right
up to the Civil War. In that sense Southern rural
inhabitants were "these new men," the Americans
who so intrigued the European observer often sceptical of America as (1) a civilization and (2) a viable
nationality. Thus if the black man has been left out
of so many history books, if the controversy over the
significance of slavery to the South seemed until
very recently a matter of no great moment, it is because a certain aspect of American historical continuity seemed to justify itself and no mere racist
conspiracy of silence could accomplish what seems
to have been imbedded within that historical aspect.
To which must be added the fundamental matter of
political organization and the effect of the South on
certain basic institutions by which an organized society emerged out of the natural wilderness. The individual planter was conditioned not only by pioneering
inland to new territories; he had to become an indi-
vidualist with a social authority larger than the
boundaries of his plantation. The reasons are as follows: The South had been originally colonized by
British trading companies licensed by the Crown. The
Northern settlements were more likely to be religious
colonies or fur-trading outposts. So that from the very
start the planter, who had to be in charge of the practical and hazardous work of founding some lasting

economic basis in the New World, was thrown into
conflict with the concentrated mercantile capitalism of
the metropolitan colonizing land. To put it succinctly,
the anticapitalist bias of the Southerner was there
from the day of his birth. It was no small thing. The
former slave—the supposedly emancipated black—
became, for lack of credit, a sharecropper. This happened because all of Southern history had prepared
somebody for that role, and the people at the bottom
of the social ladder fell into it and remained there,
some unto this day. To make up for their embattle-
ment as regards the shortage of capital, the Southerners would compensate with (a) their geography,
strategically considered, (b) the fixed position of the
main section of the laboring force—the slaves, and
(c) a type of politics which would guarantee the via-
bility of (a) and (b).

All these things add up to a "nativist" outlook that
is not that of country bumpkins, but one characterized by a sophistication that was constantly changing
by the very reason of its taking place in a nineteenth-
and late eighteenth-century setting that was becoming rapidly modernized. Slavery is a peculiar institution not only because of its horrors but because it was
something-unto-itself. The Southern attitude seems so
often a matter of temperament—unformed character
expressing itself against a general trend in worldly
affairs which opposed the fixed investment of wealth
in land and human chattel. In other words, the South
produced "personality" rather than minds of singular
or original power. But the personalities are of a singular and sustaining force: Patrick Henry, Jefferson,
Jackson, Calhoun, Clay, Stonewall Jackson, Tom Wat-
son, Huey Long are personae who will interest the
public imagination until possibly they are surpassed
by the characterization of the lives of the obscure
slaves and indigent blacks. This tends to be the on-
going matter of interest in our own day.

There is a material basis for the Southern produc-

tion of men and women of outstanding temperamental
force. (The fictional Scarlett O'Hara or Blanche DuBois
convey that the matter is not limited to the male
gender.) Despite all geographical rationalizations, the
commodity crops—tobacco, rice, sugar, cotton, and
hemp—were not limited to the South by climate. The
planters were a class capable of taking over matters
of national interest: they had warred against nature,
against the Indian; they had warred against the
blacks on the plantation, against the British, the French,
and the Spaniards. Their experience had a certain
cast by virtue of the international nature of their products—human flesh and large-scale commodity crops.
Such large-scale experiences do not lead to the production of small-minded men. So they participated in
the formation of an original American nationality.
The historical claim can be substantiated that they
produced more figures of national distinction than did,
say, by comparison, the robber barons. All this com-
bines to make the controversy about the impact of
slavery on American civilization such a pregnant and
vital intellectual confrontation.

Certain mundane matters have to be mentioned at
least in a preliminary way. It was the boredom and
harshness of plantation life that ensured that not general activity, but politics was the only matter of
universal interest and appeal. If the rural character
of their life induced in the planters, or at least in some
of them, a certain respect for plebeian democracy in
other sections of the population, it had to be by the
nature of the planter's own setting, an abridged version of popular participation in decision-making. The
father of the political party of any mass status in
American life was the planter-political philosopher,
Thomas Jefferson. The father of popular participation
in political office, apart from mere suffrage, was the
planter Andrew Jackson. The head of an army having
the popular militia as a section of its base was the

planter George Washington. Yet the halfway houses to genuine democracy which each of these figures created remain America's bones of contention unto this day.

What of social vision? The early accomplishments of these men corresponded to the formative period of American nationality. They could not go beyond. The results were imbedded in the American mentality but not anywhere in self-generating institutions. The popular militia is now the not-very-progressive National Guard. The political parties resting on mass suffrage are now in a state alternating between paralysis and crisis. The spoils of office distributed to members of the population are now a source of perpetual scandal and parasitism.

The Southern figures of the mid-nineteenth century vacillated between accommodation and hopeless fanaticism. Clay was a genius of the first order. He could never win actual leadership of the country as a whole, though he was persistent and colorful enough to engage the political attentions of his countrymen. Calhoun was a different sort. He sought to make the American Constitution a protector of the South's position in national life, invulnerable to changing national majorities. And of Jefferson Davis it can perhaps best be said that though he failed in the Southern rebellion, he was saved from hanging by the long tradition of Northern-Southern accommodation—a tradition punctured only by the actualities of the Civil War.

Some of the bobbling of the minds of the planters was due to the very fact that they stood on a tripod of vital revolutions in the then-known Western world: the Puritans in 1642, the War for Independence in 1776, and volatile France of 1789. The Clays and Calhouns lived to consider the realities of the continental-wide European Revolution of 1848. Their situation was one of Anglo-Saxon nativism turning against itself. Immigrant New York might celebrate 1848, Puritan

New England might relate revolutionary antislavery
sentiments to the wars between Cavaliers and Round-
heads, the democratic yeomanry of the western territories might enjoy the sight of crowns falling all over
Europe. The Southern planters had no comparable
frame of reference. They stuck by Constitution and
Compromise.

And when that did not last they went to war to protect geography. It was not all that simple. The border
states which did not produce commodity crops but
which had domestic slaves were the geniuses of accommodation right up to the last moment and beyond.
The idyllic notion of domestic servitude, patriarchal
chatteldom, originates from those Kentucky, Tennessee, upper Virginia, Maryland, and even Delaware
manors. If American politics became entwined with
a style of life rather than a manner of thought, we
have no difficulties discovering why. In short, the
Southern position was that of a provincialism entwined
with American nationality as a whole, but defenseless
against the universal trends of revolutionary democracy of the nineteenth century.

Nevertheless the effects of the planters were immense: The location of the nation's capital in the
borderline South; the creation and manipulation of
national political parties; the fielding of armies and
the tradition of militant armed conflict; the specializa-
tion of the South in politics as maneuver and divaga-
tion; the bias in favor of the notion that agricultural
wealth was real, and commercial wealth always
fraudulent; the sense of the manor not as parasitic
but as a center of human community; the assertion
that the concreteness of the manorial community was
superior to the impersonality of the large Northern
city; the impulsiveness of the Southern personality as
more appealing than the social discipline seemingly
inherent in industry and commerce; the general link-
up with the rural-romantic character of America's past

—all of this seems irrevocable and untouchable by general intellectual argument.

The only way to deal with it is by taking up its foundations. The Southern planter could engage in politics on a much larger scale than many Northerners or Westerners because he was of a leisure class, born and bred—a commander of the fate of men, women, and children of a different color with a more permanently fixed status. Suckled by a black nurse, attended by black servants, often encouraged to sexual experiments in the slave quarters, accustomed to the sight of blacks caring for all business involving manual labor; encouraged, even inspired, by the succession of Southern Presidents, the ambitious Southerner could see politics, even statesmanship, as destiny's decision, and cast himself in the role of fortune's darling. Furthermore, for the isolated manorial communities, politics was the prime form of social communion, whereas in the North religious revivals swept all before them in periods in between political excitement. In today's parlance, the prebellum white planter gives the impression of having found an early answer to the problems of the "lonely crowd" in the solidity of his native tradition, the fixity of his social status and the values of an inherent and irrevocable individualism.

The availability and accessibility of having things always at hand extended itself to the vast virgin lands and the supply of slaves. If capital and credit were in short supply, then the curse was on the head of the mercantilists—be they tyrannical Englishmen or grasping Boston Yankees. Social status had taken on an overweening importance; but even greater was the display of public personality—elections as jousting contests, a codified individualism rather than the self-expansive effluvia of the Northern Transcendentalists.

The rationalizations for the Atlantic slave trade and

American slavery, whether borrowed from the Bible
or the instances of Greece and Rome, raise a com-
pelling challenge to the whole matter of what indeed
constitutes a civilization. It is safe to say that the
majority of Western scholars seem to have placed a
gloss on the manner and the matter of this case.

Great Adventures In Propaganda

presents

Cab Calloway Stands In for the Moon

---

featuring papa la bas & his newfoundland hoodoo 3¢

from

D HEXORCISM OF NOXON D AWFUL

or

from boogerman to metal polisher the

story of how come

a fiend became guaranteed by goodhousekeeping

another

one of those

mean incoherent frequently nonsensical

hallucinogenic diatribes by

Ishmael Reed

---

from the forthcoming book *Mumbo Jumbo*

Some say he is the long JuJu of Aro in eastern Nigeria. A descendant of that line of conjurers who taught Greeks to oracle. [Ask yourselves why the Oracle of Delphi is known as the Pythoness when this particular snake does not thrive in Greece naturally.]

Kidnapped by pirates he was en route for sale in America's slave markets when in mid-Atlantic a rescue ship found their evil craft deserted; except for this lean elegant African.

Members of the rescue vessel reported hearing a chorus of wailing from beneath the sea as they sailed away from where they found the stranded ship. But this can be dismissed as the babblings of ignorant sailors.

There are, however, other strange items in this African's career that those who are devoted to Law and Order will find less easy to ignore or attribute to superstition.

He was bought by a Slavemaster who was found hanging a few weeks after purchasing this handsome prize. A long succession of slave-masters met a similar fate as his legend spread. Finally there were no takers and he was free.

There were other mysterious episodes. A drunken white man called him a rude name and he was dead the following Saturday. A little boy kicked his Newfoundland HooDoo 3¢ and was never heard from again.

A warehouse refused to deliver a special variety of herbs he needed for his little shop, St. Louis #2 and burned to the ground.

*Around these parts he is known as Papa La Bas.
He has a mahogany face and speaks in a nasal
voice. Some say he is 200 years old. His shop
sells jewelry, astrology charts, cards, herbs, in-
cense, potions, candles, amulets, talismans, and
books of the occult. Sometimes there are more
cars parked in front of St. Louis #2 than the
town's leading hotel. He is a familiar sight in his
old threadbare frock coat, his opera hat his
smoked glasses and cane.*

*He is making a delivery of garlic, sage, thyme,
geranium water, dry basil, parsley, saltpeter, bay
rum, and verbena essence of jack honeysuckle.*

*He chuckles to himself as he leaves his shop
with the dog 3¢ on the leash. He has every reason to be pleased with himself because the night
before he brought off one of the most difficult
feats of sorcery.*

*He entered a man's dream and walked all over
as if he owned the place. He moved the scenes
around with the deftness of a director from the
Hollywood Pantheon.*

*He called the shots, edited the script and gave
the demons their cue.*

Back there aways he had shook off some mighty
nasty crocodiles. He tried to slip them a fiver, a brand
new crisp bill, under the rock, but that didn't do any
good. The crocodiles, thrashing about, wouldn't quit
flaying him with their tails. He managed somehow to
dodge the mummy by hiding in this huge jar over
near the Temple door. You see, he had run into the
Temple trying to escape from this HooDoo locomotive

swinging up the tracks on him. He took a piss. He
didn't mean no harm. He saw this jeweled scarab and
was going to take it to his sweety. He was willing to
come up with some good old American dollars for it.
Nothing happened. Perhaps his nightmares knew more
about the gold situation and how America was *fixed*,
than he. I dunno, I dunno Noxon thought.

He took off down this long corridor of smiles and grins
coming at him. Snapping their teeth. He thought of his
daughter's picture hanging over the bathtub. Then he
was off again. Gee, I wish someone would leave me
off with a hotdog Noxon thought. With lots of mustard
on it. And hot peppers. Boy O Boy Noxon thought
seeing red. Let me at em. Let me at em. You want to
fight, a nervous Noxon the Noxious of Ob said. I mean,
do you want a sock right in the mouth Noxon thought.

Suddenly he was on an ocean floor. Some of the fish
were swimming this way and some another way.
Noxon simulated their movements with his hand. He
stuck out his forefinger and thumbs like the time he
built this paper airplane. Noxon grinned. Being at the
bottom of this ocean was better than being in that
Temple buster. There can be no 2 ways about it.

He didn't leave no tip because the sarcophagus
opened and out come this hand wrapped in dirty
bandages. He didn't like the service and was reaching in his pockets for a world-wide credit card when
he found some black cat bones (longhand for mojo).

Noxon started to float to the surface of this ocean in
which he found himself. Using his arms the way he
had seen turtles use their flippers in the cartoons he
lived in. What a way to go Noxon thought. What treatment. Here he was the MC of the USA in the year
2000 and PROPERTY OWNER. For crying out loud

Noxon thought, I can go on and on and this was in Africa.

> Noxon was born in a bin beneath the freezer
>   however some
> Historians say he hails from Yonder
> Slobovia a patch of cowdung somewheres in EUROPE
> Noxon is married to Minnie D Moocher John Phillip
> Sousa's daughter
> She is a hard working astrofiend who escaped
> from Venus in a dogpound (more later)
> Noxon likes messy gooey things especially when
> they have nice clean tails
> Noxon gave at the office
> Noxon is an all around
> Noxon won world war II with single hands

Somebody wrote a hit record on him. Noxon once took part in an experiment.

> Geez, how am I going to get Africa off me Noxon
> thought. I dunno, I dunno he thought.

The nightmare rollercoastered towards the day.

> 10 He was wrapped up with a lot of snakes
> 9 He was putting his wife thru the 3rd degree
> 8 He was sitting on Ike's lap licking a lollipop
>   and Ike was telling em bang-bang stories
> 7 He was imprisoned in this big bottle of Jim Beam
> 6 He was signing a hip's death warrant
> 5 He was saying can't we negotiate this matter
> 4 He was marching in an American Legion dinner his
>   shoes knee deep in turkey and mixed metaphors
> 3 He was saying lets win this thing and get out
> 2 what thing?
> 1 He was taking the sewer to work

Great gugga mugga was I dreamin Noxon thought. He put on his sailor suit and went into the bathroom. He took a shower and bruised his molars. All at once a blackhead popped on the mirror. It sat there all defiant like. It seemed to have eyes like a bullfrog. Noxon took a swipe at it and tried to wrestle it to the

floor. He squeezed and squeezed until some kind of
green stuff squirted on the mirror. Noxon drew a funny
picture in it. He drew a picture of Elmer Fudd and it
was real funny. Gosh Noxon thought. Wasn't bad.
Wasn't bad at all. He looked at the picture of his
daughter who had been kidnapped by the Galloping
Dick and Noxon said a little prayer until a tear come
down.

Noxon's wife Minnie D Moocher poured some milk
from the pitcher on some dog feces she had maneu-
vered into oatmeal. Smart girl that Minnie. Noxon
packed the little brown rascals on his breakfast spoon
and made it all sugary. Boy O Boy Noxon thought
throwing in a couple of Gee Whizzes. This is mighty
good grub.

He thought about the time he was a kid
He thought about the time he pushed this nigger woman
    out of the way
He thought about the time he landed on the moon and the moon
    died of fright and had to be put on ice
He thought about how they had to rush in an understudy
    for the moon as it underwent repairs
He thought about his dream

Noxon —Dear, I had a dream last nite that Africa
        was all on top of me.
Minnie —You did Noxon?
    N —Yes dear I was dreaming about Africa and
        then things. Well, things got dizzier and diz-
        zier until the last dream I can't remember
        how it shaped up.
    M —You will dear Noxon don't worry you will.
    N —Minnie, I want you should go out and tell
        Meathead Sam my Chauffeur that I won't
        need him today. I feel like breaking tradition
        —perhaps sewering to work.
    M —Sewering to work. How nice. You haven't
        sewered to work since the time we crawled

from this place that was so dark and cold
inside.

N —That's show nuff the truth to use the parlance of the ghetto wife. Why I'm celebrating us. Simple folk and how we will out.
Just plain you and me and our squaky
teeny words and our ilky itsy lookers. We
soil the Universe with our snot and turd up
the heavens with our shit. Why the whole
solar system already is becoming one big
commuter tie up.

M —O Noxon you're so professionally awful
why you even made your TV debut as an
actor last nite on that horror show. How did
you swing that one dear?

N —As you well know Minnie, good buddy and
fellow american I was in the studio debating
the opposition when all at once the wrong
booth got ahold of me. Well this disaster
had a happy ending because the nice man
there noticed the canineism of my teeth,
those large black circles around my eyes
and with my sinister grin it all added up to
a natural for the part. How did you like the
way I carried the coffin all over the place?

M —It was tremendous dear. I also liked the way
you took care of that punk planet Mars and
put it away. Got it off orbit and stuff. What
are you going to do with Mars when the
chemicals get hard dear?

N —We're going to convert Mars into a parking
lot and athletic field in case anyone gets
hungry good buddy.

M —That's really progressive dear, I wish I
could have given you a son to carry on
your work who would be like you a threat
to all life in the Universe, instead of that . . .
that thing in the closet.

N —I told you never to bring up that subject again Minnie. It's so unpleasant.

M —I know Noxon but medical science (Jake, the Butcher of Bellevue) could come up with no explanation about that thing up there born with 5 o clock shadow herringbone hide and a hard way to go. For an umbilical cord there was a telephone cable. Strange, strange as it can be. Maybe we should have signed it up for that road show Ike suggested. Speaking of Ike, what kind of chemicals did you have them spray Mars with anyway Noxon?

N —Rocky Mountain Scarlet Fever, you won't have to worry about safety in the streets up there Mother, which reminds me, I have to phone the Cape and find out the situation on other planets.

M —How's that, dear?

N —As it stands now: Jupiter has been dragnetted; Pluto is still at large; and there's an all planet bulletin out on Saturn. The air force is hushing up Uranus and *Marioprocaccino* wants the 2 satellites of Neptune named after its Mama and Poppa, seeing as how they started off from scratch.

M —*Marioprocaccino*, what's that dear?

N —Some kind of disease that New York City coughed up. I'm telling you dear I don't know what I'm going to do with that headache on the Hudson. This *Marioprocaccino* started off as a one-liner and then it grew larger and larger until now its taken over 20 tables in Toots Shor and has threatened to call up reinforcements. I think I'm going to convert New York into a warehouse and then maybe it will shut up and behave. Why some colored writer named Calvin Coolidge

Hernton has read the riot act on it and the
George Washington Bridge has become a
junkie—stays high all the time. I think I'll
change its name to No Dancing or Keep Out
From Behind The Counter. But enough of
me whacking my noodle about the important affairs of the USA which I am MC-ing,
sometimes known as Noxon D Awful or as
the boys in the newsroom call me, Scoop-
up Noxon.

M —Dear of all of your aliases that one turns me
off the most. It sounds as if your nickname
is out to get you isn't it supposed to be
Scoop Noxon?

N —Let the boys have their fun dear and let me
sewer to work. Here are a few ten dollar
bills for hashing up such a good breakfast.
I'll leave them under the plate so that you
will never forget your climb from a simple
waitress in a roadside diner full of 3 week
old apple pie to your ascent to the first lady-
ship of the USA and hostess of this 20 room
home Spiralling Agony.

With this Noxon slipped 2 tens under the plate and
went into the basement of his 20 room mansion Spiralling Agony. He lifted this custom made manhole he
had installed in case . . . well in case his horrorscope
got the best of him.

It was all shiny and dark below, but he couldn't resist the fumes and he missed the rats and as any
student of human behavior will tell you when you
neglect your misses she will come up with awful
ways. Or somethin to that effect.

The United States of America in the year 2000 is the
same old rigmarole. All the cars have american flags

on them. The men wear crewcuts or have their hair done up in waves which shine like stinking dead bass in the moonlight. The women wear pincurlers the size of lightbulbs and don't know where their children are this time of night. Willy Mays had just popped out a grand slammer and who knows what else. All the old timers still gather beneath this portrait of Custer The Tomahawked, founder of the United States of America and inventor of the Clairol empire. And O yes, by the way, the Hudson River is over.

There are 2 maybe 3 stories or maybe 1, 2 many on how the United States of America came to be: One is that USA worked as a shortorder cook on the byways of nationhood and Walt Disney drove in one day and signed it on the spot. Another is that it's not a country at all but the remainder of a set discarded by the great Zigfield of the Zigfield Follies. But these stories are crazy. Just crazy. They defy all of our Aristotelian categories—they arm wrestle these categories and make them shout Uncle.

So somebody should ought to come up with the truth quick. As our great leader the Noxon of Noxious of Ob captain of the great yacht *Awful Aint He* put it:

> Those who have no tradition are like whiskey without the sour, pizza without the cheese a golf course without the 18th hole.

There is a story circulating among some degenerates in the underground that the true story has been found. The United States was discovered a long time ago when the townsfolk marched up to the house at the top of the hill to see what all the fuss was about. They found the USA stretched out on a table as this mad scientist was giving it a huge electrical dosage. They caught the mad scientist but the USA escaped and is now crouched upon the midnight of the world ready to spring and howling its head off.

Noxon was thrown up through the manhole by a friendly ratpack he had joined during his journey to work. He walked to his shower he had installed in his office in case his horriblescope got the best of him. It contained all of the new fangled technological devices. You see when Noxon slapped the sleeping pooch on the head the dog awoke and the string tied to his nozzle yanked open the curtains. Another string tied to the dog's paw tipped over the bucket and the water poured. Noxon bathed himself. All of the crap started coming off of him. He felt good and do you know what? Ronnie Reagan was being had for lunch.

Rin Tin Rover The Gov of New York State put his foot down. Shoot, said Rin, here I have donated 3000 objects of African and Oceanic art to the Met they've escaped to Harlem where they are partying and catching Ruby and the Romantics at Sugar Ray's. My wife has run away with Chief Showcase a man I invited to my Estate to discuss the Injuns and some nitwit has sunk my boat. The squatters have located my vast Estate and to add to that the computer that's ticking me off is taking over the whole show. What a wicked no account week it has been for me and to think my Grandfather founded the United States of America and was the first man to come over here. Barry was right—right he was. I'm coming over to his side. I must call Arizona but first a word to Noxon.

He dialed Noxon's private number 666.

He didn't like to do business with Noxon whom he considered a vulgar man who didn't even know how to hold a fork, flunked French and couldn't ski nor ride a horse. And that wife of his Minnie. Oy Vey what a dog why the bitch had sunk his boat with her Evil Eye. For a brain Noxon had the will call department of Macy's and on especially dark nights he glowed. He decided to call Noxon without identifying himself

so that the MC of the USA wouldn't think he was trying to exert influence.

Noxon —Hello Hello Hello this is Noxon D
Awful here state your business friend.

Rin Tin Rover —This has been a rough week for me
Noxon maybe you can turn a few
knobs for me some colored writer is
at large and where I can't keep my
eye away from him and now they've
nabbed my African objects.

N —African objects who is this African
object. Whaddya think bothering me
with some African objects shaddup,
you just shaddup and don't bother
me.

RTR —I'll expose that deal you made, forty
miles of white castle restaurants on
Venus and I'll spill the beans about
that thing in your closet. I am Rin Tin
Rover and my grandfather founded
this country so you'd better be careful
fella.

N —Well why didn't you say so. I didn't
know some bigtime rich american was
on the phone. Rin why didn't you tell
me it was you gabbing away. Speak
up man and bother me some more.
By the way thanks for inviting me
and the misses over to that swell
shindig you chucked the other night.
Sorry she sunk your boat. That was
the swellest thing I've been to even
though I did spill the food all over
me lap. Why I use to be nothing but
a poor supermarket clerk asking my
clients such lofty questions as "do
you want that in an 8 lb bag or a 12
lb bag," and now look at me. Just

look at me now. What can I do for
you Rin?

RTR —I want you to recover my 3000 objects
from Africa even if it means closing
down that nightclub and make my
boats well again I like to fool around
with them. I want the Federal government to step into this case about my
wife and that redskin too—last seen
heading towards the Mexican border
in an old 1938 Oldsmobile shooting
everything in sight.

N —If I can't take care of these matters
Rin I'll have my brother No Nox Zu-
fuksky, head of the F.I.B., look it up.
He can add as many as 3 numbers at
a time. He was the real genius of the
family and should be sitting here in
my chair.

RTR —O I didn't know you had a family
Noxon, story has it that you climbed
out of a washing machine and
started from there that you were mere
stains on a funky t shirt before you
got all riled up.

N —The press has always been unkind to
me Rin that will be $18.50 . . .

RTR —$18.50?

N —Forgive me Rin, sometimes my humble origin won't leave up.

It was 4 o clock and the hard working Chief Executive's day was drawing to a photo finish. Miss Better
Weather his secretary came into the room with last
minute details.

Miss Better Weather —The students are cutting up the
campus.

```
Noxon  —Steel them!
   BW  —A group of tenants have been
         waiting in your office for 3
         weeks about the housing situ-
         ation.
    N  —Stale them!
   BW  —People are threatening to go to
         Chicago.
    N  —Still them!
   BW  —The National Rifle Association
         thanks you for the whooping
         crane, the elk, the rhino, the
         wildbeeste, and the last sur-
         viving Ethiopian leopard. Now
         they want a go at the rats.
    N  —Stall them!
```

The Left Hand Path is a secret society of aging white adepts who dwell in caves located high in the Swiss Alps. [We know you're up there Left Hand Path.] You have decked out these quarters with an elaborate communications system which keeps you to the pulse of the worlds. This vast outlay of electrical energy has short-circuited the world which explains the power failures that have taken place in the United States and Soviet Union in recent years. In addition to this, your satellites circle the globe and scan the Universe for signs of deviation from your rule. At present there are 4 unidentified satellites orbiting this planet alone. (The New York Times has carried reports of this fact in recent years usually buried as a filler on the entertainment page.)

The Left Hand Path is using the earth as a mere stepping stone to higher things: complete domin-ion of the Universe. You have put our own be-

loved Milky Way into hock for your stooges who rule it as your gag. These ward heelers have befouled it so that it is becoming a celestial pigsty: an ecological shithouse which is giving the heavens a blackeye.

Department stores ring Saturn; instead of its moons which were exploded by nuclear weapons in order to make way for progress. 55 baseball teams use the earth's moon for spring training and Mars is slated to become a retiring home for the old; Youth 2.

You treat the citizens of the world with contempt secure in your knowledge that a large middle class, your coolies, will keep them in line. Pollution disease famine have taken the lives of millions. So have the wars you instigated to serve as entertainment for your guests as you wile away the time imbibing spirits and exotic hallucinogens. You have drained the world of its youth so that although some of you are over 100 you have the appearance of 30 year old men. Millions have been maimed and tortured and the ages 18–24 are memories stored away on the microfilm. You have imported women from all over the world to serve your twisted carnal pleasures. You bind them, flog them and use them as your prey; humiliating them by tying rabbit tails to their asses. The rooms set aside for these orgies resemble one great issue of the Evergreen Review—minus the militant poetry [but you are working on that].

All species of animal have been wiped out save the cunning rat, spared as a concession to Noxon D Awful, D Noxious of Ob, who eats his own and carries dirt in his heart.

Now, the Left Hand Path, your hideout is not as secure as it once was. The wastes of the world are slowly climbing the slopes of your mountain so that even you are no longer safe.

You have your eye on 3 resort planets of eternal spring located in another Galaxy. Your scientists work away into the night in a secret compartment of this factory attempting to devise the secret formula for fuel. This fuel will be used in the great White Spaceship resting in one of the mountain's craters for the day when you will lift off to the stars.

But for now, you read your codes and have your fun. At the moment you watch the man you set up to rule America. Noxon keeps you in stitches. Of all of your legmen, your soldiers, he is the one who gives you the deep laughs. He is fumbling across a TV screen one of many you have set up in your hideout to see how the world is coming off. Noxon just waded through a heap of balloons. He is smeared with Blackface and is waving goodbye with his white gloves. The writing on the screen That's All Folks means that America is signing off after another day of vigorous cartooning.

It was the end of the day. The hard working Chief Executive let his hair down. He was so tired that he told Meathead Sam, his driver, that's ok I'll walk the rest of the way. He was about a mile from his Chief Executive Mansion, Spiralling Agony, when the statesman just collapsed and knuckled under a chicken coop alongside the road. The crickets were chirping. The hoot owls hooted. The boats went foggy and the trains went woo woo. Crowds went Ra Ra Ra in Yankee Stadium because they were enjoying themselves. Fat buttery popcorn floated across the heavens. Noxon was almost asleep. He pushed aside the buzzard bones so as to make more room for his hide. He thought he smelled roast duck. Imagine that, he thought roast duck in the red rooster. The Miracle of The Rooster I shall proclaim a day. Roast Duck of the Red Rooster. Heh heh heh. Up in the sky Cab Calloway stood in for the moon.

Hi di Hi di Hi di Ho went the thunder. Cab Calloway stood in for the moon like the trouper he was. The moon faded away into the pale when Noxon landed. The aging cootie of hoochie coochie pinch hitting for old shine on and no one knew the difference. Thats it, Noxon thought as he pulled up the collars of his coat to protect him from the rain. The Miracle of the Rooster—

Papa La Bas stroked his Newfoundland HooDoo as he stood next to Minnie D Moocher in the living room of Spiralling Agony. They were looking out of the window where the rain splashed against the pane.

Papa La Bas —Nice work Minnie, you have him sleeping out in the rain.

    Minnie —He dove into the sewer this morning and swam to work so I thought that by now he would come down with a case of the rams.

      PLB —Excellent excellent. It's time for the next step.

        M —What's that master?

      PLB —Take him off the diet of dogshit and start him on pins and needles.

        M —But master isn't this working backwards from the procedure you taught us?

      PLB —He is a hard nut to crack Minnie, a man whom I suspect may not even be of this world. I am going to have to

turn the procedure around and let it
loose.

M —O master you're so wise, where do we
meet for our celebration of Osiris, res-
urrection?

PLB —The coven will meet at my place at 12
o clock and don't forget the new pass-
word.

M —Nix on Noxon?

PLB —Correct you are—Nix on Noxon.

IN THE BACKSEAT OF THIS SOLAR SYSTEM IS THE
PLANET OF OB. IT HAS 5 O CLOCK SHADOW AND
A THOUSAND SKI-JUMP NOSES FOR MOUNTAINS.
ITS ORBIT IS SO SNEAKY AND WISHY WASHY
THAT IT DEFIES THE ASTRONOMER'S CALCULA-
TIONS. EVERY DAY ON THIS PLANET IS BLUE
MONDAY AND EVERY SEASON THE FALL. ITS SUR-
FACE IS THE SIZE OF BROOKLYN. ITS CRATERS
WERE ONCE FILLED WITH CHICKEN SOUP BUT
THAT NEEDN'T BOTHER US HERE. IT IS A BUG
AMONG PLANETS AND LEAVES IN ITS WAKE A
TRAIL OF BROWN STAINS. AS IT MOVES CLOSER
AND CLOSER TO EARTH A DYING RACE OF
NOXONS AWAIT THE SIGNAL OF THEIR NOXIOUS.
IT HAS ALREADY BEGUN, I MEAN, YOU KNOW
THE NIGHTMARE FOR OUR SOLAR SYSTEM.

At about 4:00 am Minnie the Moocher awoke.
Something was butting against the front door.
She put on her nightgown and went downstairs to put
the needle to Stars and Stripes Forever.

next week—

The Invasion of the Subway People

Blood of the Lamb*
and
A Fiery Baptism

by Calvin C. Hernton

BLOOD OF THE LAMB

The Ordeal of James Baldwin

> SINGING HALLELUJAH!
> BLOOD OF THE LAMB!
> LET YOUR VOICES RISE! . . .
> —From a song Bessie Smith
> used to sing

This essay was written during the early part of 1964. James Baldwin was then at the zenith (and decline) of his fame in America. His name was on the lips of almost everybody who read serious litera- ture in this country (probably less than ½ of 1 per cent of our popu- lation). Great numbers of whites were raving about Baldwin not only as the literary genius of the times (a period of about three years) but also as the most astute interpreter of and spokesman for the plight of twenty million black Americans. While many Negroes fol- lowed suit, there were a great many more who spoke and wrote about Baldwin with sheer hatred and jealousy. For instance, Syl- vester Leaks, a Harlem writer whose writing does not equal his political rabble-rousing, published a "letter" (Freedomways, 1963) called "James Baldwin—I know his Name." It was nothing more

---

* The first portion of this paper, "Blood of the Lamb," along with parts of the second portion, "A Fiery Baptism," was first published in *White Papers for White Americans* (Doubleday, 1966). The augmented portions of "A Fiery Baptism" are indicated.

than an impoverished attempt to discredit Baldwin's genius and a
downright expression of sour-grape jealousy. All of this—this essay
as well as many similar comments by others—made me mad. All
of it! So I decided to write "Blood of the Lamb."

I

The romance of our times is the one currently going
on between white Americans and a highly photogenic
Negro. The Negro is James Baldwin. I am not being
giddy. When I say romance, I mean just that; I mean
love affair.

No other Negro writer has ever been admired by
whites as Baldwin is. Nor has any Negro ever before
been so popular in the American press. Within the
last year, Baldwin's name and face have appeared
in almost every worthwhile (and some not so worthwhile) publication in America—from the crisp, pseudo-
factual pages of *Time* to the slick, feminine sheets of
Harper's Bazaar. Although Negro leaders, academicians, intellectuals, and writers are familiar with Baldwin's works, more white people than Negroes love
him, especially liberals and white women. Many Negroes, especially writers, express ambivalence about
Baldwin. Quite a few of them envy him or "put him
down" for no reason I can see other than that he is
famous and successful. On the other hand, I have yet
to meet a white person who has not expressed his
"empathy" for Baldwin; who has not confessed his
rapture over *Another Country* or his longing for the
eloquent, baptismal flames of *The Fire Next Time.*
With white Americans no other Negro writer, past or
contemporary, stands a chance, be he Ralph Ellison,
Langston Hughes, John Killens, or the late Richard
Wright.

What lies behind this?

Much too much has been written about Baldwin.
But for all that it is worth, hardly anybody has probed
the nature of Baldwin's phenomenal appeal to white

Americans, and the ideological atmosphere that has made possible his affluent popularity in the American press. Norman Mailer has scratched the surface somewhat. Irving Howe's discussion (September 14, 1963), "From Richard Wright to James Baldwin," over WBAI showed insight, but did not go far beyond the usual "literary criticism."* Julian Mayfield's "And Then Came Baldwin" (*Freedomways*, Spring 1963), and Colin MacInnes' "Dark Angel" (*Encounter*, July 1964), are the best essays I have seen so far. Indeed, Baldwin has enchanted and outraged the American literati with his great, eloquent syntax, his seemingly boundless honesty, and with his terrible but well-disciplined anger. At least one white writer I know of has imitated Baldwin's honesty with a fair degree of success. Norman Podhoretz's article, "My Negro Problem—and Ours," (*Commentary*, February 1963), reflects the current "climate of honesty and soul searching" on the race problem by blacks and whites that I am certain Baldwin's writings have precipitated. Beyond this, however, in the avalanche of articles and reviews on Baldwin, there has been too much talk about "style," too much commercialism and mechanical description, too much false imitation, too much petty jealousy, and not enough analysis. In his envoi to *A Quarter Century of Unamericana*, edited by Charlotte Pomerantz, Baldwin wrote: *"I . . . does not refer so much to the man called Baldwin as it does to the reality which has produced me, a reality with which I live, and from which most Americans spend all their time in flight."*

II

There is a phantom, an enigma, that haunts most of Baldwin's writing. The "enigma" is Baldwin's father. When I read *Go Tell It on the Mountain*, I found

---

* This discussion was later published as an essay titled "Black Boys and Native Sons" in *Dissent* (Autumn 1963), on which Mr. Howe serves as editor.

it difficult at times to discern whether the narrator was talking about the principal or about his father. The two figures, in certain passages, seemed to merge, blur, and break away in a most laborious rhythm, like tortured lovers. In *Giovanni's Room* the hero saunters through his love affair, but not without haunting recollections of the father. The father seems to have something to do with the hero's predicament; yet one cannot completely figure out what it is. Again, in many of Baldwin's essays (*Notes of a Native Son* in particular), the father is discussed and rediscussed, always in a vague, rather metaphysical fashion. No matter how smoothly the writing flows, there is an uneasiness that bores through whenever the father is brought up.

The constant involvement with the father constitutes a "hang-up." Baldwin wanted so desperately to love and be loved by his father; but, alas, he was shipwrecked upon a sea of fear, pity, and hate. In one passage of *Notes of a Native Son*, Baldwin writes that his father was ". . . very handsome . . . proud . . . chilling in the pulpit and indescribably cruel in his personal life . . . Yet there was something which lent him his tremendous power . . . blackness and beauty." In the same essay Baldwin states clearly that he hated his father, and that his father was certainly "the most bitter man" he had ever met.

To what extent, in Baldwin's mind and in reality, is the father, as much as the Harlem ghetto, responsible for Baldwin's feelings of inadequacy? My opinion is that the father symbolizes the phallic deprivation of Baldwin's childhood and the, to use his word, *conundrum* of his manhood. And Baldwin has had to labor with this "hang-up." Being a writer, he has sought clarification and resolution in the best way he knew how: by writing about it.

But the father enigma goes further than Baldwin's biological father. In the struggling days of Baldwin's career, it extended and projected itself onto the most powerful black man in literature, Richard Wright.

Why not? After all, we get glimpses of Baldwin's
father as being a "pork chop," bible-belt cripple of
the white man's world, a mendicant of the Protestant
ethics of white supremacy. "I could see him," writes
Baldwin about his father, "locked up in his terrors;
hating and fearing every living soul including his children. . . . I began to wonder what it could have felt
like for such a man to have had nine children whom
he could barely feed. . . . He used to make jokes
about our poverty, which never . . . seemed very
funny to us . . ." And as the father lay dying, Baldwin
describes him as: "All shriveled and still, like a little
black monkey!"

On the other hand, Richard Wright was a black
power structure unto himself. There was nothing weak
about him. He rejected the communists at a time when
it was not altogether fashionable to do so; he thumbed
his nose at the Confederate flag; wrote like a pneu-
matic drill; went to Europe and had people like Sartre,
Camus, Gide, and Nkrumah come to his home and
listen to what he had to say. What better symbol
would a young Negro wish to identify with? Many
budding Negro writers thought, and still think, of
Wright as their hero, their idol.

It is also interesting to note that Baldwin's early life
reminds one in many ways of the early days of
Richard Wright. Both Wright and Baldwin were born
in poverty; both had a drive to become somebody
and met with disapproval from their families as
well as from their particular Negro communities. The
only thing Baldwin could become in Harlem was a
preacher; he did this to some degree in an effort to
win the love of his father, and at the same time he
did it to compete with his father. The ministry, however, proved to be little more than a minor balm for
Baldwin's agony. So, after his father died he left
Harlem and moved to, or better still, "hung out" in
Greenwich Village. His escape from the ghetto may
be compared to Richard Wright's flight from Missis-

sippi. Both later exiled themselves in Europe with no intention of ever coming back.

Baldwin's "hang-up" with Wright, however, stemmed not from the mere fact that he identified with and idolized Wright. Owing to the flaw in the relationship between him and his father which was, in Baldwin's words, "a murderous relationship," owing to this flaw, Baldwin wanted something more than identification with Wright; he longed for something deeper; he wanted from Wright what he did not get from his own father. Although the following words are spoken by Baldwin with reference to his father, they very well express what he desired of Richard Wright—"What I really wanted was for him to *love* me. For me to be able to *prove* myself to him."

The crisis of this desire occurred when Baldwin went to Europe. Nothing happened. Or, in Baldwin's mind, what did happen was closer to denial or indifference than to love on Wright's part. Baldwin had written a piece called "Everybody's Protest Novel," in which he took Wright (*Native Son*) to task, and Wright considered the piece a direct affront. Rebuffed and angered, Baldwin took up his pen and, with hydrochloric pathos, dealt an avenging blow to perhaps the only black man he ever really loved. "Many Thousand Gone" and "Alas, Poor Richard" resolved (or dissolved), for the time being, the mean affair with Wright in Europe.

The "pater-fallacy" and the "hang-up" with Richard Wright are not dichotomous; they are interdynamic, they make up a syndrome. This is evident in Baldwin's encounter with the Black Muslim leader, Elijah Muhammad. Several times in the essay, *The Fire Next Time*, Baldwin tells us that Elijah seemed to him like the father. "He made me think of my father and me as we might have been if we had been friends." And at one moment during the course of the meeting, Baldwin slipped into an adolescent reverie: "I felt very close to him [Elijah] and really wished to be able to love and honor him as a witness, an ally, and a father." But when Elijah's smile seemed to ask: "Whose little boy are you?" Baldwin could not respond, "Why, I am your little boy," as he had done twenty years before because, Baldwin writes, "There are some things that one cannot do twice."

There is another ingredient in Baldwin's syndrome. It is the fact (and myth) of Baldwin's color. He is heavy-laden with the immense agony of being black. Always, more than anything else, it has been this "hang-up" that has played havoc with Baldwin's soul —first as a man, second as a writer, and third as an autonomous individual.

Baldwin was, or is, a rather short, puny, and dark Negro. According to white standards (which are predominantly the standards of the Negro world), he is ugly. He was not only rejected and mocked by the white world but, more significantly, he was hated and derided by other Negroes, and most of all by his own father. Thus, Baldwin hated Negroes because they hated him. He hated his father because his father hated him. Psychologically, he embraced the white world and especially identified with young, handsome, blond males. Realizing, however, that this was no solution to his agony, he confessed that one day he could hate white people as much as he did Negroes, that is, if God did not change his life.

We must understand that to Baldwin the race problem has been *his* problem. While it is easy to see in everything written by a Negro on the subject of race that which is universal to all Negroes, it is more difficult to discern that which is uniquely the writer's own personal suffering. To repeat what Norman Mailer has already observed, in everything Baldwin writes, more than about anyone or anything else, Baldwin is writing about Baldwin! His ordeal has been to transcend the cripple in himself and the realities which have

produced or allowed that cripple to develop in a
so-called healthy civilization.

III

When Baldwin went to Europe, he was confused, a
"cripple"; to use his phrase, he was crippled both as
"an honest man and a good writer." And he knew it.
During the days in Greenwich Village he admitted
that he got into trouble with everybody—cops, land-
ladies, white girls, pimps, faggots, the lot. Recalling
how he felt prior to his flight to Paris, Baldwin says:
"I could not be certain whether I was really rich or
really poor, really white or really black, really male
or female, really talented or a fraud, really strong or
merely stubborn . . ." In Europe he hoped for some
kind of salvation; he hoped for wholeness, or for what
some people call "identity."

What happened to Baldwin the eight years in Europe is best described in his essays—*Notes of a Native
Son*—and in an article that appeared in the *New York
Times Book Review* shortly after he returned to this
country. One thing is certain: Baldwin had expected
too much of Europe. His meeting with Wright, for
instance, had proved disillusioning at the least. Moreover, the general climate of Europe was not so out-
going to Baldwin at first. He was an anxiety-ridden
man, disgruntled and hard to get along with. He was
poor and he was suffering. And his ego was bleeding
from self-hatred—for, since he was "black" and "ugly,"
how could he hate his race without loathing himself?
He admits that oftentimes he was drunk and lonely.
He plundered dives and streets inhabited by beat
men and women, pimps, faggots, prostitutes. In all of
this, however, Baldwin had one thing in his favor.
Perhaps the most important thing for any writer to
remember when he has sunk to a low level, and the

one thing that sets a writer apart from the dereliction in which he finds himself, is the constant *sense of himself as a writer*, for this is the only thing that can save him. Baldwin had (and still has) this inside himself.

Somewhere in a lonely room in the middle of Europe, Baldwin labored over his typewriter, while in the background the plaintive, atavistic blues of Bessie Smith stirred and soothed his soul.

> Woke up this morning
> When chickens was crowing 'fore day
> Felt on my pillow
> My man had gone away . . .
> By his pillow he left a note
> Reading: "I'm sorry, Jane,
> You got my goat . . ."

And he struck a chord somewhere in his psyche. Deep within, he wrestled with the ambiguous illusions that plagued him, and which had driven him beyond the physical and psychological regions of his native land. In this alien region, Baldwin met himself face to face.

> Some people call me a hobo
> Some call me a bum
> Nobody knows my name
> Nobody knows what I've done.

When I read *Giovanni's Room* I knew Baldwin had achieved what all writers must long for—the mastery of the contradictory powers within himself. It is by these powers that one is consumed or one is consummated. *Giovanni's Room* was not only an unnoticed masterpiece in literary style, eloquence, and finesse, it was also a conquest of the nameless fear that lurks in the hearts of all men and women, the dark, existential riddle of our nature that makes us tremble with ontological terror when we are in the arms of those we dare love.

> I'm as good as any woman in your town
> I ain't no high yellow
> I'm a deep bitter brown
> I'm going to drink good moonshine
> And run these browns down.

James Baldwin had come of age. Meanwhile, he was also working on *Another Culture, Another Country*, which has been released as *Another Country*. But before he finished that novel, he knew Europe had done all it could do for him. The old "hang-ups" had been more or less transcended, all except one—the most agonizing one—the "hang-up" of being a black American. The Negroes and Africans that Baldwin met in Europe ("Encounter on the Seine") had offered no solace for his problem. Europe offered no solace. In a secluded, all-blond village where no black man had ever been ("Stranger in the Village"), Baldwin discovered that the guilt and immorality, the sense of humiliation he had internalized in this country for being a Negro, lived yet within *him*, and would forever leap out to attack him no matter where he was. Flight could not assuage the sickness that was his color. He had to return to the scene of the crime, return to the soil where the fires that had produced him were ablaze. For Baldwin the problem of his color was indigenous to American soil, and it was therefore in America that it must be fought out ("A Question of Identity").

> See that long lonesome road
> Lord, you know it's got to end.*

So, Baldwin returned, a native son, to wage one of the most heart-rending literary struggles for his dignity to which we have ever paid so much attention. And what has happened?

---

* The above lines and those preceding are from "Young Woman's Blues" by Bessie Smith. Copyright 1927, © 1955 by Empress Music Inc. Used by permission.

IV

A romance has ensued. A perverse love affair between white Americans, especially the communications industry, and James Baldwin. It is marvelous, for such a public love affair with a black man is unprecedented. Yet it is hazardous, not only for whites but for Baldwin as well. An analysis of the social and psychological ingredients, precisely on the part of the whites, is revealing and alarming.

A full-page advertisement in the *New York Times Book Review* (June 17, 1963) contained a large photograph of James Baldwin. In big, black, capital letters running beside Baldwin's photograph are these words:

ACTUALLY I DON'T WANT TO MARRY YOUR DAUGHTER.
I JUST WANT TO GET YOU OFF MY BACK.

A significant statement for all Negroes. More significant, however, is why this statement appeals to so many white Americans; so many liberals, both men and women. It is the "promise" of a Negro who has been called "effeminate." It seems that American whites are disposed to love, yea, to suffer with Baldwin not in spite of, but *because* of his lack of "masculine aggressiveness." In the psyches of most white people, Baldwin does not symbolize the historic fear of the great, black phallus which lurks to rape and pillage. This is why whites feared Richard Wright (or fear any aggressive Negro). Dick, in their minds, in their emotions, was perceived as a powerful, black phallus, threatening their guilt-ridden, lily-white world. On the other hand, Baldwin is a sweet, exotic, black boy who cries for mother love (nay, *father* love!) somewhere out in the metaphysical realms of being. Indeed, *Time* (May 17, 1963) described him as "effeminate" in a rather compassionate way. Baldwin "is a nervous . . . almost fragile figure, filled with frets and fears. He is effeminate in manners, drinks . . . smokes

cigarettes in chains . . . loses his audience with over-
blown arguments."

It is immensely revealing that the first Negro to get
his face on a full page of the very feminine *Harper's
Bazaar* (April 1963) is James Baldwin. The wrinkles of
his lips and the pores of his dark skin are intimately
revealed. Across from the photograph, on the opposite page, is a three-column article: "Letter From a
Prisoner." It is supposed to be about or on Baldwin.
It begins with "Call me Ishmael," and goes on in a
senseless jargon about "Black and White," "I and
You," "They and We," and some mystical, moral
"voice" speaking both for and to "Us and Them."
Sheer nonsense! The article is not signed. I know,
however, that a white woman wrote it. I also know
that *Harper's Bazaar* was very particular about select-
ing the "right" person to write the kind of slick, effeminate nonsense they wanted. For instance, of all the
writers, black and white, who could have said something meaningful—Ellison, Algren, Lillian Smith—
they came up with "Secret Ghostwriter OOX" who
not only knows nothing about Baldwin, the race problem, but who does not give a damn.

What all of this adds up to is that the American
"literary mafia" is bootlegging, or better yet *prostitut-
ing*, James Baldwin in the wide open. The "compassion and sympathy" whites feel for the "suffering
boy" stems from the white man's denial of the black
man's masculinity, which whites fear and secretly
envy. "We can love Baldwin because he will not
screw our daughters," says the white man. "We can,
at last, publicly go to bed with a Negro, have him
soothe our guilt and we his wounds, without actually
giving up anything of our sweat, sinew and loins."
This is probably the most accurate psychoanalytic
formula for the readiness with which white men and
women open their arms to James Baldwin.

Even white "moderates" (Southerners) who find it

impossible to accept the Negro as a human being say they "sympathize" with Baldwin; they feel they can "talk" with him more than with any other Negro. There is something weird about the whole affair. Several white acquaintances have called my attention to the photograph of Baldwin which accompanied the advertisement for *The Fire Next Time* and have compared James Baldwin's smile with Mona Lisa's. And they were drawn to him.

V

Sociologically, the national character of the white man in America is ripe for James Baldwin. With the Negro upheaval that is sweeping the country, whites have no alternative but to accept and put on display a man such as Baldwin who speaks of love, torture, agony and forgiveness. Simply, the national character of America is effeminate! And here, by *effeminate*, I am not so much referring to sex (although one may do well to include it) as I am to political, social and moral spinelessness. This is especially true in the area of our lives where black is clashing with white. The national, state, and local officials of this country have done (and are still doing) everything possible to withhold from the Negro the full rights and dignities of a citizen, of a human being. Some of us are trying, but our efforts are gainsaid by our psychology. The leadership in Washington lacks backbone for decisive, authoritative action. When Kennedy was alive, he and his administration had to be pushed, had to "politic around" until "mobs and dogs clashed in the streets." John F. Kennedy proposed a Civil Rights Bill, and all hell broke loose. He went on radio and pleaded with us that we were and are facing a "moral crisis." No such thing! We were and are facing a crisis of the power structure in American race relations. Any sycophant knows that the honest, forthright thing which this crisis necessitates is a thorough change in the way POWER is distributed on the basis of color in this country.

But the white man—North and South—is acting, for the most part, in the tradition of the Uncle Tom epoch, when the Negroes themselves did not select their leader but the white men did it for them. Repeatedly, I hear whites (and some middle-class Negroes) telling me that Baldwin is a leader, or that he is verbalizing the "mood" of contemporary black masses. The fandango that Robert Kennedy pulled during May 1963 illustrates this type of misconception about the current Negro upheaval. Bobby Kennedy called in "the leaders" for a friendly chat on what to do about his brother's moral crisis. Baldwin was the most representative of these "leaders." The late Lorraine Hansberry and Lena Horne were others whom the *New York Times* (May 25, 1963) called "Angry Young Negroes."

First of all, Lena Horne is anything but young! Next, Baldwin and Hansberry were not leading any Negroes. They are great prestige figures, but they have not led any sit-ins, freedom rides, picket lines, street demonstrations, nor have they been beaten over the head by mobs and cops or bitten on the buttocks by dogs. Baldwin, Hansberry, and Lena Horne represent the compassionate type of attitude on the race question. What they do and what they write does not represent an activist, militant point of view, a point of view that more and more Negroes are adopting. If Robert Kennedy wanted to talk to the real leaders of the Negro masses, why did he not summon people who were and are actively involved in the struggle. The only Negro at Robert Kennedy's little tryst who represented the actual leadership of the masses was Jerome Smith. He lives in the South and has been arrested and beaten over the head many times. But no one wanted to listen to him. And Bobby just could not understand why James Baldwin became indignant at this.

The fact that whites automatically assume that Baldwin, because he writes about being black, is a Negro leader reveals two things: (a) whites are not yet willing to accept the *masses* of Negroes into the mainstream of our society, and (b) whites are still victims of a historic self-deceit by thinking they can hand-pick Negroes who seem to advocate some milk-warm program as leaders, and thereby actually circumvent the true demands and needs of the Negro masses. This is one more reality explaining the white man's "love" for James Baldwin. In large measure, it is this reality that shall wreak more havoc upon the whole of America, South and North.

VI

But what of Baldwin? Has he actually achieved his ambition of becoming a "good writer and an honest man"? I think so. After reading *Another Country* no one can argue about his honesty, and no critic of the present "literary establishment" would dare deny Baldwin's literary maturity and his complete mastery of the essay form. Recognizing all this, we must raise the question of why James Baldwin is not satisfied. Why does he continue to bombard the white world with his bleeding words? The answer to this leads back to the reason Baldwin returned to America—to level a ceaseless assault on the forces in this culture that have instilled in him (and all Negroes) an onto-logical sense of guilt and masculine outrage, all because of black skin. The final "hang-up" must be resolved. In every word Baldwin writes he is crying for one thing—love, genuine love that, because of having been hated, must involve the quality of humility known as redemption. The essays of James Baldwin constitute a mandate: *White man, we have got*

*to forgive one another once and for all for being black
and white, so we can love each other, or our hatred
will now destroy us, like a hungry flame!*

In this regard Baldwin is not expressing the "mood"
of the masses of Negroes who are, for the most part,
concerned with the tangible barriers to their freedom.
Baldwin is dealing with the anthropomorphic. Remember, he was a religious man, and obviously still
is. In fact, Baldwin seldom writes about the political,
socioeconomic aspects of the Negro question; he does
not know that much about sociology or economics.
James Baldwin's protocol is a more spiritual, a more
existential exigency. He wants to be rid of the myth-
like iniquity that is associated with his blackness, and
which plagues his self-esteem incessantly. He does
not want to be "tolerated," nor does he want merely
to go to bed with our daughters, since such a barbarian
notion of his integrity enrages him. He wants MORE,
much more than whites ever dreamed of. He wants
you, white *man*, to repent and forgive yourself for the
nameless horrors you have committed against him
and his people. He wants to be *loved* (or appreciated)
for his genius and for the gifts of his color to this
civilization, with no strings attached. James Baldwin
wants to be cleansed "white as snow."

This puts Baldwin in the class with Camus, Sartre,
Jaspers, and other existentialists. Baldwin is writing
about the blood of the lamb, about sin and redemption. He is perhaps at the categorical head of the
newly emerging young black writers, artists and intellectuals in this country that I call Existential Negroes.

It is significant for the white man to understand this.
At present the white press is making money off James
Baldwin, and is congratulating itself on its "liberal-
ness" for publishing and displaying this sweet, nervous
black boy. No young Negro can write a book without
the publisher sending it to Baldwin to get his im-
primatur for advertisements. He is riding on the crest
of the commercial literary tide for black writers. There

is much speculation among Negroes as to how long this will last, or who will "take Baldwin's place," for we know that historically America has accommodated only one Negro writer at a time no matter how many other great ones were around, starving. (This represents one more form of tokenism.) Many fear for Baldwin—"Where will he go from here?" they ask.

I have no such fears. Baldwin will change. He will be forced to. He will massage the white man's conscience less, and become more militant. His exotic style, his perfumed words, will undergo a metamorphosis, or should I say a turbulent baptism! When this happens, James Baldwin will not be less eloquent but more crude and brute; his pen will begin to draw blood and not merely tears. Already Baldwin has "alarmed" some whites by certain militant statements he has made. Recently he said on the Barry Gray program that he might well prefer Havana to Miami. And since the March on Washington, he has spoken with increasing bitterness and cynicism about national politics on the race problem. In Foley Square (September 22, 1963) he delivered a fiery preachment that made all the others on the platform shake and squirm, including Norman Thomas. Baldwin is beginning to see that the white man in America will never hand over to him what he wants. He (like all Negroes) is going to have to take it by force; perhaps not by violence (I hope) but definitely by coercion. To the extent that this is more and more realized by and demonstrated to Baldwin, his writing will become increasingly similar to Richard Wright's. Ironic? Baldwin was critical of Wright for having too much violence in his work and not enough love. Well, as time goes on (as time does), we may find an increasing quantity and intensity of violence in James Baldwin to the diminishing of sex, or love-making.

When this happens the current romance that whites are carrying on with Baldwin will quietly cease. It is happening already.

POSTSCRIPT

A FIERY BAPTISM*

I

In "Blood of the Lamb," I made several analytical predictions. One was that Baldwin's writing would undergo a fiery baptism; I also asserted that when this happened the vicarious and pornographic romance that white Americans were carrying on with him would quietly cease.

The truth of this assertion was confirmed when James Baldwin wrote his play, *Blues for Mister Charlie*, and by the manner in which the white world reacted to its production. The play was brute, crude, violent, and bold, more in the fashion of Richard Wright (or LeRoi Jones whom I will come to later) than of the usual suffering, pleading, metaphysical Baldwin of *The Fire Next Time* and prior works.

Unlike most plays written by Negroes, *Blues for Mister Charlie* is not about civil rights or any of the other "acceptable" subjects on Negro-white relations. The play is based on the Emmett Till murder case of

* Sections I and II of this postscript were written during the latter part of 1965 in New York, one year after I wrote "Blood of the Lamb." Four years later, in 1969, I revised and augmented this postscript in London. I have dated the sections.

1955, and it deals with the sexual variable, which is perhaps the most hushed-up and yet the most explosive factor involved in racism in the United States. And Baldwin's treatment of it is so straightforward, realistic and secular that whites found it difficult to face what they have been hiding and gliding over for centuries. Moreover, this Baldwin—the *Blues for Mister Charlie* Baldwin—is an aggressive, a masculine Baldwin. Add to this the fact that the sexuality of the Negroes in the play is earthy, rich, full of power and human animalism—all of which Baldwin does not apologize for, but affirms with dignity and prowess. It was simply too much for the majority of whites to accept or seriously consider.

For instance, both times I saw the play there were as many, if not more, whites in the audience than there were Negroes. One could not help but feel the negative vibrations radiating from the whites during the major portion of the evening. They seemed to squirm throughout the play and grow little in their seats; many tried to hold a straight face (face of chalk), but one could see and feel the hot charge boiling beneath their white masks. Upon two occasions—(a) when Richard (the Negro hero), back down South telling his friends how many white girls he has slept with up North, is showing a photograph of a girl with long hair and remarks, "Man, you know where all that hair's been"; and (b) when Richard tells Lyle, (the Southern bigot) who has been threatening him, "Man, are you scared I'm going to get in your wife's drawers?"—I thought half of the white audience might jump up and storm out of the theater. But they held onto their seats. Again, after Richard has been murdered by Lyle, and Juanita (Richard's sweetheart, played by Diana Sands) in lamentation delivers her speech on how Richard made love to her, describing it in plain but powerful language, telling how she took Richard into her womb and how she "grind" him and how meaningful the act was—again, I saw the theater

faces of white people twist and contort in agony and
revulsion. In fact, the white ladies sitting next to me
began gossiping very rapidly about the careers of
Rip Torn (Lyle) and Pat Hingle (Parnell, the Southern
liberal) as if nothing was happening on stage at all.
And the applause of the whites—one got the impression that it was as much out of nervous reaction to
cover up embarrassment as it was an expression of
honest enthusiasm.

On the other hand, Negroes seemed to be enthralled
with delight and moral vindication to see for the first
time the true nature of their lives, and their plight,
played back to them with dignity and no beating
around the bush. Many Negroes were there with white
companions. I recall one tall dark Negro who is a
famous man. He came in with his white girl and sat
down as if he was out for the usual "highbrow"
theater evening. Before the play was half through,
the Negro had unbuttoned his collar, had reared back
in his seat, and was looking around as if he himself
had written *Blues for Mister Charlie*. Pride was burst-
ing on his face and chest.

Not only did whites in general recoil from the play,
but the press, in most cases, reviewed something other
than what the play was. The majority of reviewers
said the play failed as a "civil rights" play. Those few
who admitted what the play was about found ways
of debunking it as far-fetched, saying that Richard got
lynched because he "asked for it" (*The Village Voice*,
April 30, 1964). Only one reviewer wrote a favorable
piece about the play. His name is Tom Driver and he
has since resigned mysteriously from *The Reporter*.
His favorable review was not printed in the magazine.

What Tom Driver said in his review (which was
eventually published in the *Negro Digest*, *The Village
Voice*, and *Christianity and Crisis*) was that the *virtues*
of the play killed it. He praised the language of the
play, which was raw, earthy, and full of four-letter

words (and caused whites to shiver in their seats).
After lauding Diana Sands' portrayal as the "best
performance any American actress has given this
year," Driver went on to affirm the essential reality of
the play: that the white man (and woman) in America
has a sexual hang-up about himself vis-à-vis the
Negro, and it is this hang-up that terrifies the white
man whenever he encounters the Negro, and that
causes so much violence and bloodshed. Most of all,
Driver viewed favorably Baldwin's stereotyped pro-
jection of Southern Negroes and whites; that is, the
"sterile and sexually insecure" white male who places
his "lily-white" wife upon a pedestal while he slips
around at night with Negro women, and the "virile
and lusty" Negro who enjoys the sex act to the fullest
without guilt or reservations. Parnell, the Southern
liberal, confesses his deep sexual involvement with
a Negro woman. Lyle, the Southern bigot who is so
afraid that Richard is after his wife, brags about how
he has taken the bodies of many Negro girls. In fact,
Lyle is really interested in Richard's sweetheart
Juanita, rather than the other way around. And Jo
(Lyle's wife, brilliantly played by Ann Wedgeworth),
the typical fragile and neglected Southern "lady" who
usually knows about her husband's clandestine behavior with black women and who herself has come
to accept all the stereotyped notions and emotions
about and toward the Negro, leaps (almost gladly!)
to comply with her husband's accusation that Richard
has "attacked" her when the latter came to Lyle's
store to buy a Coke. In reality Richard never touched
the woman and she knows it; yet in court she testifies
to the contrary, and Lyle is set free *for* murdering
Richard. After which Lyle brags again, "Hell yes, I
killed that nigger," and is glad of it.

We "liberals" in America always want justice to
win out in the end. Well, in the South there is no
justice when it comes to the Negro. And Baldwin wrote
it as it really is. The murderers of countless Emmett

Tills are still running amuck throughout the entire South.

As I have indicated, many of the reviewers accused Baldwin of not writing a play, "technically" speaking. Well now, several of the plays of Arthur Miller, Eugene O'Neill, Clifford Odets, and others (*The Deputy*, by Rolf Hochhuth, for instance) are not plays, "technically" speaking. Yet such plays enjoy successful runs on as well as off Broadway. Any art form, I say art *form*, that deals with man's inhumanity to man and does not end with "justice winning out" or "crime does not pay" is viewed and reviewed in America as "controversial." Let's come closer to home. In regard to the Negro, when the white man is portrayed as a barbarous, unmitigated bigot, we not only label the art form as "controversial," we also cry out that it is not "art"; we call it "propaganda." Specifically, *Blues for Mister Charlie* hits white America between the eyes, and does not apologize for doing so. Evidently to talk about the white man's sexual fears and guilts is to strike him in the most vulnerable corners of his ego. And he loses all rationality, all objectivity. He either goes blank or he tries to absolve his guilt by simpleminded rationalizations. For instance, Michael Smith (*The Village Voice*, April 30, 1964) claims, ". . . Lyle kills Richard not so much because he is a Negro as because he asks for it." Later Smith asserts, "Lyle, more in defense of his sex-self-respect than of his race, murders Richard."

Unfortunately (or is it fortunately?) these remarks reveal more about Mr. Smith than they do about *Blues for Mister Charlie*. First of all, Richard does not behave around whites (Lyle and his wife) according to the "bowing-and-scraping" pattern that bigoted whites demand in the South. No, Richard walks and talks like a man who is aware of his dignity and inherent equality as a human being. To the psychotic white in the South this takes on a sexual meaning; it is perceived as sexual assault. Secondly, the only sexual self-respect Lyle has is a false one, a guilty one shot through with and based on white male supremacy! Doesn't Mr. Smith know that sexual guilt and paranoia are intricate aspects of racism in America? James Baldwin does! And thirdly, if Richard is "mean and tormented and looking for trouble," why is he mean, by what is he tormented? But most of all, Mr. Smith, like his Southern counterpart, seems to interpret Richard's "talking back" and standing up to Lyle and his wife as "looking for trouble."

I suppose that great numbers of Negroes in the South today are standing up and talking back and demanding human respect and in the process are "looking for trouble." I suppose that their endeavoring to secure their God-given rights and make America a better place in which ALL Americans can live means, with reference to their lynching, that Medgar Evers and James Chaney and countless others "asked for it." And finally, while throughout the decades the sexuality as well as the general behavior traits of Negroes has been thought of and portrayed as vulgar, subhuman and derogative, it is a telling thing that only when these same traits are portrayed with prowess and dignity against the barbarity, both sexual and otherwise, of whites, that only then (only now!) white men rise up to shout down intrusions. My grandmother used to say, "The ones who yell the loudest is the culprits with the mostest to hide."

In fact, there seemed to have been, at one time or another, an inside move to kill *Blues for Mister Charlie* before it came to its natural end, if indeed its end was natural. One day, an editor of a New York magazine called the box office for ticket reservations and was told by someone that all seats were sold out. The same editor waited several hours and called again, for he had been told such would happen and, behold, he was informed this time by another person that there were plenty of tickets available. I also understand that someone significantly connected with the play was quoted as having said, "Before I will have the things said about white men that are being said upon that stage, I'd as soon go broke."

Now, what does all this mean in terms of Baldwin's development as a writer and as a Negro? First, as a writer he is no longer addressing a predominantly white audience, at least no longer in the guilt-soothing terms that characterized most of his previous essays. In *Blues for Mister Charlie* he was no longer dealing exclusively with the subjective or moral co-efficients of the white world's inhumanity toward the Negro. Rather, Baldwin was dealing with the raw, brute, objective facts of the white man's barbarity toward black people in America. Along with the terrible facts, there are the white man's fears, anxieties, and most of all, his guilt! *Blues for Mister Charlie* plowed deep into the very psyche of white America; with justified animosity and vindictiveness it hurled all of his atrocious deeds and horrible guilts solidly back into the white man's face! And seemingly it was too much for whites to bear. But Negroes loved it.

Which means that Baldwin, as a Negro, is writing less to soothe white folks' guilt and more to enlighten, dignify and anger American Negroes. With *Blues for Mister Charlie*, Baldwin plunged into the position of being a true spokesman not just for the middle class but for the masses of his people. Michael Smith of *The Village Voice* made this observation and added that it was "unfortunate," claiming that being a spokesman for the Negro nearly prevented Baldwin from being an "artist." Why is it that after the production of *Blues for Mister Charlie* appeared the very same whites who used to praise Baldwin now rise up to put him down!

Baldwin is not merely a writer. He is a Negro writer, and we Americans—especially white Americans—have seen to that and no doubt will continue to see to it for a long time hence. The question of

whether *Blues for Mister Charlie* was artistically a
bad play is about as relevant to the real issue as
saying that *Crime and Punishment* is artistically a
bulky, sloppy novel, which it certainly is. To wit,
Another Country is so bad artistically that I am
relatively sure its publication had little to do with art.
But the critics "raved." They did not talk about the
artistry of the book, but about how "bold" it was. With
drooling mouths the public consumed it to the ticker
tape of the best-seller lists. I saw them on subways,
on buses, at lunch counters and midtown Madison
Avenue restaurants—especially the young, up-and-
coming, clean-shaven, no-mustached, gray-flanneled.
Coming and going, I saw them reading about the
country of A-not-her! Talk about art vs. propaganda.
Another Country was almost nothing but propaganda;
propaganda for homosexuality. I am definitely not
making a moral judgment about homosexuality as
artistic subject matter, or about James Baldwin. I *am*
making a moral analysis of the character of white
Americans in regard to their good faith when it comes
to facing up to the social, political, economic and sexual horrors, in artistic presentations as well as in
reality, that have been and are being heaped upon
the American Negro. It seems—and this is the real
issue—that whites in *this* country, despite an abun-
dance of liberalism, are not yet morally capable of
accepting any open presentation, on the one hand, of
their sexual feelings regarding black men, and on the
other hand, of the sexual depravity that white men
(especially Southerners) have historically inflicted
upon Negro women, the guilt stemming from it. This
is what killed *Blues for Mister Charlie* and, in my
opinion, severed the romantic involvement between
James Baldwin and white America, forever.

Although James Baldwin may not sell as many
books and will not be so affectionately discussed in
white circles, or for that matter in lily-nice, middle-
class Negro circles, the cessation of the romance rep-

resents a step forward rather than a stumble backward. Characteristically, Baldwin has written of the race problem, or of Negro-white relations, with a deep burning love (submission) that was rooted in the religion of the long-suffering. Repeatedly, incessantly, James Baldwin has pleaded with passion for forgiveness and love between whites and blacks as the solution for the nightmare that makes havoc of our lives. But, I believe, it has become apparent to Baldwin that the probability of a cleansing love and forgiveness between Negroes and whites is long in forthcoming. America is one of the most spiritually bankrupt countries in a world where it is, as Baldwin must know by now, terribly difficult to create and maintain a personal love, let alone love of mankind. But this is not to say that we will no longer see in Baldwin's work the influence of a deeply religious man. Emile Capouya, a former editor at Macmillan who once shared an apartment with Baldwin, pointed out in 1963 in a lecture at the New School for Social Research that James Baldwin is not really a deep thinker in the sense of an academic or even a rugged intellectual; rather, he is a provincial preacher with a grand intelligence for literary style and eloquence—and he is at his best, as can be seen by comparing his essays with his fiction, when he is writing out of the depths of his spiritual background. And this background will continue to echo in his labor—no matter how charged otherwise with secular rage—until he lays his pen down and saunters into elemental peace.

II

One final contention must be resolved. While James Baldwin was being called, with reference to the race problem, the "conscience of the nation," I wrote that as a writer he stood at the head of a group of emerging black artists and writers, in particular those whom

I called the Existential Negroes. First of all, Baldwin's existentialism is rooted in religion, in spirituality, in the metaphysical. This means that (a) in analyzing the race problem Baldwin has dwelt primarily with aspects such as *hate, anguish, guilt, conscience, internal torture, sin* and *iniquity*—his favorite term, I believe, is a word which applies a "riddle" or a "mystery" to race relations: *conundrum*; (b) when it comes to alleviating the race problem his key concepts include *love, redemption, cleansing the heart, forgiveness, endurance* and so on. If the elements of a situation are viewed in religious terms, then it follows that the resolution of the situation must come in and through religious measures such as, for instance, forgiveness.

Specifically, James Baldwin is a *religious* existentialist. His task, whether he intended it or not, has been, as it were, to clear the air of all moral or metaphysical issues and cobwebs, and to define, in the realm of spirituality, what must be done to end the nightmare of our lives. Notice, he always speaks in terms of "our"—which is to say both white and Negro.

Baldwin has performed (and only God knows how!) his task excellently. He has made our hearts tremble, his words have filled us with compassion, and the genius of his consternation has enthralled and whiplashed our consciences. In a word, James *The Fire Next Time* Baldwin has caused us to weep. But beyond this nothing more has ensued. And that is as it should be, for as we all know Americans have a peculiar kind of religion whereby we go to church on Sunday and weep and confess our guilts, only to go the rest of the week and commit the same crimes. But do not play Baldwin cheap. He has, perhaps inadvertently, proved his point masterfully—no amount of mere preaching is going to cause white people to go out in the real world and undo the objective sociopolitical and economic conditions which they have instituted in order to prevent the Negro from realizing

the fruits of American democracy. And the awareness of this has inspired, has necessitated, on the part
of other Negro writers, the assumption of a secular
rather than religious frame of reference when handling subject matter that deals with the race problem.
These writers—no matter what they say—owe James
Baldwin, as he owes Richard Wright, a great deal.
Before we get to them though, let us consider Baldwin's latest major work and see what observations
can be made in the light of everything I have said
about the man and his writing so far.

III

London, 1969

The big four-hundred-page novel *Tell Me How Long
the Train's Been Gone* (published in 1968) left me
rather disappointed. Baldwin, as I have stated, is one
of the best essayists in the world. He is also a novelist who toils like a ditchdigger. *Tell Me How Long* is
full of labor and it works, although I personally find
it void of the stuff that grips me in the gut and makes
me want to move. But this is Baldwin's business. Any
writer worth his typewriter will write what he alone
chooses and not what somebody tries to dictate to
him, and that's cool by me. I, moreover, do not demand that an artist top himself every time. A writer
may write about the same things involving the same
elements for as long as he lives. Edna O'Brien,
Erskine Caldwell, Mickey Spillane, Frank Yerby,
Pearl Buck, to name a few, are classic examples. But
each time there should be a new dimension, a new
depth, a new *something*; the same people and the
same general problems, all right, but the nature of
the specific problem must somehow emerge as a qual-
itatively new or different story. No matter how skillfully rendered or disguised, rehashing the same joke

or the same sob story becomes a drag for a lot of people after a while. Unless the writer and the people are hooked on the vicarious enema of the soap opera.

Richard Wright is dead now. Baldwin's father, I assume, has long been dead. Yet once again the dead is resurrected—he is the same father, the same decrepit nigger that has appeared in almost everything Baldwin has written. Only now the father is *multiplied* (more fathers to kill?). After the real father is denigrated to death, lo and behold up jumps the hero's older brother, Caleb, who turns out to be not much more than a metamorphosized version of the same Harlem pork-chop nigger preacher that the original father was. Before this happens though, the hero (whose name is Leo) and his brother are not only wedded together by virtue of their common front against the father and against the terror-laden streets of Harlem, but they are seen as boyhood lovers. Leo loves his brother with such compassion that he comforts him by making love to him one night as they lie together in their bed. Later—on the battlefield of war —the brother undergoes a conversion experience and comes away from the war a transformed man.

Leo (his last name is Proudhammer) is struggling to become an actor. His brother, who has now become God's humble black representative, frowns on the life Leo is leading (with those immoral actor types) and cannot see any future in Leo's pursuing such an ungodly and unheard of profession—unheard of, especially where a Negro is concerned. Caleb castigates Leo for not getting a "real" job and settling down to lead a decent God-fearing life among his own people. The gulf between the two brothers, the late-boyhood lovers, is widened and can never be bridged. Leo hates God and curses Him not only for what He has done to his brother, who now is a replica of their despicable father; but also for the role that God, or religion, has historically played in molding all but a few black people into obsequious Bible-jibbering nonentities (Uncle Toms) in the unmitigated grip of oppression and terror. The relationship, however, is maintained symbiotically, but with hidden resentment on both sides, mainly out of reverence for the tenderness of their childhood love, and more significantly because Leo does actually become a superstar on the stage—"nothing succeeds like success!"

It seems to me that what I have termed the "paterfallacy" in Baldwin's writing (if not in his actual life) is much more than a mere hang-up, for now the obsession with the father comes across as nothing less than Patricidal Mania. The hopelessly eternal recurrence (as in Freudian mythology, or as in the Bible) of the son's scheming and struggling to take the father's place by first having him and then destroying him. But with Baldwin it is repeated over and over again. How long must the characters in his works go on blaming and hating and loving and killing the *same* father?

Moreover there is the exact repetition of certain other motifs: (1) incest homosexuality; both in the restricted and the broader sense, the hero usually has a love-hate relationship with the father. But now this relationship occurs with the brother also, and eventually the hero goes on to have it with everybody, especially men; (2) the hero is inevitably narcissistic —he worships himself, his body, his desires, his ambitions, his sensitivities, his pains, his joys with an all-consuming passion; (3) although the hero might screw a few women, such occasions are never as meaningful or as powerfully felt as the relationships he has with men; (4) the hero is self-riddled—while he loves himself, he also loathes himself; while he loves his race, he also feels disgust toward it; while he hates white people, he also is haunted by love for them; (5) the hero is always alarmingly honest, thus he is virtuous; and (6) everything always harks back to the same set of background circumstances. The repetition of these things in *Tell Me How Long the Train's Been Gone* makes the book resemble too closely nothing but a reshuffling of the same old cards in the same old games.

I do not take back what I said about Baldwin's having become a great writer—I've said it enough. But no matter how great he is, he does not seem to have anything new or different or progressive to say anymore. This could very well mean that, among other things, Baldwin has unwittingly or wittingly written himself into the very species personage that he has seemingly been trying to destroy, the species personage of The Father. Whether this is true or not, or whether it is true for a certain period, it is clear that he has necessitated if not nurtured into being a radically different set of black writers from himself and, alas, has been eclipsed by them.

Let me make one thing absolutely clear. These writers are not in competition with James Baldwin, nor are they in conflict with him. Nor can anyone take Baldwin's "place" as a writer, and certainly not as a black writer. Baldwin is an individual writer in his own right. (All writers are individual writers in their own right.) The sooner this is recognized the sooner black writers will stop falling for the white man's trick of "Who's Going To Be Our Next Great Token Nigger Writer While the Rest of You Fight Among Yourselves!"

Certain writers may be distinguished from each other according to how much they differ in terms of style, subject matter, point of view, and so on. What I am saying here is that a revolutionary new genre of black writing has arrived on the scene. The new artists are doing their thing, which extends beyond and is categorically distinguishable from the characteristic manner in which Baldwin has been doing his thing. The results, in terms of response and effect,

are and will continue to be markedly different from
the way whites and blacks have been affected by, or
have responded to, James Baldwin.

IV

*When I first wrote this postscript back in 1965,
section III, the section you've just read, was not included, since Baldwin had not then published* Tell
Me How Long. *I ended the original postscript with the
following five paragraphs:*

1. The *secular* or *nonreligious* existential black artists, especially the writers, do not deal in the metaphysical or the moral abstractions of race relations.
They deal with the brute facts of oppression—with
murder, lynching, discrimination, segregation, castra-
tion, riot, bloodshed! They do not speak of "love,"
"forgiveness," "cleansing the heart," or any of the
rest. They speak of revenge—*black* revenge! They
"run things down" in terms of the "nitty gritty"; they
are not worried about the "art" of their calling; they
employ such terms as "motherfucker," and "white
sonofbitches" whenever they feel the need to do so,
which is very often. Unlike Baldwin, they are not
ashamed of eating watermelon or collard greens or
any of the other "soul" foods. They are not troubled
by the fact that Negroes have not produced a Rembrandt; many of them conceive of their work as being
far better than Rembrandt's. And while many other
writers, such as Baldwin, write to and for white audiences—which restricts their works in scope, power,
and aggressiveness according to what they think
whites will accept—the black writers in question may
write to white people, but what they are saying is for
Negroes.

2. Specifically I have in mind LeRoi Jones. In his
poetry, fiction, drama, criticism and scholarly works

there is but one constant hammering—to be BLACK in America is to be REVOLUTIONARY. In *Dutchman*, *The Toilet*, and *The Slave*, three plays by LeRoi Jones, there is all the hatred, venom, brutality, profanity and downright insanity that whites have traditionally heaped upon the Negro; but now turned back upon whites. Whitman once said, "A poet enlisted in a people's cause can make every word he writes draw blood." Jones, and those gathered about him, are not begging white society to love them. No. They are out to take their freedom and dignity as black men and to harass the white world while, at the same time, inspiring the masses of big-city Negroes to the affirmation of their inherent beauty and worth, not as middle-class-oriented integrated Negroes, but as Black People.

3. With slightly less emphasis on "blackism," the same may be said of writers and poets such as Harold Cruse, Ishmael Reed, and David Henderson, and a few others who are associated with the magazine *Umbra*. All of these men are talented and young. They do not write lily-word sonnets. Their works are affluent with the kind of language that smacks of the brute exigencies of day-to-day Negro life in America. Distinctively, as opposed to James Baldwin and others like him, I call these writers Secular Existential Negro Writers.

4. But it is LeRoi Jones who stands, for the present at least (1965), as the master of these writers and of the movement. The white literary establishment (along with the literate public) is reacting to him in mixed fashion—with praise, sensationalism and awe, on the one hand, and with caution, castigation, and absolute put-down, on the other. Of the first instance, the *Herald Tribune* magazine has called Jones the "King of the Lower East Side." Of the second instance, Richard Elman, in his review of *The Dead Lecturer* which appeared in the *New York Times Book Review* wanted to know why Jones always talked about hating white

people and accused Jones of not being an "artist," calling for the "real" Mr. Jones to come forward. In still further instances, not only are a great many white critics putting Jones down for being an "antiracist-racist" (whatever that is!) rather than a "true artist" (whatever that is, also!), but some white-establishment-oriented Negroes are finding excuses to put him down also—Ralph Ellison, for instance, in reviewing Jones' *Blues People*, a brilliant study on the origin and development of the blues, side-lashed Jones with the cute remark that Jones's sociological treatment of the blues would "give the blues the blues." Well, with reference to Ellison, his negative remarks seemed to be over-criticism rather than prompted by the facts of the book. The case is clear with Elman—before he could call Jones an artist he wanted to hear Jones say: "White man, I love you."

5. In the midst of all this—the sensationalism and the put-downs—I discern a hazard if not a trap for LeRoi Jones, first as a creative writer and second as a Negro concerned in his work and his life about the situation of black people in America. Jones is running two risks. In America it is so easy, because of the Hollywood interpretation of success and the universal commercialism, for a dynamic and talented artist and his works, no matter how seriously rendered, to be expropriated as a "show" for the sensationalistic appetite that seems to characterize the American Public. For a Negro this is doubly true. What ensues is the making of the individual artist into a cult. And, make no mistake, it does not matter who does it or for what reasons, a cult is short-lived; but more important is the fact that when somebody or something makes one into a cult, it is for the function of eventually destroying (sacrificing) the individual around whom the cult has risen. Finally, creative brilliance and unmitigable convictions are no guarantees against insanity. In fact, the entire spectrum of the Negro-white situation in America is littered with persons and forces that pull

toward psychopathy. And this is a thing that the talented Negro artist who is bitterly but authentically involved in or concerned with the destruction of the racist nightmare in America should watch with the vigilance of a Mahatma Gandhi.

V

We are now bopping down the corridors of a new decade, the 1970's. Much of what I wrote during the 1960's has come to pass. LeRoi Jones has continued to do his thing. Back around 1965 at every poetry reading Jones started off by reading a poem which began with: "LYNDON BAINES JOHNSON IS A MASS MURDERER AND HIS MAMMA LOOKS PECULIAR." More recently he published a poem in *Evergreen Review* which encouraged black people to come out of the ghettos, break open the stores, and take everything they have ever needed and wanted. But Jones' thing is a complicated thing, his bag is a mixed bag. While he writes acid black verse drawing white blood with every brutal word, he also writes a great deal of what I would call personalistic crypto-cultist literature. Jones got many bags, one of which harks back to when he was the only accepted Negro high up in the beat generation cult of the Black Mountain faction, of which W. C. Williams was the idol, with the whole gang including such poets and writers as Ferlinghetti, Ginsberg, Olson, Kerouac, Duncan, Dorn, Di Prima, Berge, Blackburn—all white boys and girls—to name a few. This was the scene that Jones was in prior to getting into his all-black bag, and the Black Mountain influence can still be felt in much of his poetry and prose.

Jones' autobiographical novel, *The System of Dante's Hell*, is cryptic as hell. This novel, along with many of the pieces in *Tales* (collection of short stories)

as well as some of the poems in *Preface to a Twenty
Volume Suicide Note* and *The Dead Lecturer*, are
stylistically of the beat generation and are preoccupied with private hang-ups of a sexual nature vehicled
by a complicated network of personalistic symbolism
and imagery. Jones has made a concentrated effort to
write for the average nigger in the streets, and he is
doing just this. But a lot of what he writes is for Jones
and Jones alone. Throughout much of his writing, there
is a search for the long lost Black Patriarch and a
constant hammering at white faggotism in America
mixed up with a fierce (sometimes *too* fierce) poetic
cry for manhood. The search for a Black Identity
(Jones' black identity) is another one of his themes.

> When they say roi is dead
> I wonder who will they mean

I submit that Baldwin and Jones, if not in their personal lives then definitely in their writings, are more
closely preoccupied with many of the same themes
than either of them would probably care to admit. Yet
Jones, no matter what bag he is writing out of—musi-
cologist, poet, essayist, playwright, scholar, novelist
(he has so many, he even comes, or used to come, to
poetry readings not with a brief case but with a bag)
—the color of it is now thoroughly BLACK. Even more
so than Baldwin, Jones has undergone a fiery baptism! It was Jones who first assaulted the white world
with what he called The Black Arts, The Black
Theater of Cruelty.

> We are the witchdoctors and the assassins
> But we will make a path for the true scientists

This long, painful baptism (conversion) can be
traced stage by stage in a collection of essays entitled
Home, covering a period of, I believe, six to ten years.

There are a lot of people who say they are just as
BLACK as Jones, and perhaps they are. They are
out there in the streets fighting. Some of them write

and refer to themselves as writers or as poets, but I don't trust most of them to be genuine artists. By my standards they are a lot of black frustrates and black politicians hustling or cashing in on the gold rush of the black explosion. Cleaver is perhaps the only true artist among them? What is so remarkable about LeRoi Jones is that he is an active, angry revolutionary black fighter who has nearly always been an artist of unquestionable genius and guts.

But for all of Jones' anger, all of his genius, and for all of his BLACKNESS, he is no longer—as he was during the mid-sixties—the master of the new breed of writers I call Secular Existential Black Writers. Most of them were virtually unknown when Baldwin made his big scene, or when, for that matter, LeRoi Jones first started coming on strong out of his black bag (although I mentioned back in 1964 that Harold Cruse, Ishmael Reed, and David Henderson would be among the new species; and now here they are). But there are more. Some I failed to mention at the time and some who were not even around then.

Who are these writers? What are they saying? What makes them the most diversified, the baddest, the fastest, the most trouble-shooting bunch of writers on the contemporary scene?

VI

One might expect any black man who has studied in a high-class white establishment finishing school (Harvard) to come out perhaps a good technical writer, but also rather brainwashed in terms of the potency of what he has to say about blacks and whites in America. But William Melvin Kelley's ivy league tutelage along with his unassuming demeanor (for he is unpeturbably cool), are totally disarming. He comes into town with no guns showing, with no loud booming agonies of black rage. His style is a quiet, easily

readable, point by point, well-tempered, traditional
form of writing. There is nothing about him to put one
on guard. Before you know it though, even at the
very instance when you are about to say, "Hey, man,
com'ere and tell us what you learnt in that white
school," he has stuffed your mouth full of cyanide.

Kelley's first novel, *A Different Drummer*, tells the
story of what happens when all the black people
vacate the South, as well as what has gone on during
the years before. This book is not a "parable," no
more than Howard Fast's *Freedom Road* is a parable.
Kelley depicts the very incidents, the acts and thoughts
of brutality and inhumanity that whites have historically inflicted upon blacks in the South. He depicts
the rage set off in the whites when the blacks, whom
the whites have repeatedly deemed unwanted, decide
once and for all to leave. He depicts the very *atmosphere* in and by which blacks are victimized, but
which has been created and enforced by whites alone.
Kelley depicts reality. In fact, Kelley is often closer
to reality as a novelist than was Howard Fast who, it
would seem, was incapable of writing anything but
masterpieces. But Kelley is often closer to reality
because, unlike Fast who was a communist, Kelley's
works are free of the restrictions of any kind of ideological feedback—Marxist, anti-Marxist, or otherwise.
In everything Kelley writes—*Dancers on the Shore*
(short stories), *Dem* (novel)—there is a time-measured
deliberateness underneath, in which flows the sure-
moving power of the documented narrative. Kelley
coldly "data-fies" the despicable character of white
America vis-à-vis the struggles and hopes of black
people.

But if Kelley is cool, with the eyes of a hawk and
the precision of a surgeon, Ishmael Reed comes into
town like a hurricane. You can hear him miles away
before he arrives, and he arrives in seconds, for he
is fast and he never misses. He *can't* miss. Reading his
first novel, *The Free-lance Pallbearers*—and even

more so in his second novel, *Yellow Back Radio Broke-Down*—you feel as though you have been ripped to threads by the blasting ejaculations of a triple barrel shotgun. With these two novels Ishmael Reed has shown himself to be the foremost heavyweight satirist of all times, and I am not barring Swift or anybody.

Moreover, I do not bar Hawthorne or Poe when I say that reading Reed is also an incomparable experience in horror, madness and black magic. With all barrels blasting, Reed takes on every aspect of our national life, from the President right on down to the latest bizarre societal fad, and reveals them back to us, shot to pieces through and through with feces and death. For this is what our national life consists of.

Yellow Back Radio Broke-Down, for example, is not merely a satire on the Old West, with a black cowboy as the hero; it is not merely a parable about the contemporary black struggle vis-à-vis the white establishment; it is not merely a parody on the annexation fight between the Union and the territory of Texas; it is not merely a realistic account of the slime, genocide, corruption, degeneracy and hypocrisy that infest American history and every institution and motive in our national fibre; *Yellow Back Radio* is ALL of these things, and more!

Ishmael Reed is a poet. Like LeRoi Jones, he has taken the American language out on a limb and whipped it to within an inch of its life. In so doing he has revitalized the American language with the nitty-gritty idioms of black people's conceptualization of what it means to live in dese new-nited states of merica. As a poet and a novelist, Reed has the imagination of a psychopath who is God, or who is Satan Himself—ghosts, voo-doo, rattlesnakes, weird rites, hoo-doo, superstitions, multiple schizophrenia, beasts, metempsychosis, demons, charms, visions, hallucinations. In fact, the novel is Reed's voo-doo doll. He once said that the novel is the worst literary form God ever visited upon mankind. Reed has risen the novel from a dead doll with pins in it into a living breathing walking talking animal. This is a thing more authentic, more difficult, more dangerous, more human than science can ever achieve. By this I mean Ishmael Reed employs the mumbo-jumbo witch-doctor experiential epistemology of the Afro-American folk heritage in combination with the psychotic semantic categories of the West to achieve a highly original, secular and existential portrait of what is going on, and has gone on, in our daily lives. Reed is not mad, he is supersane; it is America that is mad and, like the other secular existential black writers Reed depicts— no, Reed *explodes* this madness before our very eyes.

Nothing to fear, John Wesley Hardin is here, Drag. My contempt for niggers is very well known. When I was 15 which is about 60 years from now I killed some insolent devil who didn't know his place. It was after the Civil War and the nigger was feeling good. Well they sent some Yankees and I blasted them over too. Next I found 5 of them coons swimming in a pond and shot them out of the water. I fired so fast the lake bounced up and down and the fish had to go to some kind of neptune analyst the next day, they couldn't believe it. . . . By the time I was 17 I had wiped out 7 men. Decided to settle down, I married to raise stock. But by then it was too late. Broke out in sweats in the middle of the night. It had become an obsession. I went out and found me a black policeman and had him on the ground wiggling and convulsing from the lead I pumped into him . . . They put me into jail, them Yankees. But I sawed out of a jail in Texas and went and found me some more happenings and lynched a Negro because by this time that was more kicks than eating, fucking, or getting stoned.

VII

The cardinal task that the new breed of black writers have set for themselves is the complete DEMYSTIFI-CATION ("telling it like it is") of what has gone on as well as what is going in every secret crevice of our history and our lives. Reed did not put the above words into the mouth of one of America's most idealized heroes. Reed *researches* everything he writes, even his poetry. Which makes one think twice about people who are going around to be way-out and progressive, while at the same time they are singing folk songs idolizing some of America's worst thieves, murderers and nigger haters.

Repeat: the secular existential black writers are not writing "fiction" that they have made up out of their own heads. Nor are they exchanging one set of false interpretations of what is going on for another set which is equally false, such as some of the black politicians are doing. John A. Williams's *The Man Who Cried I Am* is the most powerful document toward the total demystification of reality being launched by the new breeds. The book is frightening!—written not with a typewriter but with a cannon. Every black man, woman and child had better read and believe it, for our lives in the very near future may well depend on heeding what Williams has written.

There is also Sam ("double agent") Greenlee's *The Spook Who Sat by the Door* which is so tough that I understand it had to be published in exile in Britain. There is Clarence Major, poet and novelist, whose *All-Night Visitors* makes what a lot of other writers are confessing and complaining about look like squirts of dried-up semen in a vacant lot. And the young poets Victor Cruz (age twenty) and David Henderson (age twenty-five). The works of the latter will within the next five years match, if not excel, the works of Lorca, Ginsberg, Pablo Neruda, Langston Hughes and Walt Whitman.

These and a few other black writers not delved into here are not preoccupied with the chic, personalized trivia of their own individual hang-ups. For instance they know who they are, what their identities are. Notice that Williams' book is not called "The

Man Who Cried . . . Who Am I?" but rather, "The Man
Who Cried . . . I Am!" Therefore, the new writers
are not engaged in any kind of petty, jealous, sibling
rivalry games among themselves in lieu of favoritism
from the white literary establishment.

More significant is the fact that among them there
is no "leader." They undoubtedly learn from each
other, but they are all good in their own right, and
will become better as they continue writing and ex-
ploring. No matter what the white critics and reviewers say (for they always say it!), the new breeds
know that they are all "masters." This is why more
and more of them are reviewing each other's works
themselves.

Finally—and this is what puts the new breeds beyond the vast majority of their recent and not-so-
recent predecessors—the secular existential black
writers are Third World Writers (Richard Wright, W.
E. B. Du Bois, Chester Himes, Frantz Fanon).

By this I mean they are writing like Malcolm X
would have written just before he was murdered, had
he been a writer or poet. The entire economic-political-
societal world system as white men and women have
constructed it must be demystified and revealed for
what it really is. White people (and blacks) must be
revealed for what they are, even in terms of their
intimate day-to-day lives. This means that certain
subjects are being written about honestly for the first
time by black writers—subjects that were formerly
taboo, or that black writers have lied about in order
to please whites (and some blacks, too). They are not
only talking about white babies being borne by black
women, for example, but about black babies coming
out of white vaginas. They are talking about the police
and the President, the FBI, international plots against
black people, as well as about their own lusty screw-
ing. They are depicting the fact that the white world
is fundamentally a great bull-dyke, faggot, drag queen
world engaged in massive licentious violence and kill-

ing. The new black artists are saying things that they should have been saying too long ago; and they are creating a fortress of literature that has been denied to black writers for centuries. They are also creating an arsenal of art which is necessitating new forms and standards of criticism and evaluation.

These black writers, the Third World Black Writers, and a few white ones, are going to set the pace for all significant writing in the next thirty years. This pace will influence and be influenced by the course of events to come in the future.

A POET
OF THE PEOPLE

by Oliver Jackman

I STILL HAVE the engraved calling card which Dacosta Payne gave me the first time we met. It reads:

Wilfred Dacosta Payne, M.A. M.Sc. (Leeds) B. Com.,
Fellow of the American Institute of Business Management.

He explained that it was "only copperplate engraving; when one is leading a life as essentially itinerant as mine, one would have to be an absolute Rockefeller to be able to afford a steel job." To underscore his point he produced from a calf-leather card case two other cards, one bearing a New York address, the other a Geneva address. "Copperplate again," he said. "Not many people can tell the difference, but one knows oneself."

I didn't feel he was trying to make a particular effort to impress me; but I was more than ready to be impressed, being in that state of shock and hypersusceptibility which classically overtakes the young man come, for the first time, to the big city. For I was then in my third disoriented day of trying to cope with the phenomenon of London, that gargantuan

agglomeration of mist and myth which had always
been totally alive and complete in my colonial imagination, but now had to be accommodated in my
actual life. Real Burberrys, genuine coppers who
actually said "'ere" to my face, palpable October
fog, the stony, audiovisual reality of Big Ben, unre-
fracted by *oratio obliqua* or the cinema screen; it
was as if on waking from one of those recurrent
dreams of flying one discovered that one could, in
fact, fly.

But I *was* impressed by the liquid, drawling vowels
of his English upper-class speech which, never mind
the black face, went perfectly with the slim, tall figure,
and the accoutrement of double-breasted camel's-hair
overcoat, tight cavalry twill trousers and dark brown
chukka boots; if there was a slightly false note it was,
perhaps, the unkempt overgrown mat of tightly curled
black hair on his head: it looked aggressively
"African." Was he, then, one of those dissolute
African "princes" in whose misdemeanors the News
of the World periodically took such profound and dis-
ingenuous delight?

"I'm Barbadian, actually," he intoned, so obvious
was my unasked question. And then, blocking the
access of patriotic pride that this piece of news had
produced in me, he added, "Originally." Of course,
I thought, deflated, that must have been a long time
ago.

"We're cousins, you know," he went on, and I
wanted to hug him. For how could I be the utter
nothing which London had begun to make me feel
I was, when there were cousins like this about?

"Actually, we're related through your mother," he
said, and went on to explain with loving precision
our relative positions on two family trees.

We were standng in the vestibule of the large,
bustling student hostel to which the Colonial Office
Students' Division had assigned me. On the white
ceiling above us Cupid had been arrested in white

plaster in the act of chasing four white plaster nymphs round a white plaster circle; from their midst the innocently phallic shaft of a chandelier emerged to light, by means of a cluster of spear-ended miniature bulbs, a severe arrangement of a dozen over-stuffed brown armchairs and half-a-dozen high, marble-topped coffee tables that served as a reception area. Dacosta Payne smoothly piloted me over to one of the tables and sat me down.

"I pop in here from time to time to see if there are any faces around I recognize," he said. He was sitting on the very edge of the chair, his hands clasped on the ferrule of a tightly rolled umbrella which he rocked gently back and forth on the floor. For me, the very posture bespoke his status as plenipotentiary of that complex, subtle and elegant world outside Barbados to the conquest of which I had so optimistically dedicated myself. Manifestly it could be conquered; Dacosta Payne had done it. But could I? "Today," he went on, "the head porter mentioned to me that three gentlemen, *gentlemen*, he said, had arrived from Barbados a few days ago. I suppose you've noticed by now how frightfully polite the English are *in England*. He let me have a look at the register, and your name struck a chord."

He set about questioning me very closely, with almost avuncular concern, about my plans for study; the news that I was on my way to Cambridge in a few days moved him to a faint sigh—of nostalgia for the delights of beginning?

"Tremendous temptations to muck around in those places," he said, but it seemed to be the voice of one who regretted not having mucked around enough.

"I came up in the early days of the war, put in a year in the arts faculty at Leeds, and then enlisted in the air force. Best thing I ever did. Worth a hell of a lot to me."

"That must have been quite an experience," I said, awed once again.

"Mmh, well, yes, I suppose it was. Not certain that that was quite what I meant, but *passons*. Where was I. Yes. Well, I got myself invalided out, end of forty-four; was doing one of those retraining larks on one of the new kites they were serving up about then. Pilot put us down in a wheat field and I got some bits of glass and assorted stuff in my eyes, d'you know? Left eye went for a complete burton, for a while anyway. I'd had enough, frankly, wasn't at all sorry to get back to university. Weren't very many of us at university in those days, you know, a few beat-up veterans like meself and lots of pimply faced young chaps straight out of grammar school. But they gave me a year's allowance and I swotted day and night and was lucky enough to pick up a first. The rest of that stuff," he waved toward the card that I found I was still clutching as if it were a good luck charm, "all that was icing."

"But what do you do now?" I asked, with the directness of my twenty years.

"Bit of this, bit of that, d'you know? I'm a kind of consultant, really. You see, English businessmen haven't the foggiest about business management, brand new over here. It's the Americans who've really got it taped. I cottoned on to that pretty early in the game, so I suppose you could say I'm blinding them with science. I do management surveys, efficiency analysis, bit of time and motion study, that kind of thing. Mostly with small firms; they're having a hell of a time getting back on their feet, you know, shortages, rationing, government controls, lack of staff. I go along and give them a few tips on how to save some money, cut some corners, streamline, find new markets, that sort of thing. Management consultant, d'you know? But the English don't like you to use that sort of title. Too pompous, they say. The fact is, they're somewhat ashamed to admit that anyone can teach the shopkeepers of the world anything about business, specially a ruddy foreigner. That's where my time in the RAF comes in useful. I may be a bloody nig, but I *was* one of 'the few'."

It was my turn, then, to give him news about Barbados—tidbits of gossip and political scandal, who was where, and the rest of it. He surprised me by the minute interest he took in it all, cross-examining me about the names of people's babies—and their legitimacy, if any. How could he care about a world that already seemed so Lilliputian to me?

"Do let me take you out one of these evenings before you commit yourself irrevocably to the cloisters of Queens," he said as he was about to leave. "Might show you a thing or two, what? London's a charming old place once you find your bearings. Shall I give you a tinkle some time soon?" I was delighted at the prospect, and said so.

Then he was off, leaving me, on the whole, more hopeful about England, a little less confused; maybe, after all, I should be able to find an accommodation with it, though surely never that mastery which he had so clearly acquired; already the porter seemed to be looking at me with slightly less pity and contempt than I had seen in his eyes these past three days.

The tinkle came two days later. He offered "a spot of dinner and a cabaret, if you care for that sort of thing, and maybe a nightcap at the house of a friend of mine afterward?" He collected me in an elegant black machine of the kind the English call a town car.

"Just a little Jaguar I picked up from a contact secondhand. It was a snip. Would have been a crime to refuse it at the price." He didn't mention the price, as I recall it.

"Would you mind terribly if I brought along the friend I was speaking about," he asked as we drove off. "Turns out she's nothing on, so I thought we'd have a crack at her liquor cabinet first, and then pay her back in provender, so to speak." I had already divined that the friend would be female, perhaps from something in his voice when he had spoken to me on the telephone and, certain that she would be as spectacular in her way as Dacosta Payne was in his, I was more than ready to spend the whole evening in her company.

As we drove through a maze of back streets toward the flat of Dacosta Payne's friend, I found myself simultaneously wondering about both the friend and Dacosta Payne himself. About Dacosta Payne I had the unaccountable feeling that if I looked away from the figure who was skillfully and knowledgeably piloting us through alleys and lanes, some of which seemed just to miss being culs-de-sac, he would no longer exist; I apprehended him no more vividly than if he had been someone I knew only by description.

But the girl I hadn't met seemed more present and real. I had a ridiculously precise picture of her; she was brunette, with soft hair cropped close to her ears, soft brown eyes set wide apart over a little nose, and a hint of freckles beneath the first, translucent layer of skin. I know that this image had not sprung full-grown from out of nowhere, and we had reached the house, a three-story brownstone building in a mews, yes, a mews, somewhere off Piccadilly, before I identified the provenance of the picture; it was part Deborah Kerr, part Ingrid Bergman of *For Whom the Bell Tolls*, and part Kathy, the freckle-faced waitress who served at table in my section of the dining hall, and who was the first white woman with whom I had ever conversed on terms of equality—she called me and all the other students, for that matter, "Sir." In a totally unconscious spasm of gratitude I had apparently given her the accolade of beauty. (To this day I don't know whether she was even good-looking; nine months later, when familiarity had bred detachment, I returned to the hostel to find that she had been sacked for making an offensive remark to a Gambian student about his color.)

The real Gillian—I never learned her surname—was, of course, far different from my patchwork image. She was blond, for a start, her head a fluffy, and probably unfashionable, mass of light golden hair; she was tall, with incredibly dark eyes that dominated a face that was too long to be oval; I suppose the black beauty spot and the tan must have been artificial, but for me they were pristine. Was she really all of a piece, as I remember her, or is it memory that distorts for simplicity's sake? I remember her voice as being like her hair, which is manifest nonsense; but that is what I remember. More objectively, I recall a pastel wallpaper and high-backed chairs, a carved wooden chest which she said came from Eastern Nigeria, a large gilt mirror (in which I watched her out of the corner of my eye) standing above a mantelpiece of stippled gray marble; a line of crystal decanters from which she offered me a choice of sherry, whiskey or six-year-old Barbados rum.

I was enchanted; and it is a fact that for a long time afterward Gillian occupied one half of the scale in which I weighed the good looks of any white woman I met. If it is true, as it probably is, that the Gillian of my memory never actually existed, the same is no less true of most of the reconstructions of memory.

Where was Dacosta Payne in all this? Foursquarely there, make no mistake about it. Amused in a detached kind of way, like a man watching—and admiring—a film of himself; elegant, courteous—a swift opener of doors for ladies, a debonair bearer of trays, a dab hand with a soda siphon, a conjurer with his gold Ronson whenever you so much as thought of having a cigarette—slightly, but not offensively, patronizing to me, as he had every right to be.

In the car, on our way to dinner, he would lean over his shoulder from time to time to bring me into the conversation or to make comments, some of which

I remember to this day: "There's a very thin dividing line between Soho and Mayfair, you'll notice, and it isn't only a matter of topography, either . . . They don't care for black people in the X Club, over there; but I could never afford to go there when I was black . . ."

Dinner was probably excellent; it seemed to me to be exquisite. We went to the X Club; being with Dacosta Payne I, too, was not black. Typically the management favored black entertainers; the American Negro folk singer who was in vogue at the time was there for a season. He saw Dacosta Payne and waved to us in the middle of a song. Later he came over and joined us, kissing Gillian on the top of the head and calling her honeylamb; Dacosta Payne he called boychile.

That year I got a Christmas card from Dacosta Payne, posted in Rome; he enclosed a note saying that he'd be out of England for most of the winter, but would drop me a line when he got back. The following spring I received an invitation to a reception he was giving at the Carlton in honor of a visiting team of American organization and methods people. On the back of the card he wrote: "Do you ever come up to town? Should love to see you if you could pop up for the weekend of this shindig; we could run down to the country the next day and lunch with some people I'm sure you'd love. W.DaC. P." But exams loomed, and common sense just prevailed over the attractions of a posh do in Town.

When I did get to London that summer I missed Dacosta Payne; I phoned Gillian, who told me that he'd gone to Finland on business. Would I care to come round for a drink anyway?

I hedged, said I'd like to very much and would call her back. I didn't go, and I didn't call her back; the self-assurance I thought I'd acquired after nine months at Cambridge simply melted away at the prospect of confronting, alone, this paragon of London sophistication.

Dacosta Payne and I met again that winter; this time it was Gillian who was missing. "She's popped off to Davos with some chums for a fortnight," he explained; but I did see the flat once again; we were going to a West Indian bottle party, and we went there for a bottle of rum. He had a key, of course.

The party showed me more plainly a side of Payne which I had barely glimpsed at our first meeting, when he had been so hungrily curious about what was going on in Barbados. The gathering was a mishmash of students, current and superannuated, a few professional men who had "made it" in England and who sported, without exception, English wives or girl friends; some entertainers who had, without exception, not made it; and one exiled calypso king. It took place in a grim, flaking, semi-detached Victorian house in Chiswick. Chased inside by the cold mist that emanated from the river and clung like a miasma to the street, we edged past the disapproving glances of two or three white residents and crowded into a large, bare, pathetically badly heated room that was shared by two law students. After Cambridge, where the top of the voice was used only for the exchange of intimacies or for drunken altercations, the noise was deafening; everyone seemed to be shouting for no reason, more loudly, I thought, than one would in the West Indies; newcomers were greeted with an impartial effusiveness that I found alien—and even somewhat shocking. Exile seemed to bear more heavily on my London-based compatriots than on those of us who inhabited the serene world of Cambridge; perhaps, to stay alive here you had to enact a caricature of being lively.

In all this, Dacosta Payne seemed to drink more, dance more, tell more jokes, laugh and talk more loudly, and eat more rice and peas than anyone else, all the while holding firmly to his English mannerisms and accent. Clearly, he desperately wanted his credentials to be acknowledged—and I suppose they were, on the whole; but he had a double set.

That was to be the last time I saw him for six years. He continued to send me postcards and Christmas cards while I remained in England; but now his base of operations was more or less definitely on the Continent between Geneva and Rome.

In my last year at university, I received from him a reprint of an article, "Quelques considérations sur les problèmes d'industrialisation dans les pays sousdéveloppés, par W. Dacosta Payne," which had appeared in a learned journal in Switzerland. On a card, which described him as "conseilleur industriel," and which bore a Geneva address, he had written, "Still blinding them with science. W.DaC.P."

II

I suppose I was happy in Nigeria. By 1956, which was when Dacosta Payne swam into my ken once more, I had discovered there a few certitudes and something of a firm outline for my life. Within two years of my arrival I had become a good, competent journalist—read, quoted, sometimes reviled; and was the regular recipient of letters from the fourth forms of secondary schools which began: "Dear Mr. Brathwaite, Could a journalist of your eminence spare a few minutes of your doubtless precious time to consider my case . . .?" The "cases" were almost invariably based on a desire to know my "professional secret." There had been, let it be said, considerable erosion of that diffidence which had caused me to shy away from accepting Gillian's invitation to have a drink.

Dacosta Payne reappeared in an item in the

French agency file. "Dr. Wilfred Dacosta Payne, the British industrial consultant," was in Togo advising certain French-based companies on the expansion of their investments in industrial undertakings in West Africa. He would be stopping over in Lagos for discussions with "leaders of industry" in Nigeria.

I knew then without the flicker of a doubt that Dacosta Payne was, and had all along been, a fraud. What made it worse was the realization that I had probably perceived this from the days of our earliest encounters, but some childishness—and cowardliness —in me had prevented me from making the admission to myself; he was such a glitteringly perfect piece of bronze that in my boyish avidity to see and enjoy real gold I had been all too ready to accept the fiction he proposed and represented. I was bitterly disappointed in myself, with the total contempt for the twenty-year-old Brathwaite that only a twenty-six-year-old Brathwaite could have.

It was obvious that I would have to see him when he came to Lagos. There would have to be a showdown, though precisely why, and precisely how, I did not know.

I learned of his arrival from our port reporter, found out that he was staying at the Grand, the only decent hotel in town, and with a full head of truculence up, went to find him out.

It was just after eleven in the morning, when the hotel was full of guests and journalists and businessmen escaping gratefully from the heat into the dark, high-ceilinged vault of the lobby bar for a cuppa or a beer. As I walked in I immediately recognized the back of Dacosta Payne's head rising out of one of the heavy, overstuffed leather chairs that stood in the passageway to the bar. I realized with annoyance that I would have recognized it even if I hadn't been expecting to see him.

I stood, uncertain of what I was going to do, near the mahogany cage that imprisoned the receptionist,

for a full minute. Then like an avenging angel who
has lost confidence in his mission, I moved over to
Dacosta Payne's chair, and coming up on his right
side I leaned over and said, "Doctor Payne?"

"Yes?" he replied, a little startled, "Yes, you
wanted . . . ?" Then he recognized me, made to get
up, and started what would surely have been a smile
of genuine delight; but both gestures must have been
arrested by what he saw in my eyes, and he sank
back into his chair, still looking at me, not speaking.
With some surprise at my own detachment, I noticed
that his hands were tense on the arms of the chair.
He looked straight at me with the tired, experienced
expression of a man who recognizes an unpleasant
corner when he sees one, but is no longer overly
excited by the phenomenon. "What do you want?"

Something told me that we had gone too far too
fast. Whatever message my intuition or newly acquired experience had sent me, this was still the
Dacosta Payne who had opened his heart, or something resembling it, to me in England. He had certainly never defrauded me of anything. Yet there I
was looming righteously over him and, incredibly
enough, clearly constituting some kind of threat to
him. Whatever I might think I had on him, I could
never say I had anything against him. But the situation had already developed its own momentum,
which I simply didn't know how to turn aside.

It was he, typically, who saved me.

"Well," he said, his voice cool and low, "cat got
your tongue?"

Spoken in purest Bajan by this adept of purest
Mayfair, this broke me up into laughter that was
only fifty percent relief. He couldn't help joining in.

The détente gave me a chance to draw a chair,
to compose myself—a little, at least—and to prepare
a tactic of withdrawal, for there was now really no
alternative to withdrawal.

"This is one hell of a reunion, isn't it?" he said

when I had settled down in my own overstuffed chair.
I could only nod. "What's it now, five years? six?
since we were last in touch? What're you up to these
days, working for Interpol?"

"*Touché*," I said, feeling not unlike the decapitated
fencer in the Thurber cartoon. "People change, you
know," I added feebly.

"Of course they change. I should jolly well hope
they change. You, for one, I shouldn't like to think
you were still as wet behind the ears as you were a
few years back, what? So what've you learnt, meanwhile? A certain cynicism, no doubt; anything less
negative along with it?"

The tone was right; we were both relieved to find
that it was possible to communicate. For my part, I
didn't need to insist too much; he understood only
too well that the days of our patron-client relationship were over.

It turned out that he was almost certainly going to
be establishing himself in West Africa in the near
future, in all probability in Lagos. Conversation became a little awkward at that stage; we were approaching tricky terrain. But Dacosta Payne glided
easily over it.

"Look here," he said, rubbing his upper lip with a
forefinger and giving me a look that was almost a
caricature of roguishness, "I *did* get a B.A. at Leeds,
and I *did* serve in the RAF." Laughter, that ambiguous unguent, rolled gratefully over us once more.

He stayed a week in Lagos. I told him that my
Hillman was at his disposal; but he didn't need it.
There was always a Buick or an Armstrong-Siddeley
—supplied by various Leaders of Industry—to take
him where he was going.

Before he left for Geneva we met once again
briefly, at his request, and had a curious conversation that, despite many obliquities, was essentially
cordial.

"This Nigerian deal means an awful lot to me," he

said. "Believe me, I'm giving up a gold mine in Europe to come into Africa. That's gen. It's going to cost me. Of course I don't plan to starve, but I think I may end up doing Nigeria at least as much good as it'll do me. You'll never understand that, I'm sure; but that's what I'd like, anyway."

I have to say that I didn't understand, but it was such an outrageous idea that I almost believed him.

About three months later he was back. He didn't get in touch with me immediately but, inevitably, I heard about his arrival, and learned that he had taken a top-floor in central Lagos, with Swedish intercom system, air-conditioning, wall-to-wall carpeting, the works. He was operating under the name of "Africonsult Inc., Industrial Consultants."

About a week after his return, he telephoned me.

"I didn't call earlier, as I've been rather tied up with all the piddling details of getting settled in. Not that I'm by any means over that hurdle, but I'm beginning to get things more or less sorted out. What say we have a session some time soon?"

It was another ten days before the session materialized, lunch—at the Grand, of course; there was nowhere else. He was one hundred per cent himself again, already on first-name terms (their first names) with the waiters, and even rating a "Good Morning, Mr. Payne!" from Rees, the unconvivial alcoholic Welshman who managed the hotel.

Over lunch we chatted amiably and aimlessly about the banalities of life in Lagos, about his settling in, about the apparent technical incompatibility of his specially imported telephone system and that of the Nigerian Posts and Telegraphs, the problems of finding the right kind of secretary—he was probably going to have to engage a married English woman, although hiring a white secretary in Nigeria

went against the grain—about the question of con-
tacts of various kinds: "I'm expecting more than a
leg-up from you there, old man," he informed me,
leaving no doubt in my mind that this was the last
thing he either expected or needed.

It occurred to me that in some ways I now knew
him too well, and that to this extent Dacosta Payne
was becoming a bit of a bore; for I knew that all this
was preamble; he wanted to say something fairly
specific, and was probably keeping it until the coffee
came.

I was completely right.

"Sugar for you?" Yes, I said, two lumps.

"None for me. At thirty-five you have to begin to
think of the old waistline. You've got a while yet
before that kind of thing starts to bother you."

We sipped silently at the watery Grand brew, he
smoking some expensive-looking gold-tipped cigarette, while I puffed on a cheroot—cheap, local, and
foul—but, like my bow tie, an essential part of the
Brathwaite image which I was then assiduously cul-
tivating.

"D'you know, it's occurred to me that you might
just conceivably find our rather curious relationship
a little embarrassing from time to time . . . I mean,
in your line of country you don't want the idea to get
about that you're too close to any particular business-
man, that kind of thing. So if you feel that you'd
prefer us not to see perhaps as much of each other
as we might have done if this had been London,
well, quite frankly, I think I'd understand."

It was spoken with the elaborate casualness of a
speech that had been meticulously rehearsed; to this
extent it was not well done, but that it was done at
all was a tribute to a sort of honesty and delicacy
in Dacosta Payne. For what he was saying was that
his line of country was such that one day there might
well be some kind of stink; and this was a friendly

warning that it might be advisable for me not to stay
too close to him, for my own good. On the moralities
of friendship, at least, he was impeccable.

Almost immediately the Dacosta Payne boom began in Lagos. There were his official receptions—part
of the contact-making process—that always developed into parties which people talked about for days
afterward; there were the Sunday luncheons which
soon got the reputation of providing the best palm-oil
chop in town; there were the "coffee breaks" at
eleven A.M. at the Grand, with a score of civil servants and businessmen and journalists, ostensibly
doing precisely the same thing they had done before
Dacosta Payne's arrival, but somehow finding in him
a focus and an ornament. It was very chic to know
and be known by Dacosta Payne; and willy-nilly, I
found that it was even more chic to have known him
longer than anyone else in town.

In any event, people assumed that, coming from
Barbados myself, I was naturally an intimate friend:
West Indians were considered, for most practical
purposes, an expatriate tribe with all the solidarity
of the native tribes. So reporters, as well as people
outside the business, would frequently question me
or gossip to me about him; one of our younger men
who never did anything for the twice-weekly column
I ran suddenly began offering me stories about the
new "industrial consulting magnate," ("magnate"
being a word very much in vogue at the time for
anyone in commerce from Henry Ford II to the owner
of four canoes plying the lagoon between Apapa and
the Marina), and was flabbergasted when I refused
to use them on the grounds of their triviality. I am
certain that it was he who started a rumor in the
office that Dacosta Payne and I had fallen out, which
had the curious effect of increasing the volume of
gossip I now heard about my compatriot.

It was he, too, who dropped the first hint about Dacosta Payne and Funke. He stopped by my cubby-hole one day about six months after Dacosta Payne's arrival and said, "I hear your countryman is nego-tiating with one of the big American hotel chains to build a luxury hotel in Lagos. Is he having any suc-cess?" I told him I knew nothing about it; I didn't get around town as much as he.

"You mean you are still not speaking to him?"

"Olapeju, why don't you go and buy some more fried plantain and leave me alone?" I said wearily. His mouth was still not completely empty, and there were palm-oil stains on his handkerchief that be-trayed the menu of his last snack. Totally unabashed, he came and sat on my desk, and leaned over my typewriter with an air of one about to impart a great confidence.

"Listen, *oga*, you know who he is entertaining these days after all the parties are finished?" he asked, his long, thin, foxy face further elongated by the con-spiratorial look it now wore. I shook my head.

"Funke!" He opened his arms wide, in a gesture of triumph: this wouldn't get into my column either, but it was certainly news. He got down off the desk and went out the door jauntily, saying, "Trust Olapeju to get the *real* news."

I didn't know what to make of it. Funke was a Lagos institution; although I had seen her close up only once in all the time I had been in Lagos, she was, like an institution glimpsed frequently but never visited, almost three-dimensionally familiar to me. In a town where sexual prudery was unknown, and would probably be incomprehensible to most people, she had made a name for blatant, even flamboyant, venality and sexual opportunism, and for shifting from patron to patron as her bank balance moved her. The series of patrons had been spectacular, and it was no exaggeration to say that there was not one—at least of those about whom I had heard—who had not left her better off and found himself worse off. There was the young Scottish solicitor who was discreetly repatriated to Glasgow before he could be charged with embezzlement; a timber merchant from Warri who had cut a swathe through Lagos social life for a whole year and had afterward simply disappeared; one of the first Nigerians to be made an assistant superintendent of police who was summarily dismissed for corruption about six months after he took up with her—and six months after his promotion; a painter who had refused a scholarship to the Slade because of her and was now reduced to carving so-called Benin busts for the airport trade: these I knew of, and although reason cautioned that there were probably more sides to all these stories than the one I had heard, yet the statistics were pretty impressive.

And yet, who better to lock horns with the local *femme fatale* than a Dacosta Payne, I thought, and more or less left it at that.

In the event, Funke had nothing whatever to do with Dacosta Payne's downfall, although it took its place easily in the corpus of the Funke legend.

We saw each other, inevitably, during his year in Lagos; sometimes he would invite me to the smaller parties, and I can vouch for the excellence of the palm-oil chop. More pertinently, he would call me up from time to time, keeping in touch, occasionally giving me useful tips on what was happening in that part of the city's business life in which he was involved. He did this, I felt, out of a sense of duty, that surprising sense of duty which I had seen at work before; for by now we both knew that we didn't particularly like one another: he found me too staid, too verveless; and I was impatient with his act now that I perceived it to be an act, however totally and unremittingly performed.

His industrial consultancy was genuine enough, it appeared. He was making something of a living—

though hardly on the scale of his spendings—by advising small industrial firms on productivity, marketing and advertising, and even ran, with the blessing of one of the international organizations, a well-publicized seminar on manpower training. By the end of his first year in Lagos, he was definitely somebody, not a heavyweight, perhaps, but a widely known welterweight in the world of commerce and society, one of the people, to boot, about whom it was felt that they "contributed something." Despite Funke, about whom everybody now knew, he was on the secondary Government House guest list, invited frequently to receptions and the larger dinner parties. Funke was not. Sir Femi Oladairo, the Q.C. whose brother was Oba of Lagos, and who was perhaps the most influential Yoruba in the West, said one night at a party that Dacosta Payne was an *omowale*, a child come back. The remark was widely repeated, not least by Dacosta Payne himself; it was not long before all references to him in the newspapers read, deadpan, "Mr. Dacosta (Omowale) Payne."

In a sense, I suppose, this is where the process of his destruction began. My own awareness of it I can trace only from a telephone call, one in the series by which we occasionally linked our separate worlds, that I received from him one day about a year after his installation in Lagos.

"St. Clair? Dacosta Payne here. Look here, old sport, I think I may be able to put you on to something fairly interesting. D'you think you could pop round and see me today or tomorrow? Preferably today, if it isn't too much of a bore?" How total a thing is language! From merely speaking like a certain kind of Englishman, Dacosta Payne had become a certain kind of Englishman, completely giving away, by a language designed to be hermetic, the extraordinary excitement that lay behind the anodyne words.

"I'll come right now," I said.

"That would be frightfully good of you, if you're sure it's not too inconvenient. I know you newspaper chaps have rather a frantic time of it . . ."

I found his iron-faced English secretary-receptionist presiding over the northern elegance of his waiting room. She informed me, in an accent a few degrees east of the Mayfair of her employer, that he was expecting me.

He met me at the door, greeting me with a two-handed grip on both my forearms, excitement flowing through his limbs like an electric current, and sat me down in a form-fitting Scandinavian armchair. He remained standing, his back to a large executive desk that was as antiseptically uncluttered as any movie tycoon's.

"Listen, St. Clair, I'm afraid even to put this into words, but I think I've got it. I *think* I've got it. Just listen to this, and maybe you'll be able to give me a few pointers." There was certainly something extraordinary in the wind: I had the impression that he genuinely wished my help.

"Anyway, it's the kind of thing you'll almost certainly be wanting to do a piece about when the time is ripe, *when* the time is ripe."

He moved away from the desk now, a lithe, predatory figure, whose present unease did not blot out a certain natural elegance, a fineness of physique that seemed to complete and continue itself in his surroundings and in the clothes he wore (he had brought his anglophile style of clothes to Lagos, the near-Edwardian cavalry twill trousers and the hats, but had changed his chukka boots for a lighter suede shoe, and mastering the spirit of Lagos as he had that of London, he wore a clever adaptation of the Yoruba *dashiki* which on him looked to be both highly original and profoundly traditional at the same time—as it was).

"Look here," he said, but he was moving away

from me toward the blue wall to my left, which displayed an enormous black and green abstract by Funke's discarded painter, "you know there's been an awful lot of cant talked about the shortages of managerial skills in countries like Nigeria, parrot stuff: why are there no Nigerians even in the middle echelons of business, why do these firms bring in expatriates at astronomical cost to do jobs that Nigerians should be doing. Practically every time I go to the G.H., H.E. takes me off into a corner and tells me how ashamed he is that nothing is being done by the Colonial Office or by the big business houses to put the situation right. If you tackle the businessmen, they give you the old dead-end answer: simply haven't got the chaps, they say; it'll take decades to train the right sort of people, dida dida dida. Well, I think old Dacosta Payne's found the answer. Just listen and see if you find any holes in it." ·

For some months now he had been working on a number of foreign businessmen, and he had finally got eight of them to agree to recommend to their head offices a scheme for training a limited number of their middle-level Nigerian employees: first there would be an "intensified" in-service orientation period of three months; this would be followed by a six-month academic type course in general business management, economics, and accountancy, all to be topped off by assignments in relevant branches in the various head offices overseas.

"It's so damned simple it's a wonder nobody's thought of it before," he said. "Of course it took some persuasion to bring them round; all the old prejudices came out about what the 'natives' can do and what they can't. I think that the magic word 'independence' did the trick. They simply haven't got around to thinking out some of the implications of independence; I pointed out to them that we'd be getting independence sooner or later, within five years at the outside, and that life might just not be as simple

for them as it is nowadays. You could see the little
wheels turning around in their heads each time I
brought this up. On the positive side, of course, they
could see that it wouldn't do any harm in an independent Nigeria to be considered as pioneers in
bringing Nigerians into management." He told me
that he had kept Sir Femi informed about all these
developments, and the scheme had his blessing.
Payne would, of course, be a consultant to the various managements concerned, and would help in ar-
ranging the training program.

On my side, his idea was that I should get up the
background on the employment situation in commerce in Nigeria, and prepare a couple of articles to
be published as soon as the formal agreement was
signed.

"You must admit that I'm handing you a scoop on
a silver platter," he said. I agreed, but pointed out
that one didn't say "scoop" these days: the word
was "beat."

It was a genuine beat for both of us. For him, of
course, it was everything: whatever he had been
before, however marginal had been his life in the
various societies where he had found a living, he had
now, through the "Payne Plan," achieved a kind of
moral rehabilitation—with material benefits in the
offing—and had found a place and a role. All this
remained unspoken between us; there was no need
for words.

I went to work on my background piece, and had
it ready in ten days. In the meantime I hadn't heard
from him, but I gave it another four or five days before calling up to find out how things were going.

He wasn't in; his secretary said he was out of town
for a few days, but refused to say where or why.
About a week later I called again, for he should
surely have got everything straightened out by now;

he was still away, and his secretary was still uncommunicative. Then, checking on his house, I got an out-of-order signal; the telephone operator confirmed that the number "had been discontinued." This was very, very odd indeed.

It is still a little embarrassing to recall that my first reaction was that of a journalist; at the smell of "a story" Brathwaite the friend gave way to Brathwaite the reporter and columnist. I went in to the editor, told him about Payne's coup, and handed over the copy I had up to then kept locked in my desk. I suggested he put Olapeju on to the story.

But Brathwaite the friend hadn't altogether disappeared: it was he who tried to find Funke—who was out of town as well. I found out that she hadn't been seen for more than a fortnight; a brother of her police superintendent who worked in Inland Revenue gave me a couple of names of people who might know where to find her, and volunteered that he had heard that "there was something on" with Dacosta Payne, but would volunteer no more.

It was comparatively easy to track Funke down; Lagos was full of people with whom her secrets were not safe. I was told by one of her former protégées that she was staying in a town in the West, which I shall call Afin, where she had relatives, but that she was living in a house by herself. Within fifteen minutes of arriving in Afin I found her. Her refuge was an unpainted lathe-and-plaster house about four hundred yards in from the trunk road that passes through Afin on its way to Ibadan. Surrounded as it was on all sides by the poor mud-and-thatch cottages of road workers, public works messengers, and roadside vendors of the one-stick-of-cigarette-and-two-kola-nut variety, it was as inescapable as the first skyscraper in Lagos.

I have never learned much about Funke's background. When I arrived in Nigeria she was already in full spate and, since she seemed to be the black

sheep of no particular family, I assumed that she was
the result of some kind of social parthenogenesis, an
Aphrodite from the provinces sprung full-grown from
the foam created by what the sociologists call the
drift to the urban areas. Now, here in Afin, it seemed
that she had a place and a family to whom she
could turn for shelter.

It was she herself who answered to my knock,
coming on to the little verandah at the front of the
house and pushing the door shut behind her.

"*Ki lo fe?*" she said abruptly. Yoruba custom,
deeply embedded in habits of language, demands
that the stranger be greeted "properly"; and the
elaborate formu'ae of courtesy are so automatic that
they come close to being instinctive even among the
most sophisticated of city dwellers. "What do you
want?" would be uttered only after the ritual remarks
about the weather, and at least one apology about
the state of the road. Funke was clearly under great
strain. She stood watching me, waiting for me to
speak, her legs challengingly apart, dressed in nothing but a *lappa* that went slightly more than once
around her body, covering her from armpit to knee-
cap, and loosely tucked in near her left breast.

"I'm a friend of Dacosta Payne's. St. Clair Brath-
waite. I think you've seen me before at his house.
I'm trying to find him," I said, almost stammering.
She had really unnerved me by her aggressiveness.

"*Ori e o bajo!*" She was shouting. "Weytin do you,
my friend, your head no good? You dey come ask
me for your friend? You think say if he get trouble,
na *Funke* go know wey side he dey?"

My God, I thought, she's right of course. I had
sought her out, on the banal principle of *cherchez la
femme*, like any tenth-rate detective—or journalist;
but this, after all, was Funke, a specialist in skinning
men, but no taxidermist. If it was obvious that Dacosta Payne was in trouble, then it was obvious that

Funke would be the last person to offer him a helping hand: it simply wasn't her style.

And yet . . . instinct told me that there was something; why *had* she left Lagos, for one thing? Why was she being so aggressive? And, inconsequential as it might seem, I found it odd that she should speak Yoruba and then pidgin to me, when I knew that she could speak perfectly good English. It was no more than a feeling; but after driving forty-five miles to find her I wasn't going back to Lagos without some kind of satisfaction. And, anyway, she had to know *something* about what was going on.

I decided to play it sentimental.

"Look," I said, "I'm a *friend* of Dacosta Payne. We're cousins, as a matter of fact; he's related to my mother." I think it was the word "mother" that did the trick. Nowhere is the mother an object of such awed devotion as in a polygamous society.

"You from Barbados, too?" she asked, but from the way her body had relaxed after my last speech I knew that I had won. I nodded.

"I know you. Come in," she said simply, and turned and walked through the door.

The sitting room into which she led me reminded me of nothing so much as one of those weekend beach houses which are rented out to the holidaying middle classes on the east coast of Barbados. In one half of a large room there was a perfunctory suite of four mass-produced Morris chairs and a settee, in the other half a dining table with four upright, cane-bottomed chairs, with an antiquated refrigerator groaning away in a corner beside them. It was already eleven A.M., but the dining table still bore the traces of breakfast in the shape of a porridge bowl, a coffee pot, a loaf of computer-sliced bread, a dish of melted butter, and a bottle of honey.

Funke waved me to a seat and, turning her back on me, leant over and unwound and rewound her

lappa around a body that was evidently nude. It was a
gesture that was more familial than coquettish. I was
truly accepted. The maneuver over, she moved in an
instinctive housekeeperly gesture in the direction of
the dining table, and then stopped herself as if realizing that she was in the presence of a friend who would
not—or should not—be bothered about the disarray
that was so evident there. I literally couldn't take my
eyes off her. Never had I heard even the bitchiest of
Lagos women ask about Funke the classic bitch
question: "What do they see in her?" For it was only
too obvious. It was the body, of course, an extrava-
gant thing, on a scale nearer to poster art than to
real life. She was tall, as tall as I, statuesque, a sculp-
ture of mahogany curves and smoothness. But it was
the face, which I had casually judged to be "good-
looking" the two or three times I had seen her, that
now held me. There was a flatness at the eyes that
was oriental, but the high cheekbones were those of
the Benin terra cottas; down the cheeks ran the single
slash of the Ondo mark, giving to the whole face a
quality that was at once exotically savage and
classic. You suspected, perhaps from something in
the eyes and from the slight pout of the lower lip,
that all her life had been one of sexual challenge,
that she took as much pleasure from men as she
gave, and that she was probably too familiar with
ecstasy to be capable of love.

I had been looking at her frankly, and she seemed
to have *paused* for the examination. "You finish?"
she asked, in a voice that was both mocking and
complacent. I was quite unembarrassed. I nodded.

"Omowale is at Alapa. He is under observation,"
she said. There was no identifiable emotion in her
voice, but she looked directly at me, waiting, I knew,
to see my reaction. Alapa, about three miles from
Afin, was the site of the most modern psychiatric
hospital in Africa.

I had been expecting something fairly shattering

but more orthodox; *this* was almost a relief. But it would have been impolitic to show this—to show anything at all, for I wasn't yet quite sure exactly where Funke stood.

"What happened?" I asked neutrally.

"He had a breakdown. They say it isn't very serious, but they want to keep him for a few weeks. It is only in the last few days that he begins to recognize me." Up to then she had been standing over me, anxiously, scrutinizing my face as if searching there for an omen. Now she suddenly moved away toward the table, stacked the crockery in a tray, and disappeared into a passageway behind us.

A moment later she reappeared, and joined me on the settee. Putting one electric hand on my knee, she said, "He has to go away. He must not stay in this country. He must go as soon as he is better." She must have seen the sign she wanted, for her tone had softened, and she spoke to me now as to a fellow member of the club, the sodality of those who had been smitten by the Dacosta Payne magic. She started to tell me the whole story.

She didn't know all the details; she hadn't been precisely an intellectual companion, but she did know about the Payne Plan, and perhaps, in the ultimate intimacy of the bedroom, he had been able to unload his whole freight of anxiety and excitement and anticipation over it. What seemed clear was that he had managed to engage Funke more deeply than any of her previous lovers, possibly because he was more articulate and, in his own way, more engaged than any of them.

One evening about three weeks before, she told me, he had come home and without even a greeting had handed her an envelope, and had gone to his room. She saw that it was from the firm of solicitors headed by Sir Femi, and contained a formal letter signed by Sir Femi himself as well as an enclosure. The letter stated that on the instructions of his clients the Nigerian Businessmen's Association, Sir Femi was transmitting to Mr. Dacosta Payne the attached note, and was informing Mr. Payne that copies of the note had been circulated to the Private Secretary, Government House, the Immigration Department, and to members of the Council of the Association. Such circulation might well be construed by the courts as publication, in the terms of the Defamation Act, and it might be that Mr. Payne might contemplate legal action as a consequence. Oladairo, Rawson, and Adedapo looked forward to hearing from him.

The enclosure was a curriculum vitae of Dacosta Payne, which included a reference to a six-month jail sentence at Nottingham for fraudulent conversion in 1946, and a suspended sentence for living off the immoral earnings of a prostitute in Leeds in 1948. The curriculum vitae noted that no trace could be found of the American Institute of Business Management of which Dacosta Payne claimed to be a member.

Payne didn't go to work the next day, or the next, or the next. He didn't speak a word to anyone, not even her, for a fortnight. Incredibly, she stayed with him, fed him, and continued to try to communicate with him. When he did start to speak again, she said, it was nearly always declamatory, to an unseen audience: he spoke sometimes in what she thought was French, sometimes in a gibberish mixture composed of the few Yoruba words he knew, of sounds she didn't recognize, and of Nigerian pidgin; sometimes in English. "I have come back, my people, I have come back," he would repeat, over and over again, when he spoke English; and among his gibberish speeches she often heard the Yoruba expression "*Omobawale, omobawale*"—"the prince is come back." It was then she decided to have a psychiatrist see him.

Irony is too much with us. For once Dacosta Payne had been playing it more or less straight; for once this promoter was promoting something other than his own immediate financial interest; for once his interlocutors should have had nothing to fear from him; and it was this one time that he came a cropper.

But of course they did have something to fear from him; and I was to learn afterward that he had been the victim of an unlikely alliance between business and government. On one side the more conservative elements of his famous "eight" had balked at the last minute at the prospects of "abdication" and "surrender to forces of nationalism" which his scheme implied; on the other, the colonial government was less than enchanted by the possibility that one private person—and a black one at that—working with private commercial interests might bring off in a couple of years a reform that HMG's own specialists had repeatedly said would need decades of gradual work. It would have been too awkward a chapter to be accommodated in the history of graceful and deliberate decolonization which HMG wished to write. So it was, I was told, that Scotland Yard was ready to give its fullest cooperation in the "research" into Dacosta Payne's background.

His recovery was comparatively swift. The psychiatrist explained to me that it was "a simple breakdown, the defenses have broken down under pressure. We've seen a similar sort of thing with Nigerian students in England; it's a question of how well and how quickly you can adjust to a new society. What's interesting, if you don't mind my saying so, is that your friend is of African origin, and one would have thought that this would have made it that much easier for him. It's rather a provocative case, this." The psychiatrist was English, and eager, and I had the definite feeling that he was going to "write it up" one of these days.

Of course, there was nowhere for Dacosta Payne to go now but out. He went quickly. Funke paid, since he seemed to have no liquid funds. He made her executrix of his Lagos interests, but when she deducted his passage money and the "loan" of £500 which she let him have, I doubt that she could have broken even.

He didn't write to either Funke or myself from England; on the day when we went to take him from the hospital straight to the docks to board his steamer, he had said scarcely a word to me. At the beginning we did have some news of him through a cousin of Funke's who was the bandleader in an African club in London, and whom she had asked to keep an eye on Payne. Soon we learned that he was hanging out exclusively with West Indians, and had become ostentatiously anti-African, apparently fluctuating between playing conga drums in a calypso band and living off the dole. Then I stopped getting news of him altogether; I no longer saw a great deal of Funke, for she had her own survival to see to.

III

Of course I have frequently questioned myself about the motives that led me to undertake my Nigerian "experience." I have no definitive answers; and, indeed, I have been obliged to discard the easy answer that puts it no higher than a mere meeting of curiosity and opportunity. There were too many other West Indians making their various kinds of pilgrimages to all parts of West Africa in the nineteen-fifties for that simplistic analysis to stand up.

What was it then that Dacosta Payne and I—and those other lemmings—had in common? Partly, I suppose, we all felt dissatisfied with that basic assumption we had inherited from our fathers—that the highest form of existence was that of the Englishman, and that as a consequence the highest form of existence for the black man was that of the black Englishman; I suppose that we were all, in our different ways, desperately trying to find alternatives. In the particular case of Dacosta Payne, perhaps he became dissatisfied even with that more flamboyant alternative which he had picked up for himself, despite its hints of universality and its roots in a hallowed tradition of globe-trotting con-men. Had he actually, a thought daring if only in its banality, gone to Nigeria in search of his own integrity?

This was, at any rate, the drift of the questions I put to Roopnarine when I began to feel comfortable with him; he himself had been lucky enough or sturdy enough or both, it seemed, to solve these problems for himself at the age of nineteen, when his first child, Vidia the doctor, was born.

"Man, the only real trouble somebody like me could have is with the people who think all Indian is coolie, and even they have a hard time with me. When you're a Trinidadian creole Brahmin, it ain't easy for people like that to really give you stick. They just don't know where to catch hold, see what I mean?"

He was teasingly condescending about the fate of West Indian Negroes in Africa. "At least under pressure I could scramble up a few words of pidgin Hindi, but it beat me how all you managed out there, boy, without word one in the local dialects!" But Roop knew well that that was among the least of the problems, although it was harshly symbolic of them.

The time was late 1959; I was back in the West Indies, in Trinidad, not Barbados, which after all was really "home"; but I hadn't been able to overcome the feeling that for me Barbados was worked-out, a lode that I had exhausted through the unconscious mining-processes of adolescence. In Nigeria a moment had come when I had known indisputably that that particular experience was over and it was time to go home; and Trinidad, familiar, yet unfamiliar, like the house of your father's twin brother, seemed to be the place to go, for a start at least.

I was still a columnist; and the paper still belonged
to a foreign monopoly; at work and away from work
I was besieged by a sense of things not quite déjà
vu. But Roopnarine was quite new, a West Indian in
the West Indies, who was running away from nothing
and in search of nothing, a homegrown adult of a
kind that I had never known as an adult and, I
suppose, had not conceived of as possible. A meat-
eater, a beer-drinker, a frequenter of brothels, a
paterfamilias emeritus—the doctor, twin air-hostesses,
and a PPE student on a government scholarship at
Balliol were all eminently self-supporting—he was a
"self-made" journalist who had taught himself to
write "in self-defense, man," when the eldest child
had won the first of a series of scholarships at the
age of ten. He pretended to be happily rid of parental
responsibilities, and to be totally immersed in the
life he was now free to live, irreverent, truly irre-
sponsible—"The children would never let their mother
starve, and me, I couldn't starve if I tried. I have too
many Chinese restaurant owners owing me for plugs
in the paper and for telling visitors how it's the best
Chinese food in the world outside San Francisco."

But his face gave the lie to this picaresque image;
it was darkened and runneled by vicarious exam
fevers, and by a too-close appreciation of the perils
of air travel; to see him walk, on his thin bow-legs,
with his head carried at that tellingly introspective
inch below the perpendicular, was to know him for
the congenital worrier and bearer of other people's
burdens that he was.

His stoop and his conversational English seemed
to me of a piece, a banner aggressively marked
"Trample on me!" When someone tried, as once
occurred in my presence when a new English recruit
to the staff made the innocently imperial assumption
that Roop was the obvious man to send for a paper-
cupful of water, Roop would straighten up physically

and linguistically, and it was the trampler who found himself flat on his back.

"A cup of water, Mr. St. John-Prestwick? Certainly. But I don't recommend the water here; local standards of cleanliness are pretty poor, you'll find. I've a better idea. Here's fifty cents. Run round the corner, over there where you see the Löwenbrau sign, and buy yourself a cold beer. Foreign, of course, the local stuff is horse piss. Would you bring me a box of matches if there's any change?"

This was the man whom the management assigned to be my assistant. At the beginning he was no more than correct, suspicious, predictably, of this younger man who had come to the paper on a transfer dictated from headquarters. Perhaps he had expected me to trample, or try to, but when I didn't and when I wrote what I hoped was a sympathetic but unsentimental series on current Nigerian affairs, he totally accepted me.

"I thought maybe that you was one of these kiss-me-ass back-to-Africa boys who was coming back to tell me how to run the West Indies," he said afterward, when he had well and truly integrated me into the void, which he clamorously claimed not to exist, that the absence of his children had clearly created.

He was very sceptical about my plan for the next series: six articles, ending the week before Carnival, on the place of carnival and calypso in the life of Trinidad.

"Man, you must be mad! You come here to tell Trinidadians about Carnival? First, to begin with all-you don't even have carnival in Barbados. And then, even if you was a *Brazilian*, no Trinidadian even going listen. All-you Bajans fast, yes?" But as he spoke he was already succumbing to the professional challenge of the thing. "A Bajan and a creole Indian writing about calypso. That is gall, father! Le' we try."

We tried. As a first step he tracked down material for me in defunct "little magazines," in books, in learned journals, even in the newspaper's own badly preserved and uncatalogued back numbers. From there we went on to talk to the survivors of earlier generations, old journalists, old promoters, old mistresses of old-time calypsonians, and even a handful of old-time calypsonians themselves, living, according to their luck, on the fringes of senile respectability or senile destitution. His own experiences and ideas and prejudices accompanied all this "objective" research like a running counterpoint.

"A calypsonian is by definition a whoremonger," he dogmatized. "I ain't asking you, I telling you. The only question is, which come first, calypsonian or saga boy? My answer to that is saga boy come first. I talking about the good ones, because anybody can put together a couple easy rhymes, steal a old melody, and it have enough coonoomoonoos in this world that he can catch a beer or a rum from them from time to time and he gone home and tell he old lady he is big calypsonian down in Port of Spain. I have a feeling the good ones don't even know they're calypsonians until something irrelevant happen to start them off. Like he lost a girl friend or he lost all his money on a horse race, and all of a sudden he listening to the radio or a juke box and he hear the Mighty This or the Mighty That singing, and right there he know that he only have to spend a few minutes thinking and he can come up with something better. And it does turn out that he right. You *have* to be a saga boy, and you *have* to be a Trinidadian."

Roop held the view that the great calypsonians were the only true West Indian poets. "All that crap they does write in these little magazines, you call that poetry? Either they trying to imitate some American or English poet, or they turning out a bunch of introspective nonsense, 'Look, boy, is suffering, I suf-

fering, but elegant for so, yes?' There should be a
law that no West Indian should publish a poem until
he write one successful calypso. You have to be a
poet of the people first!"

By this time the precarnival season was in full
swing, most of the labels on the jukeboxes were
handwritten, a sure sign of the fast turnover in nine-
day wonders, and three or four definite contenders
for the title of calypso king could already be identified, including a new singer called Lord Beguiler.

"I think Beguiler is the man this year, boy," Roop
told me one day. "Leh we make a rounds by the New
Ca'iso Tent tonight and hear how he shaping." He
went on to talk about Beguiler, about whom nothing
much was known except that he had spent a fair
time in England probably as a merchant seaman,
and had come back to Port of Spain the previous
year with some small fame as a result of a calypso
called "Beguiler is a Beast" which had climbed fairly
high on the English hit parade.

"The boy really got something," Roop said. "I hear
this Beast thing a couple times last year, and it call
to mind some of the good old-time calypsonians, Lion
and Killer and them. But where he beat them, to my
mind, ain't so much that he up-to-date in style and
all that, because everybody nowadays making records with echo chamber and amplified guitars and
jazz-up arrangements. Is the *line*, man, the line. He
taking a line and bending it and stretching it and
filling it with assonances like if he was one of them
post-Victorian poets." By now I knew Roop well
enough not to be startled by the reference.

"The boy really clever; if you hear that Beast song
you'll really take off your hat to him. He singing
about how he is a savage from darkest Africa, and
he have to start the day with a sacrifice, but is only
farm-fresh English chicken he using. First he does
clip their wings, then he does strip them down, and

then he does eat them raw. I don't have to dot the
i's for you; but maybe the English didn't catch on.
Anyway I hear they was playing it on the BBC on
Housewives' Choice."

He laughed the sad, almost reluctant laugh I now
knew well, the stifled unpracticed guffaw of a man
who has only recently been able to afford the luxury
of laughter.

"As a matter of fact, the boy in trouble right now,"
he went on. "The police arrest him at a bar in Coco-
rite over a girl, they say. I hear he's a very fast man
with a broken beer bottle, and that he hate white people. Anyway, he out on bail now, and I willing to bet
he have a calypso on the case already. I think
maybe we should do a little interview with him after
the show. From our point of view that's the man with
everything. I mean he modern, and yet you can see
that he got roots in the old tradition. I hear he driving
a Mercedes some company give him on credit; he
building a house with swimming pool and thing, on
credit too. This must be the first calypso singer to
have he own lawyer, and yet he can't keep out of
whorehouses and he can't keep out of the police station. The boy is brand new, but you can still see the
old pattern coming out."

The New Ca'iso Tent was the most modern in town.
In the off-season it served as the assembly hall for
one of the largest unions in Trinidad; a prestige affair
in the American union tradition, with cantilevered
roof; seating for a thousand and—this the mark of
true affluence—a plenitude of modernistic toilet facilities.

" 'Nice' people love to come here even if the calypsonians are second-rate because their wives can go to
the toilets in comfort," Roop explained as we sat in
the front row press seats and watched the common

herd being tortured by the sports-shirted ushers. The proceedings had already begun, and a thin Indian boy was singing a deary single entendre song about a battle he had with a hairy monster at the dead of night.

"It even have Chinese calypsonians these days," Roop observed in a low voice; and indeed one did come on later to sing a self-regarding and strictly nonessential ballad about the problems of being a Chinese calypsonian.

"All this is just the preliminaries," Roop told me in the first interval. "People does come to hear one or two singers, and sometimes, once in a blue moon, one of these young ones does come up with a hit. But tonight is strictly Beguiler, Lord Fantasy, and maybe Exciter might spring a surprise." Exciter had been much in evidence as Master of Ceremonies, introducing his colleagues and competitors with remarks of varying snideness as to their chances of beating him for the crown, and making cutting remarks about latecomers, especially those who had to run the long gauntlet down the aisle to the cheaper seats.

The interval over, Exciter reappeared leaning over the wooden barrier that enclosed the stage, and speaking through a negligently held hand-mike, "Ladies and gemmen," he intoned, "did you ever hear of a English calypsonian? Well, I in the business all these years and this is the first time I ever run into one. The New Ca'iso Tent takes great pleasure in introducing the London Beast himself, the one and only, ever-popular, Mighty Beguiler. He is going to sing for you his latest composition, and I understand his lawyer is in the audience to take it down word for word to be used as the defense case in a forthcoming trial. From what I hear, Beguiler may not be in the competition this year. Certain people planning for him to do his singing in a cage. But meanwhile give the Beguiler a big hand, ladies and gemmen, and lend an ear to his new calypso, 'UNTOUCHED BY HUMAN HAND'!"

The ten-piece band broke into a fast jump-up rhythm, a voice was heard through the public-address system shouting, "Taint me, taint me, I never touch the Yankee man!" and a tall, spade-bearded black man, wearing a well-cut gray italianate suit, and swinging a ten-gallon hat in one hand, appeared at the wooden barrier.

The beard was new to me, but the rest was Dacosta Payne.

> I don't know, your worship, I don't know.
> Don't ask me, your worship, who beat up the Yankee so.
> The last time I see he, he was getting in the police van,
> And up to then I swear, your worship, he was UNTOUCHED BY
>   HUMAN HAND!

The chorus came first, and then Beguiler/Dacosta Payne moved into the narrative: he had been sitting in a bar sipping a lemonade and waiting for a friend. It was a low bar, full of people with whom he ordinarily didn't associate, in particular a number of ladies whom he understood to be "Businesswomen," although he was not certain what kind of business was meant. It was very noisy, and he presumed that the ladies were discussing contracts in their line of business. Suddenly a well-dressed white man came in, escorted by some Trinidadian men whom he took for tourist guides. What was a man like that doing in a place like that?

> Could be a anthropologist
> Checking on the local practices

because he had heard that anthropology could be practiced only in black people's country. Anyway, he didn't pay too much attention, and the next thing he knew a fight broke out, and as a supporter of nonviolence he retired to a corner to wait for the whole thing to blow over. But the police arrived

and started to act ignorant,
catching on to the guilty and the innocent

and that was where he found himself being hustled
into a police van. And back into the chorus.

The audience, which had been little more than polite in their applause for previous singers, now went
wild; by the time Beguiler was ready to sing the
fourth chorus they were singing with him. In the back
rows people were jumping in the aisles. Everyone,
including Roop and me, was shouting "Encore," although a traveled wit near us preferred *"Bis!"*

"As of now," Roop shouted in my ear, "that is the
calypso king, and that is the Road March for this
year. The others might as well don't bother. What I
tell you, man?"

It was true. Even a total stranger would have been
able to sense the great, swelling pressure of unanim-
ity that washed over the audience in the tent. The wit
and the rhythm and the dipping melody had sharp-
ened and sweetened our awareness of the poetry of
our daily existence; the disenchantment with white
people and the disrespect for what we still considered, deep in our hearts, "the white man's law" was
now codified and slotted precisely and unforgettably
into our consciousnesses, and it was Beguiler who
had done it for us. For months—perhaps for years—
to come we would be singing this song, or remem-
bering snatches of it; without question this was the
song we would be calling for from the steel bands
on Jouvet Monday morning when, exerting our right
to possess ecstasy before death possessed us, we
would make the annual march of weary triumph
through the streets of town, greeting the dawn as if it
was our first and might be our last.

The applause and the shouting went on, and Beguiler stood at the rail, sweating under the fluorescent lights, smiling, a look of exhaustion and
achievement on his face like that of an athlete at the
end of a race, fanning himself with his Stetson, wait-

ing until the shouts of "encore" should die down to
sing the encore we wanted.

"That is a giant, yes," Roop said, and I noticed
that he was sweating almost as much as Dacosta
Payne. Passing my handkerchief surreptitiously over
my forehead I found that I too was sweating gener-
ously.

I nodded my agreement with Roop's judgment, and
wondered whether to tell him that the Mighty Beguiler was Dacosta Payne. It was the kind of thing
that would appeal profoundly to someone of Roop's
turn of mind. But I decided against it: Roop would be
unable to resist the temptation to do a big story on it,
and who knew what he might find out? Perhaps that
Gillian was a whore, and that Payne had never been
anywhere near Leeds University or the RAF; what
was the point? Dacosta Payne is dead; long live the
Mighty Beguiler!

BEYOND CHAOS

Black History and the Search for the New Land

by Vincent Harding

I have tracked my bleeding countrymen through the widely
scattered documents of American history; I have listened to
their groans, their clanking chains, and melting prayers,
until the woes of a race and the agonies of centuries seem
to crowd upon my soul as a bitter reality. Many pages of
this history have been blistered with my tears; and, although having lived but a little more than a generation, my
mind feels as if it were cycles old.

—George Washington Williams, 1882

The American Negro must remake his past in order to make
his future.

—Arthur Schomburg, 1925

. . . the plunge into the chasm of the past is the condition
and the source of freedom.

—Frantz Fanon, 1956

WHEN THE POET Don L. Lee lately wrote of his commit-
ment to a new integration "between Negroes and
Blacks," several things were already clear. One was
that he spoke for a significant part of the black generation which has been coming to intellectual matu-

rity since 1954. It was also evident that he dealt not in semantics, but in the hard, often jagged personal and political differences represented by those two words—Negro and Black. Finally, those who know him (and others young with him) realize that he spoke not as a provocateur but as a healer who had seen our wounds, and desired our wholeness.

For within the heart of the black community in America there exists today a set of agonies which apparently are part of the necessary inheritance of any community that has been engaged in prolonged struggles for radical change, true freedom and lasting justice. In the realm of academic affairs no less than in the arena of political action the extended nature of the struggle and the modern reality of telescoped generational change have created gaps in understanding and intensities of feeling which are too often marked by bitterness and hostility.

One of the most significant examples of this painful division can be found in the movement which has transformed the traditional approaches to Negro History into Black History and now burgeons into the search for Black Studies. Some of the hurt is necessary, for it grows at once out of the nature of the struggle and out of the natural tendency of the sons (especially with Westernized training) to seek to devour their fathers. (Indeed, this essay is itself an attempt to come to terms with the fathers and to understand the nature of the new paths we younger black historians have begun to walk. As such it is a tentative set of suggestions, a brooding over the past and present in search of meaning, form and possibly hope.) But some of the pain is unnecessary, and part of the motivation for this work is the hope that it may enter into the healing process simply by suggesting briefly the larger historical perspective in which we have moved from Negro History to Black History and now stretch out into the yet undefined ground of

Black Studies. For this is part of a larger process extending over much of the world, for which no man here can claim praise or take blame.

It is impossible, of course, to speak of the "intellectual" pilgrimage toward blackness without mentioning the political one—even in a sketchy way. As is the case with the intellectuals of any hard-pressed and colonized people, black intellectuals in America have had their inner lives inextricably bound up with the life of the "outer" struggles of our people.

The initial (and still overwhelming) struggles were, of course, for unimpeded citizenship rights, for the recognition of our manhood and for the opening of the American society to full participation by its black builders. But a key to this struggle was found in the fact that it was, by and large, a battle in which we sought to be accepted on the terms by which this nation defined itself. This meant not only that the majority of us who struggled accepted the idea that the myth of American democracy was a great truth —except for us—but we also accepted on various levels of our consciousness the fact that only a minority of us would actually make it into the mainstream. For only a minority was "ready" for integration at any given time, as the keepers of the society defined "readiness."

Fortunately this view was always questioned by some black persons. In the twentieth century their views began to be expressed most eloquently by W. E. B. Du Bois, who compared black people to would-be passengers on a train. Du Bois said that blacks were like passengers who had spent all of their time and energies trying to prove to their fellow passengers and to the conductor that they had a right to be on the American train. Indeed, he said that we had given so much of our attention to this task that we had never bothered to ask about the train's destination. Finally, said Du Bois, after a few seats had been

commandeered and some of the immediate attacks
had died down, a few black persons began to ask
(and he was surely foremost among them): "Where,
by the way, is this train going?" What is its destination? Most often no one knew. When answers were
supplied some of us began to wonder if we really
wanted to go, especially if our destination would always be determined by the people who had fought
for centuries to keep us off, or confined to the Negro
car.

As important as anything else for the political
story, however, was the rising surge of anticolonial-
ism throughout the nonwhite world. With it developed overwhelming movements toward self-definition,
self-determination and liberation. Those whose institutions had been controlled by the white West were
demanding more autonomy than assimilation. This,
too, was part of the development of a ground for
American black-consciousness, and the ideology of
the postwar mood was most clearly expressed for
American blacks in the writings of Frantz Fanon.

At the same time significant numbers of middle-
class young blacks were experiencing the levels of
relationship with the white world for which their fathers had lived and sometimes died. This was especially so after 1963. In the midst of this encounter with
white America they discovered an atmosphere that
often suggested tiredness and death and dying.
Often the newly arriving black people found that individual prejudices, institutional racism, and the colonialism of the society had not in any way abated
simply because token blacks were present and accounted for. The desperate searches for new levels
of black solidarity and for the "integration" of
Negroes and blacks came out of a host of such
experiences. One of the young poets simply said:
"America, we've found you out."

So a movement which began largely as a struggle

for inclusion in America as America defined itself increasingly became a political struggle for the power of self-definition and self-determination and for the ability to make America "ready" for the coming of black men. (Whether that can happen short of revolutionary changes remains to be seen.)

The movement from Negro History to Black History has amazing parallels to the political encounter, partly because they are both really a part of the larger issue. In a profound sense, the intellectual struggle began with the appearance of George Washington Williams, the first substantial scholarly historian of blacks in America. Though Williams, a minister turned politician and scholar, should well be considered a father of Negro History, the seeds of the entire struggle for Black History also rested in his work, especially in his sense of mission.

It was in 1876 that Williams began his profound encounter with Negro History. He was only twenty-seven at the time. Significantly enough, he had been asked to prepare an address on the occasion of the centennial of the Declaration of Independence. He chose to speak about black people to his Ohio audience, and began his research. Six years later (after many speeches) he had published the important pioneering work, *History of the Negro Race in America 1619–1880.* To understand Williams is to understand many of the issues involved in our agony.

In the Preface to the first of the two volumes, he told why he wrote the *History.* It was done, he said, because blacks "had been the most vexatious problem in North America, from the time of its discovery down to the present day." He wrote, too, because he wanted to reveal how "the Colored people had always displayed a matchless patriotism and an incomparable heroism in the cause of Americans," whenever the nation was attacked "from without or within." But his labor was not simply for others, to

give them "more correct ideas of the Colored people." It was also done, Williams claimed, to "incite"
the black population "to greater effort in the struggle
of citizenship and manhood." Finally, he claimed
that he was writing "not as the blind panegyrist of
my race, nor as the partisan apologist, but from a
love for 'the truth of history,'" and had therefore
striven "to record the truth, the whole truth, and nothing but the truth."

Within that range of comments much of the story
of Negro History is told: its attempt to reveal the
"contributions" of blacks to the American saga; its
emphasis on black heroism in the wars; its call for
racial pride and for continued struggle to enter the
mainstream of American life; its claim to be primarily interested in objective truth, while writing history
through tears. All of these were so clearly present in
Williams' work that it was hard to realize that other
seeds were present too.

Though George Washington Williams, the young
minister turned politician, set the major directions for
the Negro History movement, it was Carter G.
Woodson, the carefully trained scholar, who represented that movement most fully to the twentieth
century. In many ways, his founding (with others)
of the Association for the Study of Negro Life and
History, his editing of its *Journal*, and his work to establish Negro History Week did more to institutional-
ize the Negro History movement than the books that
he wrote. Nevertheless, the books are important, for
they indicate the many ways in which he carried on
the tradition of Williams in a far less emotional, far
more meticulous, but essentially faithful way.

One of his most influential works was a volume for
secondary schools called *The Story of the Negro Re-
told*. First published in 1935, it contained segments of
earlier works by Woodson. In this volume he included a clear statement of his approach, one that
illuminates much of the traditional assumptions of

Negro History. Under the subtitle "Truth not to be Neglected," Woodson wrote:

> In our own particular history we should not dim one bit the lustre of any star in our firmament. Let no one be so thoughtless as to decry the record of the makers of the United States of America. We should not learn less of George Washington, "First in War, First in Peace and First in the hearts of his Countrymen"; but we should learn something also of the three thousand Negro soldiers of the American Revolution who helped to make this "Father of our Country" possible. We should not fail to appreciate the unusual contribution of Thomas Jefferson to freedom and democracy but we should invite attention also to one of his outstanding contemporaries, Benjamin Banneker, the mathematician and astronomer. . . . We should not cease to pay tribute to Abraham Lincoln as the "Saviour of the Country"; but we should ascribe praise also to the 178,975 Negroes who had to be mustered into the service of the Union before it could be preserved, and who by their heroism demonstrated that they were entitled to Freedom and citizenship. We should in no way whatever withhold assistance from the effort to make the world safe for democracy, but we should teach our citizenry history rather than propaganda and thus make this country safe for all elements of the population at home.

Much of Negro History took this tack. It did not intend to threaten the established heroes or the basic values of America. It would not dim any luster. Rather it sought only to guarantee that the black presence was properly acknowledged, assuming that blackness could be contained within the confines of the American saga. It was an obvious parallel to the efforts to include a special minority of "ready" Negroes into an American society which would not be basically changed by their presence.

There were, of course, intellectual tensions in the movement for Negro History, just as there were tensions within the individual works. For instance, when John Hope Franklin published the first edition of

From Slavery to Freedom in 1947 he made it clear that the American story could not quite remain unmoved by Negro History. In the preface to his masterly work he wrote, "It has been necessary . . . to retell the story of the evolution of the people of the United States in order to place the Negro in his proper relationship and perspective." In the text of the work one constantly feels that Franklin knows far more than he says about the ways in which the story of black people might need to rip apart the white fabric of American History. Indeed, he often comes to the brink of such total reevaluation and then draws back. (This was especially apparent in his section on "The Negro and American Imperialism.") The final impact, though, is still one of optimism about the movement of blacks into the mainstream of America, carrying with them certain gifts, but bearing no essential threat to the status quo.

Writing in the midst of the Civil Rights movement, Benjamin Quarles, another of our fathers in this pilgrimage, wrote with even more optimism—about the power of Negro History and the future of American society. He brought the older themes into that present moment when he wrote that

> A proper perspective of Negro History would be of value to those well-meaning persons who believe that the colored man has an unworthy past, and hence has no strong claim to all the rights of other Americans. Books which seek to present an accurate picture of the Negro's past are, in effect, bridges to intergroup harmony—*the Negro would be more readily accepted into the full promise of American life if his role in our history were better known.* (Italics mine)

Part of Quarles' optimism was obviously created out of the fact that he finished his work just after the March on Washington of 1963 (and just before the Birmingham bombing which left four black Sunday school children dead). But it may be that the source of his hope was more accurately described within his own pages when he wrote near the end of the book about the Nation of Islam and its refusal to hope for black equality in America. Quarles noted that the Muslim view was a minority opinion, saying, "To most Negroes outside the Muslim movement, the vision of the founders of this republic was still a vital force." Then he added:

> Americans to the core, [Negroes] believed that freedom and equality for all could be achieved in their native land. This belief they would not easily surrender, for it had been their lodestar.

This was perhaps the most crucial source of the faith of our fathers in Negro History. They believed because they had internalized America and its "promise." They believed and wrote out of belief because they had come so far through "clanking chains and melting prayers" that they could not afford to consider unbelief as a live option. Essentially America was a great land, and one day its greatness would overwhelm it, partly as a result of black struggle, partly because of "well-meaning" whites. Then blacks would be received into the greatness of the land, to contribute their own variety to be sure, but not as rulers and controllers. Out of this paradoxical past and into this future much Negro History was written. What else could they believe? To wrestle with the demonic elements in American history might bring them too close to the chasm, to the void, to the point at which men must seek for totally new meaning and truth.

Of course, the tensions continued. As always, Du Bois was near the heart of them, and is clearly one of the fathers who cannot easily be placed within the stream of Negro History. Ever since his first major work, *The Suppression of the African Slave Trade to the United States of America, 1638–1870*, Du Bois had a skewed vision which kept moving to radical depths. Dealing in his *Suppression* with one of the major corrupting forces in American society, he spoke of the nation's failure to act in moral courage as "discreditable to a great people." For him, he said, the key question which grew out of his study was: "How far in a State can a recognized moral wrong safely be compromised?"

As he played his many roles over the next decades Du Bois became an increasingly critical viewer of the American nation, and much of his experience seemed to answer for him the question which he posed about the compromising of a moral wrong. Thus by the time he developed another major historical work, *Black Reconstruction in America*, he claimed it was necessary to rewrite almost all of the "received" American history for that period. For up to then, the story had been totally falsified, told in such a way as to "make pleasant reading for Americans."

It is in this context that we can expand on his comments about blacks and the American train. For his question is not only a matter of where we are going, but where have we *really* been? Du Bois brought a deep concern to that last query, for he knew that the issue of the future could not be disassociated from an answer concerning the past. A people's vision of where they have been will deeply affect their convictions concerning the pathways really open before them. So Du Bois was far more ready than most historians of his generation to raise profound questions about the nature of American civilization. Indeed, it was probably not accidental that he finished *Black Reconstruction* about the same time that he worked out his program for Black Solidarity (1930–33), a clear anticipation of much of the Black Power–Third World spirit of autonomy and self-definition.

This step beyond Negro History which was so often symbolized by Du Bois' life and work was caught up in a pregnant phrase by another of the crucial fathers, Arthur Schomburg. Writing for Alain Locke's collection, *The New Negro*, Schomburg said, "The American Negro must remake his past in order to make his future." This was 1925, at the height of the Negro Renaissance. It clearly stated the new emphasis which would increasingly characterize the groping toward Black History. Its focus was on the initiative of black men in the shaping of their future and their past. Its search seemed to be less dependent upon the opening of America to them. Perhaps the excitement of the black affirmation and fulfillment of the twenties was enough to encourage a new definition of black manhood. Perhaps this capacity to stand in the kaleidoscopic present with a firm grasp on the making of the past as well as on the movement of tomorrow was at the heart of the new black manhood, the New Negro. That was certainly the theme sounded by Langston Hughes for the artists when he wrote in 1926:

> We younger Negro artists who create now intend to express our individual dark-skinned selves without fear or shame. If white people are pleased we are glad. If they are not, it doesn't matter. We know we are beautiful. And ugly too. . . . We build our temples for tomorrow, strong as we know how, and we stand on top of the mountain, free within ourselves.

Whatever their fullest meanings, the words of Schomburg and Hughes were clearly part of the new mood brought on by World War I, its holocausts and its aftermaths all over the colonized world. This was the mood partially shaped and partially caught by black America on the political level, and it was no less relevant in the realm of ideas. It proved to be an inexorable movement, constantly grasping at the past and future while seeking a foothold in the present. It declared the need of all the oppressed to control their past as part of their struggle for the future. It moved with an air of independence which had not characterized the heart of the Negro History movement. It carried a mood of black celebration which would have been considered too subjective by the Negro scholars.

World War II heightened the process immeasurably. On the surface it seemed in America to do little more than shake the system loose for the presence of more blacks and to create renewed optimism within the writers of Negro History. But there were new spirits abroad in the world. In Paris in 1956 the First Congress of Negro Writers and Artists heard an embodiment of that new spirit, Frantz Fanon, speak on "Racism and Culture." One major portion of his theme was set forth as the need of the colonized peoples to face with courage the truth concerning the ways in which the representatives of Western power had totally distorted the nonwhite past. Fanon demanded of all colonized people a struggle with that past, a grasping of all its ambiguous scattered parts, and a remaking of its center. Indeed, he declared then, "The plunge into the chasm of the past is the condition and the source of freedom."

Black History in America is that plunge. Almost all of its proponents have come into their intellectual maturity under the tutelage of the fathers of Negro History, but unlike them we have lived most of our adult lives since 1954. We have lived through the politics of the sixties, through all of the promises and betrayals, through the discomfiting of the West. We have seen ourselves as part of a new people, the formerly colonized, the wretched of the earth. We are unique, but we also share a common history with the colonized.

We who write Black History cannot track our "bleeding countrymen through the widely scattered documents of American history" and still believe in America. We cannot see luster when we must glimpse it through oceans of tears. We cannot—do not wish to—write with detachment from the agonies of our people. We are not satisfied to have our story accepted into the American saga. We deal in redefinitions, in taking over, in moving to set our own vision upon the blindness of American historiography.

Black History is that plunge which refuses to fall prey to the American dream, which is romanticism and childlike avoidance of tragedy and death. We have tasted too much of these, known too much chaos and uncertainty and struggle and survival and overcoming and prevailing to walk away from the gates of death.

Black History does not seek to highlight the outstanding contributions of special black people to the life and times of America. Rather our emphasis is on exposure, disclosure, on reinterpretation of the entire American past. We want to *know* America at its depths, now that invitations to its life are besieging us. And it is clear even now that the black past cannot be remade and clearly known without America's larger past being shaken at the foundations. While Negro History almost never questioned the basic goodness and greatness of American society, while it assumed its innate potential for improvement (provided it was ready to read additional volumes on Negro History), Black History has peeped a different card.

Black History suggests that the American past upon which so much hope has been built never really existed, and probably never will. We who have been forced to be both black and white in America have seen the society from the dark side, and are therefore dangerous, just as our street brothers are dangerous when they refuse to be absorbed into the corruption they have seen around them since childhood. We are dangerous because we suggest to the society that we are simply the vanguard of all those who must one day awake from the dream of America. What will happen when the dream opens into nothingness? (We are, of course, also dangerous to ourselves, for what can a man do when the goal for which he fought all his life becomes no goal, becomes antilife, becomes nothing worth having?)

As it moves into the chasm of the past, Black History is clearly more than the study of exclusively black things, for since the days of our slavery we could not be understood in an exclusively black light. So that Black History which seeks to deal with America begins with its European heritage, assesses the "Rise of the West." It asks how much of this ascendancy came at the expense of the death and degradation of our fathers and other nonwhite peoples of the globe. When it is clear that the "greatness" of Europe was built under the shadow of our ancestors' deaths, how shall we view this Western world and its major child—America? Black History is the reassessment of an unrequited love affair. It is the exposure of the strange foundations of Western power. Therefore it might be an intimation of things to come.

Black History looks upon America with little of the affection and admiration which was obviously carried by our Negro History fathers. We look at the paradox of Black indentured-servitude/slavery being introduced into the colony of Virginia at the same time that the House of Burgesses came into being. So slavery and "representative government" were planted together. We ask: Which defined the reality? Or did both? From the perspective of Black History, the greater freedom which was gained for local government in the English colonies actually turned out to be freedom to embed the slavery of our forefathers deep into freedom's soil. So we are forced to begin to ask whether it was ever freedom's soil.

Black History looks at the slave codes of the seventeenth and eighteenth centuries and it reminds a society obsessed by pseudo-law-and-order that the first law and order we knew was the law of our repression and our bondage, the order that comes naturally out of death. So the introduction of black men to American law was not auspicious. Black History bears long testimony to this.

Indeed, a black reading of America is weighted with testimony—and perhaps this is why our fathers avoided dwelling on certain matters; the burden was too much to bear—even against the original religious sense of mission of the first white settlers. For it suggests that if there were men who sensed a calling from God which was more than arrogance, a sense of being sent on an errand into a new land for an opportunity to encounter new righteousness, then those men and their mission were almost immediately corrupted upon contact with the new land. For blacks must read history with Indian eyes as well, and cannot fail to note that many of the New England "fathers" participated not only in the forced migration and decimation of the original inhabitants, but gave full strength to that trade in men which brought other dark men to these shores. The treatment received by both blacks and Indians cannot fail to shape the black approach to New England history, a history which set in motion an American dream of "Manifest Destiny" which may yet bring to the world its ultimate corruption.

Indeed Black History is forced to press on to ask about the meaning of America itself. (This raising of questions did not mark Negro History. Perhaps our fathers lived too close to the brutal experiences of black life to allow such a luxury.) When the spirit and institutions of the nation were so fully formed and defined by the leaders of Massachusetts and the rest of New England—slave traders on the one hand, slaveholders on the other—what indeed is the nation's meaning? Whose founding "fathers" were they, and what does their creation mean for the children of their slaves?

Black History is not satisfied with telling how many black men fought in the Revolutionary War. We are not among those who lift the banner of Crispus Attucks, for we are caught in painful dilemmas. While we recognize their heroism, we recognize too that a revolution which ended with more than 700,000 persons still in slavery was perhaps no revolution at all, but essentially a war among colonialist powers. So the children of the slaves who fought might better mourn rather than rejoice and celebrate, for it is likely that our fathers were no different than the millions of nonwhite pawns who have been pushed about by the military leaders of the colonizers for centuries. (And we save our energies and our wits for the exposing of this delusion and the encouraging of the heirs of the slaves to refuse to be pawns any longer.) In this way the experiences of our forefathers and the developments of this generation coalesce into a totally different reading of America than is usually known.

By the stabbing light of Black History the Declaration of Independence becomes something close to mockery. For what is such a declaration signed by slaveholders, and what did it mean to their slaves—our forefathers? We know why the Declaration did not mention slavery. We know why the Constitution not only mentioned it, but protected it so carefully that it had to be exorcised from the heart of the nation by blood. Black History looks at the "great historical documents" and realizes that we are a people of the future so far as "official" America is concerned. For we cannot look back to the masters of our fathers for the "wisdom" that our friends seem to find when they turn in the direction of the nation's founding documents. We can only mark the corruption written into the origins of the Republic and reflect on the comments of one of the few radicals of 1776, Thomas Paine:

> Now is the seed-time of continental union, faith and
> honor. The least fracture now will be like a name
> engraved with the point of a pin on the tender rind
> of a young oak; the wound would enlarge with the
> tree, and posterity would read it in full grown char-
> acters.

Black History suggests that we are the name (that
nobody knew), we are the wound (that nobody saw
—or saw and refused to heal), we are the letters of
judgment growing fuller every moment. Black History is an attempt to read them clear.

Such a reading of America presses us to ask
whether it was ever a democracy, demands to know
whether it is possible for a democracy to exist where
one quarter of the population of the land is either in
slavery or being steadily driven off its ancient
grounds. Black History is not simply "soul food" and
"soul music" as some of its misinterpreters have suggested. Black History is the history of the Black Experience in America, which is the history of black
and white—and Indian—inextricably, painfully, rarely
joyfully, entwined. So Black History explores Henry
Adams concerning the American nation at the
beginning of the nineteenth century and hears him
say that America in 1800 was a healthy organism.
Then in the same work we read that the one major
problem in America in 1800 was "the cancer" of slavery. In that set of statements America is diagnosed
for black eyes: Healthy—except for cancer.

Black History is the constant demand that the cancerous state of America be seen and known. Sometimes it hopes, as Martin King used to hope, to
expose the sore and thus move to its healing. King
(who would have fitted more easily among the
Negro Historians for most of his life) was more op-
timistic than most of the generation just below his.
For they are not sure that national cancer can be
cured. So, listening to the historian Henry Adams,

they shape their own political question: Who wants
to integrate with cancer?

Black History cannot help but be politically ori-
ented, for it tends toward the total redefinition of an
experience which was highly political. Black History
must be political, for it deals with the most political
phenomenon of all—the struggle between the master
and the slave, between the colonized and the colo-
nizer, between the oppressed and the oppressor. And
it recognizes that all histories of peoples participate
in politics and are shaped by political and ideological views.

This happens for instance when Black History fo-
cuses on Andrew Jackson and "The Age of the Common Man." When one of my students wrote that
phrase in an essay, I wrote in the margin: "Which
common man? The Indian who was being driven off
his land in North Carolina, Georgia and Alabama
with the blessings of Andrew Jackson? The black
men who were losing the franchise in the North as
part of a bargain struck by Jackson and his support-
ers who sought for expanded white male suffrage?
Who were the Common Men: his slaves?"

But Black History is also black men and women
and children. If contributions are stressed, they tend
to be contributions to struggle and to new hope and
to the enduring pilgrimage of black people in America. So those who have from the beginning struggled
for integrity in a thousand ways are remembered, as
individuals and in groups. Black History comes closer
to the significance of the black folk creations than
much of Negro History. It encompasses more of the
literature and the music than Negro History. Its tendency is to deal with the Black Experience, to shake
off the more narrowly defined discipline-oriented
understanding of history (thus it approaches Black
Studies). But Black History especially remembers
those who have stood in judgment upon America,
like David Walker, Nat Turner, Martin Delaney, Har-

riet Tubman, Henry Highland Garnet and hundreds of others.

Black History is also another look at Frederick Douglass and an attempt to understand his deepest dilemmas, unavoidable struggles for all who would be at once black and honest in America. We remember his words late in 1849 as black people moved toward that brutal decade that was just upon them. He said to his readers in the *North Star*:

> We shall neither die out, nor be driven out; but shall go with this people, either as a testimony against them, or as an evidence in their favor throughout their generations.

We know what Douglass hoped, for we know that he loved America deeply, and yearned that black people would one day be that joyful, affirming testimony. But even Douglass wavered in that hope before he died almost four decades later; and we who write Black History today simply cannot hope as he did. We can neither hope in America (for we know its origins and its movement), nor can we love America and love our bleeding forefathers as well.

Black History is constant reassessment, sometimes considered harsh, epecially when the heroes are highly placed—like Abraham Lincoln. But we cannot see him as anything more or less than did the black man who knew him, Frederick Douglass, and who said of him, "He was preeminently the white man's President, entirely devoted to the welfare of white men ... In his interests, in his associations, in his habits of thought, and in his prejudices, he was a white man." Black History knows him not only as a white man but as one who believed sincerely that this was a white man's country, set out under a divine destiny as the world's "last, best hope." He was therefore willing to do anything with blacks which would make it possible for that destiny to be fulfilled —including sending us out of the country. Black History is hard on national heroes. It allows us no hope in white saviors. It insists that we grow up—black. Our fathers in Negro History still generally lived in an age of belief in white deliverers. Our maturity and our fulfillment demand unbelief.

They demand such unbelief partly because we remember with utmost clarity the hopes and betrayals of Reconstruction. Here we can read at once through the eyes of Du Bois and Franklin as well as through the documents they called to our attention. We can read the clear evidence that most white Americans shared Lincoln's conviction that this was a white man's country, and that reconciliation between whites was far more important than full manhood and citizenship for blacks. Black History coldly recognizes that a tier of Northern states which were denying the franchise to most of their black men would not risk long periods of discomfort, controversy, expense and even the possibility of renewed open conflict in order to guarantee black participation in the shaping of the nation's destiny. Indeed, Black History looks at a cancerous America and imagines that there may be no destiny but death as long as whites are the major shapers of the future. The evidence seems to allow no other conclusions. (It is this shock of recognition which forces those who write Black History to the only logical conclusion: black-led, radical, perhaps revolutionary change for America. We see no evidence that anything less is sufficient.)

The Black History that emerges out of the debacle of Reconstruction's betrayal suggests that it would be wise again to see America through Indian eyes. From this angle of vision we realize that the first time the armies of the South and those of the North were joined together again after the Civil War was in the destruction of the Indians of the Western Plains. So reconciliation came. (With the participation of the usual black pawns as well.) But recognition comes too, for it becomes increasingly apparent that there was only one major difference between the nineteenth century experiences of blacks and Indians: the Indians had a commodity—their land—that whites could use without them. Blacks were required for the use of their commodity—labor. (What happens in the coming day when black labor is no longer needed is a chilling but necessary thought.)

George Washington Williams began his monumental history in the midst of a period when it seemed to some persons as if blacks were immediately scheduled for the Indian fate. So as he wrote he hoped that America would fully appreciate the heroic contributions of black men to the defense of the nation. Perhaps he hoped because he, like so many of the fathers, could do nothing else. Whatever his reasons, he set a pattern and pioneered a path for two generations of scholars in the Negro History movement, and one of its most important characteristics was the act of withdrawal from the edge of chaos, from the chasm of the American black-white past, from the logical conclusions of white American behavior. The overall mood of the movement was to stand with Frederick Douglass, to confess love for a land that refused to love, and to believe that the Black Experience would ultimately be recorded as an evidence in favor of America.

Black History is the new mood. Black History says to Douglass: We are judgment and testimony against the American society. All the world now knows that. We are witnesses to the fact that America never really existed. (America, you've never been America to me.) Nor are we certain that it ever will. We say in love to Williams and his many followers: You told your story, often burdened and filled with tears, so that we might continue the struggle for full citizenship and full manhood, never dreaming that we might have to choose between them. As we read the black past and meditate upon our present, we sense that our manhood will not ever be fulfilled through full participation in *this* America, through entry into *this* mainstream. We see America as counter-life, counter-joy, in league with ultimate nothingness and death.

So we have seen the emptiness. Black History is our journey into the void where our fathers believed America to be. Black History plunges us into the chasm, into the darkness, where we can depend upon no sagas called America. Black History insists that we be men, that we refuse to live like American escapees from tragedy, pain and struggle. Black History reminds us of the conversation in *Invisible Man*, between black Mr. Trueblood and the white trustee, Mr. Norton, after Mr. Norton realized that Trueblood had struggled with some of the same demons which he had sought to escape. It was then that Norton exclaimed in wonder, "You have looked upon chaos and are not destroyed!" And Trueblood replied, "No suh! I feels all right."

In the darkness of our new gropings with the past and our plunging toward the future, we reach out, and we touch, and we grasp our blackness. We discover that it means, perhaps above all else, endurance in the face of hell, and we begin to "feel all right." Indeed, as we touch the black experience in its depths for the first time, as we handle our blackness, we are tempted to fondle it, to worship it, to lie down in its beauty and sleep a long black sleep of rapping and joy. But our brother Fanon and our fathers and our children press us on, suggesting that while our blackness is absolutely necessary it is not sufficient. For if there is to be any hope for some living, moving, growing experience beyond America's long dying, we sense that we must enter fully into its coming.

It is at this point that Black History moves into Black Studies and becomes part of the search for the new land, the new society, the new being. As those who have no assurances of justice and full humanity in an American Eden behind us, we are pressed by

Black History beyond the chasm into the future. It is in the midst of this turn toward this future, this movement into newness that we are able to hear best the continued calling of our brother Fanon:

> It is a question of the Third World starting a new History of Man . . . we must invent and we must make discoveries . . . For [America] for ourselves and for humanity, comrades, we must turn over a new leaf, we must work out new concepts, and try to set afoot a new man.

Black History, then, is the facing of the chasm, the hard and unromantic reading of the experiences of black people in America. It is the groans, the tears, the chains, the songs, the prayers, the institutions. It is a recording of the hopes, even if we no longer participate in them. It is seeing clearly not only what we have done, but what has been done to us. It is the grasping of our history out of the hands of others and taking the responsibility of men for the reshaping of our own past. For we insist on the future.

Black History is refusal to give over our lives, our creativity, our history, our future into the hands of white America, for they have proved themselves totally inadequate and ultimately dangerous. So we demand hegemony over our institutions. We seek for control of the telling of our story. Negro History Week becomes passé, for we move toward controlling the total definition of the society. Racial pride becomes black consciousness, no longer focused on how we look to the white world, but centered on our preparedness to move for a new world. Our fathers in Negro History (and Negro Politics) do not understand us. After their long struggle to be accepted by the keepers of the American scholarly establishment, they painfully watch us demand the keys—or turn our backs to build or rebuild on black grounds. Sometimes all we can do is ask for their trust, for our own time has come to build for tomorrow, "strong as we know how."

It is at this point that we are faced with one of the most frightening aspects of the search for hope, for the new land, for the new man. For out of the distilled experiences of the anticolonial struggles elsewhere, Fanon leaves a last word with all who consider themselves pilgrims toward the new land. To us all, he wrote shortly before his death:

> The colonised man who writes for his people ought to use the past with the intention of opening the future, as an invitation to action and a basis for hope. But to ensure that hope and to give it form, he must take part in action and throw himself body and soul into the . . . struggle. You may decide to speak about everything under the sun; but when you decide to speak of that unique thing in man's life that is represented by the fact of opening up new horizons, by bringing light . . . by raising yourself and your people to their feet, then you must collaborate on the physical plane.

For those of us who seek to create Black History and Black Studies and a newly defined world, this is the most sobering of words. (For now, it must be accepted in silent meditation, otherwise we might be foolishly tempted to speak before we ought.) When the words are heard by the guardians of the academic and scholarly status quo—or their reformist friends—they are even more frightening, for they threaten ancient shibboleths about detachment and objectivity.

Nevertheless we must move on beyond the chasm, recognizing that we have always frightened the keepers of the gates when we have decided to rise up with our grave cloths flying like a pennant behind us. (We note, for instance, how our new musicians have been frightening; how their eastern-oriented, often martial refrains, filled with the complexities of new life, have troubled many persons, and have stood in sharp contrast to the new white singers of the Blues. And perhaps the white Blues singers are among the most sensitive of white Americans, and are approaching the tragedy of their lives with honesty for the first time, watching wistfully—not fearfully—as we move onward toward the future which we must shape with our own black hands.) The most important thing is that we should not be terrified by our history, or our future. Instead, we move, becoming participants in the search for a new Black Body, a full body which will receive and give love to all who need it. And in this body we may be granted the grace to become the builders of a new land whose place and shape and time are still unclear. It is nothing we have known here in America. It is nothing we have been promised here. Black History tells us that. But it also tells us that we can build, and we begin with an entirely new understanding of ourselves and our surroundings—Black Studies, Black creativity, Black hope.

If this happens, Black History then becomes a means toward an end, a movement into Black Studies, Black creativity, a search for a land in which the best of blackness has prevailed, where men need not live in agonizing fear or need or in the absence of undying love.

If we find the strength, the vision, and the courage to move beyond the chasm and to build, then it may be that our brothers and sisters of the centuries, and of our generation, whose heads were broken and whose lives were taken in search for citizenship and manhood will be vindicated. For there will be a new city and new men growing out of our plunge into the chaos of America, and citizenship and manhood will be defined in ways that break beyond all old, strictured and dying pasts.

If we move, following the intuitive leadings of our poets and musicians, we shall perhaps redeem the fathers who wrote Negro History with tear-flooded eyes, filled with desperate hope (and the fathers who blew their horns in the night, and the mammas who sang till their hearts broke).

If we allow our history to liberate us, our past to press us on, our blackness to embolden us beyond our wildest midnight dreams, then we may finally begin to answer that magnificent call of our older sister Margaret Walker, who has worked through many stages and still calls out,

> For my people standing staring trying to fashion a better way from confusion, from hypocrisy and misunderstanding, trying to fashion a world that will hold all the people, all the faces, all the adams and eves and their countless generations;

> Let a new earth rise. Let another world be born. Let a bloody peace be written in the sky. Let a second generation full of courage issue forth; let a people loving freedom come to growth. Let a beauty full of healing and a strength of final clenching be the pulsing in our spirits and our blood. Let the martial songs be written, let the dirges disappear. Let a race of men now rise and take control.

Whenever we are tempted to say that such things are too poetic and can never be, simply remember Imamu Ameer Baraka who cried out, "Let all the World be a Black Poem." Then we shall face chaos, and know that we "feels all right."

The Kitchen Crisis: A Rap

To Be Read Aloud

by Verta Grosvenor

en *la casa de verta*
for Verta

for on monday   in 1969   on the streets
was diamonds.   downtown society   bodegas   one
right after the other.   avocado & tomato juice
spaceships parked in front of Vertas house/ sparkling
yellow medal   with stickers from Venus Airlines
Moon   Shuttle   Jupiter Car Service   Mars heliport
& all on monday by a bridge. 1969 year of the rooster
hot sauce / street beans . . .

caribean rice on the fire
with african beans warming
whow
the centuries & centuries
of sea exploration & mixing.
but here we all are
in vertas   soul space kitchen
taking off.

Victor Hernandez Cruz
1969

EATING IS A VERY PERSONAL THING. Some people will sit down and eat with anybody. That is very uncool. You can't eat with everybody. You got to have the right vibrations. If you don't get good vibrations from someone, cancel them out for eating (other things too). That is the only way to keep bad kitchen vibes at a minimum. Tell those kind of folks that you will meet them in a luncheonette or a bar. Even at the risk of static from family and friends. PROTECT YOUR KITCHEN.

It's hard, though. Sometimes look like in spite of all you do and as careful as you try to be, a rapscallion will slip right in your kitchen. I can't stand rapscallions. Among other things they are insensitive. You ask them, "May I offer you something—some coffee, tea, juice, water, milk, or maybe an alcoholic beverage?" They always answer, "Nah, nuttin for me" or else they say, "I'll have tea—if you got teabags," or "Coffee if it is instant—I don't want to put you through no trouble." What the rapscallions are really saying is don't go to any trouble for me 'cause I wouldn't go to none for you. Rapscallions don't mind taking the alcoholic drink because it is impersonal. Nothing of you is in that. All you got to do is pour from a bottle. They don't feel that you have extended yourself for them so they don't have to go to no trouble for you in return. In most other cultures when you enter a person's home, you and the host share a moment together by partaking of something. Rapscallions love to talk about culture, but their actions prove they ain't got none. They don't understand that it is about more than the coffee, tea or drink of water. It's about extending yourself.

So watch out for rapscallions. They'll mess up your kitchen vibes. PROTECT YOUR KITCHEN.

Which leads me to WHERE HAVE ALL THE KITCH-
ENS GONE.

Gone to closets nearly every one. In some apart-
ments the closet is bigger than the kitchen. And them
that are left are out to lunch. What is happening?????
At a time when Americans are putting the flag on
the moon, kitchens are taking the rag off the bush.
That is to say that kitchens are going to pot. We got
to put some law and order in the kitchen.

I am concerned 'cause I love kitchens. I got a small
apartment but my kitchen is big. My kitchen is full
of things. The walls are covered with pictures. Pots
hang from the ceiling; the shelves are filled with pot-
tery; there are two tables and they are usually filled
with papers, the typewriter, the sewing machine, the
children's homework, the record player, the tape recorder, records, books I plan to read while I'm on
the phone. It's a real mess. Sometimes we have to
eat out of paper plates on our laps cause things are
so bad. But I love my kitchen. My kitchen is so bad
that a poet friend wrote a poem about it. This all
might sound a little conceited. I mean—I don't want
you all to think that my kitchen is better than anyone else's, but shit if you got it—flaunt it.

The Kitchens that are still left in the home are so
instant they might as well be out to lunch too. Instant
milk, instant coffee, instant tea, instant potatoes, instant old-fashioned oatmeal. Everything is prepre-
pared for the unprepared woman in the kitchen. The
chicken is precut. The flour is premeasured, the rice
is minute. The salt is preseasoned, and the peas are
prebuttered.

Just goes to show you white folks will do anything
for their women. They had to invent instant food because the servant problem got so bad that their

woman had to get in the kitchen herself with her own
two little lily-white hands. It is no accident that in
the old old south where they had slaves they was
eating fried chicken coated with batter, and biscuits
so light they could have flown across the Mason-
Dixon line if they had wanted to. There was pound
cake that had to be beat eight hundred strokes. Who
do YOU think was doing this beating? It sure wasn't
Missy. Missy was beating the upstairs house nigger
for not bringing her mint julep quick enough. Massa
was out beating the field niggers for not hoeing the
cotton fast enough.

Meanwhile up in the north country, where they didn't
have no slaves to speak of, they was eating baked
beans and so-called New England boiled dinner. It
ain't no big thing to put everything in one pot and
let it cook.

Black men and women have been whipping up fine
food for centuries, and outside of black bottom pie
and nigger toes there is no reference to our contribution and participation in and to the culinary arts.
When they do mention our food they act like it is
some obscure thing that niggers down south made
up and don't nobody else in the world eat it. Food
ain't nothing but food. Food is universal. Everybody
eats.

We've got to have some sort of kitchen control. I
have been trying for years to do something about
the kitchen crises: A friend of mine named Ragde J.
Revooh is working with me and we hope to get the
federal government to step in. We want to establish
a House Untogether Kitchen Committee to investigate
food crimes and racism in the kitchen. We want to
get Flo Kennedy to head the Committee on Racism.
There is enough evidence of racism in the kitchen to
indict a whole bunch of well-known chefs.

We are setting up a kitchen brigade. We need you. You can be a Double-O SOUL kitchen spy, and to qualify you have to be:

> black or white
> male or female
> over thirty
> able to make a good cup of coffee
> able to cook rice until every grain stands
> to itself
> able to fry the hell out of chicken

All you have to do is report on the state of the kitchen. Say—you go to one of them home-cooking places and the food is awful. The job is easy. All you do is report on the state of kitchens. For instance, if you eat in one of them "home cookin'" joints and the food is bad, you report that they got a bad home and we send some kitchen help. If you eat at someone's home and they commit a food crime—you squeal on them. Report them to us and we will use the evidence and your opinion to indict them.

We feel very strongly that certain standards will have to be set and at least have a seal of good practice. One of the first set will be a good coffee standard. WHO DOES OR DOES NOT WASH THEIR COFFEE POT? Coffee ain't good if you have a dirty pot.

And we are going to do something about cookbooks. Cookbooks ain't nothing but a hustle. Everybody got a name but us (not counting nigger toes and black bottom pie) . . . Russian Dressing, French Fries, Spanish Rice, Jerusalem artichokes, Bavarian Cream, Dutch Apple Pie, Canadian bacon, Brussels sprouts, Swedish Meatballs, Danish pastry and so on. They even name things after their heroes . . . Lobster Rockefeller, Peach Melba, Waldorf Salad and so on and on. After the revolution don't you know we

gonna have Neckbones à la Moms Mabley, Nina
Simone Eggs, Hotel Theresa Salad, Muhammad Ali
Soufflé, Rap Brown Ragout, and Brown Betty will take
on a different meaning—

REAL BROWN BETTY

First off you need real lemons and real butter,
margarine won't do. What you do is take the butter
—you got that? Butter! I ain't talking about margarine. I'm talking about Butter! Butter! Butter! And
you stir it until it's soft.

Then get a couple of slices of whole wheat bread,
not the Wonder shit. But whole wheat! And you cube
the bread and stir the butter with it. Cover the ??????
of a big black skillet with four pared and sliced
apples, alternating with the bread and butter mixture. As you alternate spread the juice of a real
lemon and the rind. Sprinkle and layer with a whole
nutmeg grated.

You should end up with a layer of whole wheat
bread.

Bake in a moderate oven.

Serve with a Roy Wilkins Sauce, commonly known
as thin cream.

A potato is a patata and not Irish as white folks
would have you believe. Watermelons are prehis-
toric and eaten all over the world. The Russians
make a watermelon beer. In the Orient, they dry and
roast and salt the seeds. When old Chris got here,
the Indians were eating hominy grits. Before he
"discovered" this country the Greeks and Romans
were snaking on collard greens. Black-eyed peas
ain't nothing but dried cow peas whose name in
Sanskrit traces its line back to the days before history was recorded. Uh, excuse me boss, I means

before you all was recordin' history. Ah know this is hard for you to believe, suh, but I got it from one of yo' history books and I know you all wouldn't talk with no forked tongue about history.

The truth will out . . . Food is colored. You take the prized bitch—sweet Miss Georgia Peach—the hussy used to pass for a Persian apple. And at one time claimed to be Indian. But them white folks ain't kiddin'. Once they start investigating you, they find out that Miss Thing is Chinese. Oh yes she is. But the truth is the old whore didn't reach America until 1571. And they say that she came with a boatload of Spaniards. Poor peach goes for bad but in fact is not that hearty. Her bud is killed by winter temperatures of 10 below and her offspring the nectarine is more vulnerable than she. Po thing—nectarine is mo delicate and got more aroma but she ain't got no fuzz. And peaches ain't the only one. Plenty is passing. At this time I ain't gonna go into it too heavy but you look for my book *The De-Mystification of Food*. And you can get all the lowdown. Anyhow, the truth will out. Yes! Food is colored. Peaches are Chinese. Watermelons are African. Mangos is Indian. Avocado is Mexican. Carrots are Arab. If you check it out, ain't too many things, food or people, REAL WHITE-AMERICANS:

REAL WHITE AMERICAN TAFFY

And for that you need

> 1 teaspoon of glycerin
> 2½ tablespoons of vinegar
> ½ cup water
> 1 teaspoon of imitation vanilla flavor
> 2 cups of granulated sugar

You boil the sugar, water, glycerin and vinegar to a hard boil.

When adding flavoring, pour onto a greased platter. When cool enough to handle, pull until very white. Stretch into a long rope and cut into short pieces.

If you feel that it is time to call a halt to food crimes; if you feel that the state of kitchens across the country is in a state of confusion—join us. And together we can combat crime and racism in the kitchen. WRITE to Ragde J. Revooh at the Black House in the State of Washington.

Long live Soul Food.

The Negro Artist
and the Racial Mountain

ONE OF THE MOST PROMISING of the young Negro poets said to me once, "I want to be a poet—not a Negro poet," meaning, I believe, "I want to write like a white poet"; meaning, subconsciously, "I would like to be a white poet"; meaning behind that, "I would like to be white." And I was sorry the young man said that, for no great poet has ever been afraid of being himself. And I doubted then that, with his desire to run away spiritually from his race, this boy would ever be a great poet. But this is the mountain standing in the way of any true Negro art in America —this urge within the race toward whiteness, the desire to pour racial individuality into the mold of American standardization, and to be as little Negro and as much American as possible.

But let us look at the immediate background of this young poet. His family is of what I suppose one would call the Negro middle class: people who are by no means rich, yet never uncomfortable nor hungry—smug, contented, respectable folk, members of the Baptist church. The father goes to work every morning. He is a chief steward at a large white club. The mother sometimes does fancy sewing or supervises parties for the rich families of the town. The children go to a mixed school. In the home they read white papers and magazines. And the mother often says, "Don't be like niggers" when the children are bad. A frequent phrase from the father is, "Look how well a white man does things." And so the word white comes to be unconsciously a symbol of all the virtues. It holds for the children beauty, morality and money. The whisper of "I want to be white" runs silently through their minds. This young poet's home is, I believe, a fairly typical home of the colored middle class. One sees immediately how difficult it would be for an artist born in such a home to interest himself in interpreting the beauty of his own people. He is never taught to see that beauty. He is taught rather not to see it, or if he does, to be ashamed of it when it is not according to Caucasian patterns.

Certainly there is, for the American Negro artist who can escape the restrictions the more advanced among his own group would put upon him, a great field of unused material ready for his art. Without going outside his race, and even among the better classes with their "white" culture and conscious American manners, but still Negro enough to be different, there is sufficient matter to furnish a black artist with a lifetime of creative work. And when he chooses to touch on the relations between Negroes and whites in this country, with their innumerable overtones and undertones, surely, and especially for literature and the drama, there is an inexhaustible supply of themes at hand. To these the Negro artist can give his racial individuality, his heritage of rhythm and warmth, and his incongruous humor that so often, as in the Blues, becomes ironic laughter mixed with tears. But let us look again at the mountain.

The road for the serious black artist, then, who would produce a racial art is most certainly rocky and the mountain is high. Until recently he received almost no encouragement for his work from either white or colored people. The fine novels of Chesnutt go out of print with neither race noticing their passing. The quaint charm and humor of Dunbar's dialect verse brought to him, in his day, largely the same kind of encouragement one would give a side-show freak (A colored man writing poetry! How odd!) or a clown (How amusing!).

The Negro artist works against an undertow of sharp criticism and misunderstanding from his own group and unintentional bribes from the whites. "O, be respectable, write about nice people, show how good we are," say the Negroes. "Be stereotyped, don't go too far, don't shatter our illusions about you, don't amuse us too seriously. We will pay you," say the whites. Both would have told Jean Toomer not to write *Cane*. The colored people did not praise it. The white people did not buy it. Most of the colored people who did read *Cane* hate it. They are afraid of it. Although the critics gave it good reviews the public remained indifferent. Yet (excepting the work of Du Bois) *Cane* contains the finest prose written by a Negro in America. And like the singing of Robeson it is truly racial.

Most of my own poems are racial in theme and treatment, derived from the life I know. In many of them I try to grasp and hold some of the meanings and rhythms of jazz. I am sincere as I know how to be in these poems and yet after every reading I answer questions like these from my own people: "Do you think Negroes should always write about Negroes? I wish you wouldn't read some of your poems to white folks. How do you find anything interesting in a place like a cabaret? Why do you write about black people? You aren't black. What makes you do so many jazz poems?"

But jazz to me is one of the inherent expressions of Negro life in America: the eternal tom-tom beating in the Negro soul—the tom-tom of revolt against weariness in a white world, a world of subway trains and work, work, work; the tom-tom of joy and laughter, and pain swallowed in a smile. Yet the Philadelphia clubwoman is ashamed to say that her race created it and she does not like me to write about it. The old subconscious "white is best" runs through her mind. Years of study under white teachers, a lifetime of white books, pictures, and papers, and white manners, morals, and Puritan standards made her dislike the spirituals. And now she turns up her nose at jazz and all its manifestations—likewise almost everything else distinctly racial. She doesn't care for the Winold Reiss portraits of Negroes because they are "too Negro." She does not want a true picture of herself from anybody. She wants the artist to flatter her, to make the white world believe that all Negroes are as smug and as near white in soul as she wants to be. But, to my mind, it is the duty of the younger Negro artist, if he accepts any duties at all from outsiders, to change through the force of his art that old whispering, "I want to be white," hidden in the aspirations of his people, to "Why should I want to be white? I am a Negro—and beautiful!"

So I am ashamed for the black poet who says, "I want to be a poet, not a Negro poet," as though his own racial world were not as interesting as any other world. I am ashamed, too, for the colored artist who runs from the painting of Negro faces to the painting of sunsets after the manner of the academicians because he fears the strange un-whiteness of his own features. An artist must be free to choose what he does, certainly, but he must also never be afraid to do what he might choose.

Let the blare of Negro jazz bands and the bellowing voice of Bessie Smith singing Blues penetrate the closed ears of the colored near-intellectuals until they listen and perhaps understand. Let Paul Robeson singing "Water Boy," and Rudolph Fisher writing about the streets of Harlem, and Jean Toomer holding the heart of Georgia in his hands, and Aaron Douglas drawing strange black fantasies cause the smug Negro middle class to turn from their white, respectable, ordinary books and papers to catch a glimmer of their own beauty. We younger Negro artists who create now intend to express our individual dark-skinned selves without fear or shame. If white people are pleased we are glad. If they are not, it doesn't matter. We know we are beautiful. And ugly too. The tom-tom cries and the tom-tom laughs. If colored people are pleased we are glad. If they are not, their displeasure doesn't matter either. We build our temples for tomorrow, strong as we know how, and we stand on top of the mountain, free within ourselves.

Langston Hughes
The Nation
June 23, 1926

GEORGE DAVIS has served as staff writer for the *Washington Post* and is at present an editor with the *New York Times* Sunday Department. He is also a member of the John O. Killens Writers Workshop at Columbia University. The current selection is from a novel Mr. Davis is writing about the Vietnam War. He was a pilot in the U.S. Air Force and flew more than forty combat missions in 1967 and 1968.

ADDISON GAYLE, JR., is a professor of English at City College. He is the editor of the anthology *Black Expression: Essays By and About Black Americans in the Creative Arts*. He is also the author of *The Sound of Angels*.

VERTA GROSVENOR is the author of a forthcoming book entitled *The Vibration Cookbook*. She is also a singer with an avant-garde musical group, Sun Ra and His Solar Arkestra.

VINCENT HARDING is a professor of history and sociology at Spelman College (part of Atlanta University). He is one of the leading essayists on the ideology of Black Studies and the director of The Martin Luther King, Jr., Memorial Center in Atlanta.

CHARLES F. HARRIS has written many articles and is an editor at Random House.

CALVIN C. HERNTON is the author of two books of essays, *Sex and Racism in America* and *White Papers for White Americans*. His book *Social Struggle and Sexual Crisis* will be published in 1970. Most recently, he has served as writer-in-residence at Central State College in Wilberforce, Ohio.

CHESTER HIMES has been widely read since 1932 when his first short stories were published. His first novel was published in 1945 and since then he has added fifteen titles to his list. Nine of these are mysteries and include *Run Man Run*, and *The Crazy Kill*. The most recent, *Blind Man with a Pistol*, was published in 1969. All of these mysteries, with the exception of the last one, were originally published in France and afterward in the United States. One of his detective stories, *Cotton Comes to Harlem*, is being made into a motion picture.

OLIVER JACKMAN is Ambassador to the United Nations for Barbados. He is a former correspondent for the BBC and for Nigerian newspapers. He has also served as Political Affairs Officer to the United Nations in Africa. His short story is from a novel titled *Saw the House in Half* that will be published in 1970.

C. L. R. JAMES has most recently been visiting professor of political science at Northwestern University and Federal City College in Washington, D.C. He is the author of *Mariners, Renegades and Castaways: A Critical Review of Herman Melville* and *The Black Jacobins*.

ISHMAEL REED is the author of two novels, *The Free-lance Pallbearers* and *Yellow Back Radio Broke-Down*. He is also a lecturer in American literature at the University of California at Berkeley.

JOHN A. WILLIAMS is the author of the following books: *The Man Who Cried I Am*, *Sons of Darkness, Sons of Light* (which will be made into a movie), *Sissie* and *Night Song*.